Friedrich Nietzche

THE BIRTH OF TRAGEDY, SEVENTY-FIVE APHORISMS & THE ANTI-CHRIST

Published By Frederick Ellis
8000 E. Girard, Suite 501
Denver , Colorado 80231

ISBN 1-934568-473

THE BIRTH OF TRAGEDY

Whatever may be at the bottom of this questionable book, it must have been an exceptionally significant and fascinating question, and deeply personal at that: the time in which it was written, in spite of which it was written, bears witness to that-- the exciting time of the Franco-Prussian war of 1870-71. As the thunder of the Battle of Worth was rolling over Europe, the muser and riddle-friend who was to be the father of this book sat somewhere in an alpine nook, very bemused and beriddled, hence very concerned and yet unconcerned, and wrote down his thoughts about the Greeks--the core of the strange and almost inaccessible book to which this belated preface (or postscript) shall now be added. A few weeks later--and he himself was to be found under the walls of Metz, still wedded to the question marks that he had placed after the alleged "cheerfulness" of the Greeks and of Greek art. Eventually, in that month of profoundest suspense when the peace treaty was being debated at Versailles, he, too, made peace with himself and, slowly convalescing from an illness contracted at the front, completed the final draft of The Birth of Tragedy out of the Spirit of Music.--Out of music? Music and tragedy? Greeks and the music of tragedy? Greeks and the art form of pessimism? The best turned out, most beautiful, most envied type of humanity to date, those most apt to seduce us to life, the Greeks--how now? They of all people should of needed tragedy? Even more--art? For what--Greek art?

You will guess where the big question mark concerning the value of existence has thus been raised. Is pessimism necessarily a sign of decline, decay, degeneration, weary and weak instincts--as it once was in India and now is, to all appearances, among us, "modern" men and Europeans? Is there pessimism of strength? An intellectual predilection for the hard, gruesome, evil, problematic aspect of existence, prompted by well-being, by overflowing health, by the fullness of existence? Is it perhaps possible to suffer precisely from overfullness? The sharp-eyed courage that tempts and attempts, that craves the frightful as the enemy, the worthy enemy, against whom one can test one's strength? From whom one can learn what it means "to be frightened"? What is the significance of the tragic myth among the Greeks of the best, the strongest, the most courageous period? And the tremendous phenomenon of the Dionysian--and, born from it, tragedy--what might they signify?-- And again: that of which tragedy died, the Socratism of morality, the dialectics, frugality, and cheerfulness of the theoretical man--how now? Might not this very Socratism be a sign of decline, of weariness, of infection, of the anarchical dissolution of the instincts? And the "Greek cheerfulness" of the later Greeks--merely the afterglow of the sunset? The Epicureans resolve against pessimism--a mere precaution of the afflicted? And science itself, our science-- indeed, what is the significance of all science, viewed as a symptom of life? For what--worse yet, whence--all science? How now? Is the resolve to be so scientific about everything perhaps a kind of fear of, an escape from, pessimism? A subtle last resort against--truth? And, morally speaking, a sort of cowardice and falseness? Amorally speaking, a ruse? O Socrates, Socrates, was that perhaps your secret? O enigmatic ironist, was that perhaps your--irony?

2

What I then got hold of, something frightful and dangerous, a problem with horns but not necessarily a bull, in any case a new problem--today I should say that it was the problem of science itself, science considered for the first time as problematic, as questionable. But the book in which my youthful courage and suspicion found an outlet--what an impossible book had to result from a task so uncongenial to youth! Constructed from a lot of immature, overgreen personal experiences, all of them close to the limits of communication, presented in the context of art--for the problem of science cannot be recognized in the context of science--a book perhaps for artists who also have an analytic and retrospective penchant (in other words, an exceptional type of artist for whom one might have to look far and wide and really would not care to look); a book full of psychological innovations and artists' secrets, with an artists' metaphysics in the background; a youthful work full of the intrepid mood of youth, the moodiness of youth, independent, defiantly self-reliant even where it seems to bow before an authority and personal reverence; in sum, a first book, also in every bad sense of that label. In spite of the problem which seems congenial to old age, the book is marked by every defect of youth, with its "length in excess: and its "storm and stress." On the other hand, considering its success (especially with the great artist to whom it addressed itself as in a dialogue, Richard Wagner), it is a proven book, I mean one that in any case satisfied "the best minds of the time." In view of that, it really ought to be treated with some consideration and taciturnity. Still, I do not want to suppress entirely how disagreeable it now seems to me, how strange it appears now, after sixteen years--before a much older, a hundred times more demanding, but by no means colder eye which has not become a stranger to the task which this audacious book dared to tackle for the first time: to look at science in the perspective of the artist, but at art in that of life.

3

To say it once more: today I find it an impossible book: I consider it badly written, ponderous, embarrassing, image-mad and image-confused, sentimental, in places saccharine to the point of effeminacy, uneven in tempo, without the will to logical cleanliness, very convinced and therefore disdainful of proof, mistrustful even of the propriety of proof, a book for initiates, "music" for those dedicated to music, those who are closely related to begin with on the basis of common and rare aesthetic experiences, "music" meant as a sign of recognition for close relatives in arbitus [In the arts.]--an arrogant and rhapsodic book that ought to exclude right from the beginning the profanum vulgus [The profane crowd.] of "the educated" even more than "the mass" or "folk." Still, the effect of the book proved and proves that it had a knack for seeking our fellow-rhapsodizers and for luring them on to new secret paths and dancing places. What found expression here was anyway--this was admitted with as much curiosity as antipathy--a strange voice, the disciple of a still "unknown God," one who concealed himself for the time being under the scholar's hood, under the gravity and dialectical ill-humor of the German, even under the bad manners of the Wagnerian. Here was a spirit with strange, still nameless needs, a memory bursting with questions, experiences, concealed things after which the name of Dionysus was added as one more question mark. What spoke here--as was admitted, not without suspicion--was something like a mystical, almost maenadic soul that stammered with difficulty, a feat of the will, as in a strange tongue, almost undecided whether it should communicate or conceal itself. It should have sung, this "new soul"--and not spoken! What I had to say then--too bad that I did not dare say it as a poet: perhaps I had the ability. Or at least as a philologist: after all, even today practically everything in this field remains to be discovered and dug up by philologists! Above all, the problem that there is a problem here--and that the Greeks, as long as we lack an answer to the question "what is Dionysian?" remain as totally uncomprehended and unimaginable as ever.

4

Indeed, what is Dionysian?-- This book contains an answer: one "who knows" is talking, the initiate and disciple of his god. Now I should perhaps speak more cautiously and less eloquently about such a difficult psychological question as that concerning the origin of tragedy among the Greeks. The question of the Greek's relation to pain, his degree of sensitivity, is basic: did this relation remain constant? Or did it change radically? The question is whether his ever stronger craving for beauty, for festivals, pleasures, new cults was rooted in some deficiency, privation, melancholy, pain? Supposing that this were true--and Pericles (or Thucydides) suggests as much in the great funeral oration--how should we then have to explain the origin of the opposite craving, which developed earlier in time, the craving for the ugly; the good, severe will of the older Greeks to pessimism, to the tragic myth, to the image of everything underlying existence that is frightful, evil, a riddle, destructive, fatal? What, then, would be the origin of tragedy? Perhaps joy, strength, overflowing health, overgreat fullness? And what, then, is the significance, physiologically speaking, of that madness out of which tragic and comic art developed--the Dionysian madness? How now? Is madness perhaps not necessarily the symptom of degeneration, decline, and the final stage of culture? Are there perhaps--a question for psychiatrists--neuroses of health? of the youth and youthfulness of a people? Where does that synthesis of god and billy goat in the satyr point? What experience of himself, what urge compelled the Greek to conceive the Dionysian enthusiast and primeval man as a satyr? And regarding the origin of the tragic chorus: did those centuries when the Greek body flourished and the Greek soul foamed over with health perhaps know endemic ecstasies? Visions and hallucinations shared by entire communities or assemblies at a cult? How now? Should the Greeks, precisely in the abundance of their youth, have had the will to the tragic and have been pessimists? Should it have been madness, to use one of Plato's phrases, that brought the greatest blessings upon Greece? On the other hand, conversely, could it be that the Greeks became more and more optimistic, superficial, and histrionic precisely in the period of dissolution and weakness--more and more ardent for logic and logicizing the world and thus more "cheerful" and "scientific"? How now? Could it be possible that, in spite of all "modern ideas" and the prejudices of a democratic taste, the triumph of optimism, the gradual prevalence of rationality, practical and theoretical utilitarianism, no less than democracy itself which developed at the same time, might all have been symptoms of a decline of strength, of impending old age, and of physiological weariness? These, and not pessimism? Was Epicure an optimist--precisely because he was afflicted?

It is apparent that it was a whole cluster of grave questions with which this book burdened itself. Let us add the gravest question of all. What, seen in the perspective of life, is the significance of morality?

5

Already in the preface addressed to Richard Wagner, art, and not morality, is presented as the truly metaphysical activity of man. In the book itself the suggestive sentence is repeated several times, that the existence of the world is justified only as an aesthetic phenomenon. Indeed, the whole book knows only an artistic meaning and crypto-meaning behind all events--a "god," if you please, but certainly only an entirely reckless and amoral artist-god who wants to experience, whether he is building or destroying, in the good and in the bad, his own joy and glory--one who, creating worlds, frees himself from the distress of fullness and overfullness and from the affliction of the contradictions compressed in his soul. The world--at every moment the attained salvation of God, as the eternally changing, eternally new vision of the most deeply afflicted, discordant, and contradictory being who can find salvation only in appearance: you can call this whole artists' metaphysics arbitrary, idle, fantastic; what matters is that it betrays a spirit who will one day fight at any risk whatever the moral interpretation and significance of existence. Here, perhaps for the first time, a pessimism "beyond good and evil" is suggested. Here that "perversity of mind" gains speech and formulation against which Schopenhauer never wearied of hurling in advance his most irate curses and thunderbolts: a philosophy that dares to move, to demote, morality into the realm of appearance--and not merely among "appearances" or phenomena (in the sense assigned to these words by Idealistic philosophers), but among "deceptions," as semblance, delusion, error, interpretation, contrivance, art.

Perhaps the depth of this antimoral propensity is best inferred from the careful and hostile silence with which Christianity is treated throughout the whole book--Christianity as the most prodigal elaboration of the moral theme to which humanity has ever been subjected. In truth, nothing could be more opposed to the purely aesthetic interpretation and justification of the world which are taught in this book than the Christian teaching, which is, and wants to be, only moral and which relegates art, every art, to the realm of lies; with its absolute standards, beginning with the truthfulness of God, it negates, judges, and damns art. Behind this mode of thought and valuation, which must be hostile to art if it is at all genuine, I never failed to sense a hostility to life--a furious, vengeful antipathy to life itself: for all of life is based on semblance, art, deception, points of view, and the necessity of perspectives and error. Christianity was from the beginning, essentially and fundamentally, life's nausea and disgust with life, merely concealed behind, masked by, dressed up as, faith in "another: or "better" life. Hatred of "the world," condemnations of the passions, fear of beauty and sensuality, a beyond invented the better to slander this life, at bottom a craving for the nothing, for the end, for respite, for "the sabbath of sabbaths"--all this always struck me, no less than the unconditional will of Christianity to recognize only moral values, as the most dangerous and uncanny form of all possible forms of a "will to decline"--at the very least a sign of abysmal sickness, weariness, discouragement, exhaustion, and the impoverishment of life. For, confronted with morality (especially Christian, or unconditional, morality), life must continually and inevitably be in the wrong, because life is something essentially amoral--and eventually, crushed by the weight of contempt and the eternal No, life must then be felt to be unworthy of desire and altogether worthless. Morality itself--how now? might not morality be "a will to negate life," a secret instinct of annihilation, a principle of decay, diminution, and slander--the beginning of the end? Hence, the danger of dangers?

It was against morality that my instinct turned with this questionable book, long ago; it was an instinct that aligned itself with life and that discovered for itself a fundamentally opposite doctrine and valuation of life--purely artistic and anti-Christian. What to call it? As a philologist and man of words I baptized it, not without taking some liberty--for who could claim to know the rightful name of the Antichrist?--in the name of a Greek god: I called it Dionysian.

6

It is clear what task I first dared to touch with this book? How I regret now that in those days I still lacked the courage (or immodesty?) to permit myself in every way an individual language of my own for such individual views and hazards--and that instead I tried laboriously to express by means of Schopenhauerian and Kantian formulas strange and new valuations which were basically at odds with Kant's and Schopenhauer's spirit and taste! What, after all, did Schopenhauer think of tragedy?

"That which bestows on everything tragic its peculiar elevating force"--he says in The World as Will and Representation, volume II, p. 495--"is the discovery that the world, that life, can never give real satisfaction and hence is not worthy of our affection: this constitutes the tragic spirit--it leads to resignation."

How differently Dionysus spoke to me! How far removed I was from all this resignationism!-- But there is something far worse in this book, something I now regret still more than that I obscured and spoiled Dionysian premonitions with Schopenhauerian formulations: namely, that I spoiled the grandiose Greek problem, as it had arisen before my eyes, by introducing the most modern problems! That I appended hopes where there was no ground for hope, where everything pointed all too plainly to an end! That on the basis of the latest German music I began to rave about "the German spirit" as if that were in the process even then of discovering and finding itself again--at a time when the German spirit which not long before had still had the will to dominate Europe and the strength to lead Europe, was just making its testament and abdicating forever, making its transition, under the pompous pretense of founding a Reich, to a leveling mediocrity, democracy, and "modern ideas"!

Indeed, meanwhile I have learned to consider this "German spirit" with a sufficient lack of hope or mercy; also, contemporary German music, which is romanticism through and through and most un-Greek of all possible art forms--moreover, a first-rate poison for the nerves, doubly dangerous among a people who love drink and who honor lack of clarity as a virtue, for it has the double quality of a narcotic that both intoxicates and spreads a fog.

To be sure, apart from all the hasty hopes and faulty applications to the present with which I spoiled my first book, there still remains the great Dionysian question mark I raised--regarding music as well: what would a music have to like that would no longer be of romantic origin, like German music--but Dionysian?

7

But, my dear sir, what in the world is romantic if your book isn't? Can deep hatred against "the Now," against "reality" and "modern ideas" be pushed further than you pushed it in your artists' metaphysics? believing sooner in the Nothing, sooner in the devil than in "the Now"? Is it not a deep bass of wrath and the lust for destruction that we hear humming underneath all of your contrapuntal art and seduction of the ear, a furious resolve against everything that is "now," a will that is not too far removed from practical nihilism and seems to say: "sooner let nothing be true than that you should be right, than that your truth should be prove right!"

Listen yourself, my dear pessimist and art-deifier, but with open ears, to a single passage chosen from your book--to the not ineloquent dragon-slayer passage which may have an insidious pied-piper sound for young ears and hearts. How now? Isn't this the typical creed of the romantic of 1830, masked by the pessimism of 1850? Even the usual romantic finale is sounded-- break, breakdown, return and collapse before an old faith, before the old God. How now? Is your pessimists' book not itself a piece of anti-Hellenism and romanticism? Is it not itself something "equally intoxicating and befogging," in any case a narcotic, even a piece of music, German music? But listen:

"Let us imagine a coming generation with such intrepidity of vision, with such a heroic penchant for the tremendous; let us imagine the bold stride of these dragon-slayers, the proud audacity with which they turn their back on all the weakling's doctrines of optimism in order to 'live resolutely' in wholeness and fullness: would it not be necessary for the tragic man of such a culture, in view of his self-education for seriousness and terror, to desire a new art, the art of metaphysical comfort, and to exclaim with Faust:

Should not my longing overleap the distance

And draw the fairest form into existence?"

[Quoted from Section 18]

"Would it not be necessary?"--No, thrice no! O you young romantics: it would not be necessary! But it is highly probable that it will end that way--namely, "comforted," as it is written, in spite of all self-education for seriousness and terror, "comforted metaphysically"--in sum, as romantics end, as Christians.

No! You ought to learn the art of this-worldly comfort first; you ought to learn to laugh, my young friends, if you are hell-bent on remaining pessimists. Then perhaps, as laughers, you may some day dispatch all metaphysical comforts to the devil--metaphysics in front. Or, to say in the language of that Dionysian monster who bears the name of Zarathustra:

"Raise up your hearts, my brothers, high, higher! And don't forget your legs! Raise up your legs too, good dancers; and still better: stand on your heads!

"This crown of the laugher, this rose-wreath crown: I crown myself with this crown; I myself pronounced holy my laughter. I did not find anyone else today strong enough for that.

"Zarathustra, the dancer; Zarathustra, the light one who beckons with his wings, preparing for a flight, beckoning to all birds, ready and heady, blissfully lightheaded;

"Zarathustra, the soothsayer; Zarathustra, the sooth-laugher; not impatient; not unconditional; one who loves leaps and side-leaps: I crown myself with this crown.

"This crown of the laugher, this rose-wreath crown: to you, my brothers, I throw this crown. Laughter I have pronounced holy: you higher men, learn--to laugh!"

Thus Spoke Zarathustra, Part IV. ["On the Higher Man," 17-20, in part.]

Sils-Maria,

Upper Engadine,

August 1886

FRIEDRICH NIETZSCHE

Preface to Richard Wagner

(1871)

To keep at a distance all the possible scruples, excitements, and misunderstandings that the thoughts united in this essay will occasion, in view of the peculiar character of our aesthetic public, and to be able to write these introductory remarks, too, with the same contemplative delight whose reflection--the distillation of good and elevating hours--is evident on every page, I picture the moment when you, my highly respected friend, will receive this essay. Perhaps after an evening walk in the winter snow, you will behold Prometheus unbound on the title page, read my name, and be convinced at once that, whatever this essay should contain, the author certainly has something serious and urgent to say; also that, as he hatched these ideas, he was communicating with you as if you were present, and hence could write down only what was in keeping with that presence. You will recall that it was during the same period when your splendid Festschrift on Beethoven came into being, amid the terrors and sublimities of the war that had just broken out, that I collected myself for these reflections. Yet anyone would be mistaken if he associated my reflections with the contrast between patriotic excitement and aesthetic enthusiasm, of courageous seriousness and a cheerful game: if he really read this essay, it would dawn on him, to his surprise, what a seriously German problem is faced here and placed right in the center of German hopes, as a vortex and turning point. But perhaps such readers will find it offensive that an aesthetic problem should be taken so seriously--assuming they are unable to consider art more than a pleasant sideline, a readily dispensable tinkling of bells that accompanies the "seriousness of life," just as if nobody knew what was involved in such a contrast with the "seriousness of life." Let such "serious" readers learn something from the fact that I am convinced that art represents the highest task and the truly metaphysical activity of this life, in the sense of that man to whom, as my sublime predecessor on this path, I wish to dedicate this essay.

Basel, end of the year 1871

FRIEDRICH NIETZSCHE

The Birth of Tragedy

1

Much will have been gained for aesthetics once we have succeeded in apprehending directly--rather than merely ascertaining--that art owes its continuous evolution to the Apollinian- Dionysian duality, even as the propagation of the species depends on the duality of the sexes, their constant conflicts and periodic acts of reconciliation. I have borrowed my adjectives from the Greeks, who developed their mystical doctrines of art through plausible embodiments, not through purely conceptual means. It is by those two art sponsoring deities, Apollo and Dionysus, that we are made to recognize the tremendous split, as regards both origins and objectives, between the plastic, Apollinian arts and the nonvisual art of music inspired by Dionysus. The two creative tendencies developed alongside one another, usually in fierce opposition, each by its taunts forcing the other to more energetic production, both perpetuating in a discordant concord that agon which the term art but feebly denominates: until at last, by the thaumaturgy of an Hellenic act of will, the pair accepted the yoke of marriage and, in this condition, begot Attic tragedy, which exhibits the salient features of both parents.

To reach a closer understanding of both these tendencies, let us begin by viewing them as the separate art realms of dream and intoxication, two physiological phenomena standing toward one another in much the same relationship as the Apollinian and Dionysian. It was in a dream, according to Lucretius, that the marvelous gods and goddesses first presented themselves to the minds of men. That great sculptor, Phidias, beheld in a dream the entrancing bodies of more than human beings, and likewise, if anyone had asked the Greek poets about the mystery of poetic creation, they too would have referred him to dreams and instructed him much as Hans Sachs instructs us in Die Meistersinger:

The poet's task is this, my friend,

to read his dreams and comprehend.

The truest human fancy seems

to be revealed to us in dreams:

all poems and versification

are but true dreams' interpretation.

The fair illusion of the dream sphere, in the production of which every man proves himself an accomplished artist, is a precondition not only of all plastic art, but even, as we shall see presently, of a wide range of poetry. Here we enjoy an immediate apprehension of form, all shapes speak to us directly, nothing seems indifferent or redundant. Despite the high intensity with which these dream realities exist for us, we still have a residual sensation that they are illusions; at least such has been my experience-- and the frequency, not to say normality, of the experience is borne out in many passages of the poets. Men of philosophical disposition are known for their constant premonition that our everyday reality, too, is an illusion, hiding another, totally different kind of reality. It was Schopenhauer who considered the ability to view at certain times all men and things as mere phantoms or dream images to be the true mark of philosophic talent. The person who is responsive to the stimuli of art behaves toward the reality of dream much the way the philosopher behaves toward the reality of existence: he observes exactly and enjoys his observations, for it is by these images that he interprets life, by these processes that he rehearses it. Nor is it by pleasant images only that such plausible connections are made: the whole divine comedy of life, including its somber aspects, its sudden balkings, impish accidents, anxious expectations, moves past him, not quite like a shadow play--for it is he himself, after all, who lives and suffers through these scenes--yet never without giving a fleeting sense of illusion; and I imagine that many persons have reassured themselves amidst the perils of dream by calling out, "It is a dream! I want it to go on." I have even heard of people spinning out the causality of one and the same dream over three or more successive nights. All these facts clearly bear witness that our innermost being, the common substratum of humanity, experiences dreams with deep delight and a sense of real necessity. This deep and happy sense of the necessity of dream experiences was expressed by the Greeks in the image of Apollo. Apollo is at once the god of all plastic powers and the soothsaying god. He who is etymologically the "lucent" one, the god of light, reigns also over the fair illusion of our inner world of fantasy. The perfection of these conditions in contrast to our imperfectly understood waking reality, as well as our profound awareness of nature's healing powers during the interval of sleep and dream, furnishes a symbolic analogue to the soothsaying faculty and quite generally to the arts, which make life possible and worth living. But the image of Apollo must incorporate that thin line which the dream image may not cross, under penalty of becoming pathological, of imposing itself on us as crass reality: a discreet limitation, a freedom from all extravagant urges, the sapient tranquillity of the plastic god. His eye must be sunlike, in keeping with his origin. Even at those moments when he is angry and ill-tempered there lies upon him the consecration of fair illusion. In an eccentric way one might say of Apollo what Schopenhauer says, in the first part of The World as Will and Idea, of man caught in the veil of Maya: "Even as on an immense, raging sea, assailed by huge wave crests, a man sits in a little rowboat trusting his frail craft, so, amidst the furious torments of this world, the individual sits tranquilly, supported by the principium individuationis and relying on it." One might say that the unshakable confidence in that principle has received its most magnificent expression in Apollo, and that Apollo himself may be regarded as the marvelous divine image of the principium individuationis, whose looks and gestures radiate the full delight, wisdom, and beauty of "illusion."

In the same context Schopenhauer has described for us the tremendous awe which seizes man when he suddenly begins to doubt the cognitive modes of experience, in other words, when in a given instance the law of causation seems to suspend itself. If we add to this awe the glorious transport which arises in man, even from the very depths of nature, at the shattering of the principium individuationis, then we are in a position to apprehend the essence of Dionysian rapture, whose closest analogy is furnished by physical intoxication. Dionysian stirrings arise either through the influence of those narcotic potions of which all primitive races speak in their hymns, or through the powerful approach of spring, which penetrates with joy the whole frame of nature. So stirred, the individual forgets himself completely. It is the same Dionysian power which in medieval Germany drove ever increasing crowds of people singing and dancing from place to place; we recognize in these St. John's and St. Vitus' dancers the Bacchic choruses of the Greeks, who had their precursors in Asia Minor and as far back as Babylon and the orgiastic Sacaea. There are people who, either from lack of experience or out of sheer stupidity, turn away from such phenomena, and, strong in the sense of their own sanity, label them either mockingly or pityingly "endemic diseases." These benighted souls have no idea how cadaverous and ghostly their "sanity" appears as the intense throng of Dionysian revelers sweeps past them.

Not only does the bond between man and man come to be forged once more by the magic of the Dionysian rite, but nature itself, long alienated or subjugated, rises again to celebrate the reconciliation with her prodigal son, man. The earth offers its gifts voluntarily, and the savage beasts of mountain and desert approach in peace. The chariot of Dionysus is bedecked with flowers and garlands; panthers and tigers stride beneath his yoke. If one were to convert Beethoven's "Paean to Joy" into a painting, and refuse to curb the imagination when that multitude prostrates itself reverently in the dust, one might form some apprehension of Dionysian ritual. Now the slave emerges as a freeman; all the rigid, hostile walls which either necessity or despotism has erected between men are shattered. Now that the gospel of universal harmony is sounded, each individual becomes not only reconciled to his fellow but actually at one with him--as though the veil of Maya had been torn apart and there remained only shreds floating before the vision of mystical Oneness. Man now expresses himself through song and dance as the member of a higher community; he has forgotten how to walk, how to speak, and is on the brink of taking wing as he dances. Each of his gestures betokens enchantment; through him sounds a supernatural power, the same power which makes the animals speak and the earth render up milk and honey.

He feels himself to be godlike and strides with the same elation and ecstasy as the gods he has seen in his dreams. No longer the artist, he has himself become a work of art: the productive power of the whole universe is now manifest in his transport, to the glorious satisfaction of the primordial One. The finest clay, the most precious marble--man--is here kneaded and hewn, and the chisel blows of the Dionysian world artist are accompanied by the cry of the Eleusinian mystagogues: "Do you fall on your knees, multitudes, do you divine your creator?"

2

So far we have examined the Apollinian and Dionysian states as the product of formative forces arising directly from nature without the mediation of the human artist. At this stage artistic urges are satisfied directly, on the one hand through the imagery of dreams, whose perfection is quite independent of the intellectual rank, the artistic development of the individual; on the other hand, through an ecstatic reality which once again takes no account of the individual and may even destroy him, or else redeem him through a mystical experience of the collective. In relation to these immediate creative conditions of nature every artist must appear as "imitator," either as the Apollinian dream artist or the Dionysian ecstatic artist, or, finally (as in Greek tragedy, for example) as dream and ecstatic artist in one. We might picture to ourselves how the last of these, in a state of Dionysian intoxication and mystical self-abrogation, wandering apart from the reveling throng, sinks upon the ground, and how there is then revealed to him his own condition--complete oneness with the essence of the universe--in a dream similitude.

Having set down these general premises and distinctions, we now turn to the Greeks in order to realize to what degree the formative forces of nature were developed in them. Such an inquiry will enable us to assess properly the relation of the Greek artist to his prototypes or, to use Aristotle's expression, his "imitation of nature." Of the dreams the Greeks dreamed it is not possible to speak with any certainty, despite the extant dream literature and the large number of dream anecdotes. But considering the incredible accuracy of their eyes, their keen and unabashed delight in colors, one can hardly be wrong in assuming that their dreams too showed a strict consequence of lines and contours, hues and groupings, a progression of scenes similar to their best bas reliefs. The perfection of these dream scenes might almost tempt us to consider the dreaming Greek as a Homer and Homer as a dreaming Greek; which would be as though the modern man were to compare himself in his dreaming to Shakespeare.

Yet there is another point about which we do not have to conjecture at all: I mean the profound gap separating the Dionysian Greeks from the Dionysian barbarians. Throughout the range of ancient civilization (leaving the newer civilizations out of account for the moment) we find evidence of Dionysian celebrations which stand to the Greek type in much the same relation as the bearded satyr, whose name and attributes are derived from the goat, stands to the god Dionysus. The central concern of such celebrations was, almost universally, a complete sexual promiscuity overriding every form of established tribal law; all the savage urges of the mind were unleashed on those occasions until they reached that paroxysm of lust and cruelty which has always struck me as the "witches' cauldron" par excellence. It would appear that the Greeks were for a while quite immune from these feverish excesses which must have reached them by every known land or sea route. What kept Greece safe was the proud, imposing image of Apollo, who in holding up the head of the Gorgon to those brutal and grotesque Dionysian forces subdued them. Doric art has immortalized Apollo's majestic rejection of all license. But resistance became difficult, even impossible, as soon as similar urges began to break forth from the deep substratum of Hellenism itself. Soon the function of the Delphic god developed into something quite different and much more limited: all he could hope to accomplish now was to wrest the destructive weapon, by a timely gesture of pacification, from his opponent's hand. That act of pacification represents the most important event in the history of Greek ritual; every department of life now shows symptoms of a revolutionary change. The two great antagonists have been reconciled. Each feels obliged henceforth to keep to his bounds, each will honor the other by the bestowal of periodic gifts, while the cleavage remains fundamentally the same. And yet, if we examine what happened to the Dionysian powers under the pressure of that treaty we notice a great difference: in the place of the Babylonian Sacaea, with their throwback of men to the condition of apes and tigers, we now see entirely new rites celebrated: rites of universal redemption, of glorious transfiguration. Only now has it become possible to speak of nature's celebrating an aesthetic triumph; only now has the abrogation of the principium individuationis become an aesthetic event. That terrible witches' brew concocted of lust and cruelty has lost all power under the new conditions. Yet the peculiar blending of emotions in the heart of the Dionysian reveler--his ambiguity if you will--seems still to hark back (as the medicinal drug harks back to the deadly poison) to the days when the infliction of pain was experienced as joy while a sense of supreme triumph elicited cries of anguish from the heart. For now in every exuberant joy there is heard an undertone of terror, or else a wistful lament over an irrecoverable loss. It is as though in these Greek festivals a sentimental trait of nature were coming to the fore, as though nature were bemoaning the fact of her fragmentation, her decomposition into separate individuals. The chants and gestures of these revelers, so ambiguous in their motivation, represented an absolute novum in the world of the Homeric Greeks; their Dionysian music, in especial, spread abroad terror and a deep shudder. It is true: music had long been familiar to the Greeks as an Apollinian art, as a regular beat like that of waves lapping the shore, a plastic rhythm expressly developed for the portrayal of Apollinian conditions. Apollo's music was a Doric architecture of sound--of barely hinted sounds such as are proper to the cithara. Those very elements which characterize Dionysian music and, after it, music quite generally:

the heart shaking power of tone, the uniform stream of melody, the incomparable resources of harmony--all those elements had been carefully kept at a distance as being inconsonant with the Apollinian norm. In the Dionysian dithyramb man is incited to strain his symbolic faculties to the utmost; something quite unheard of is now clamoring to be heard: the desire to tear asunder the veil of Maya, to sink back into the original oneness of nature; the desire to express the very essence of nature symbolically. Thus an entirely new set of symbols springs into being. First, all the symbols pertaining to physical features: mouth, face, the spoken word, the dance movement which coordinates the limbs and bends them to its rhythm. Then suddenly all the rest of the symbolic forces--music and rhythm as such, dynamics, harmony--assert themselves with great energy. In order to comprehend this total emancipation of all the symbolic powers one must have reached the same measure of inner freedom those powers themselves were making manifest; which is to say that the votary of Dionysus could not be understood except by his own kind. It is not difficult to imagine the awed surprise with which the Apollinian Greek must have looked on him. And that surprise would be further increased as the latter realized, with a shudder, that all this was not so alien to him after all, that his Apollinian consciousness was but a thin veil hiding from him the whole Dionysian realm.

3

In order to comprehend this we must take down the elaborate edifice of Apollinian culture stone by stone until we discover its foundations. At first the eye is struck by the marvelous shapes of the Olympian gods who stand upon its pediments, and whose exploits, in shining bas-relief, adorn its friezes. The fact that among them we find Apollo as one god among many, making no claim to a privileged position, should not mislead us. The same drive that found its most complete representation in Apollo generated the whole Olympian world, and in this sense we may consider Apollo the father of that world. But what was the radical need out of which that illustrious society of Olympian beings sprang?

Whoever approaches the Olympians with a different religion in his heart, seeking moral elevation, sanctity, spirituality, loving kindness, will presently be forced to turn away from them in ill-humored disappointment. Nothing in these deities reminds us of asceticism, high intellect, or duty: we are confronted by luxuriant, triumphant existence, which deifies the good and the bad indifferently. And the beholder may find himself dismayed in the presence of such overflowing life and ask himself what potion these heady people must have drunk in order to behold, in whatever direction they looked, Helen laughing back at them, the beguiling image of their own existence. But we shall call out to this beholder, who has already turned his back: Don't go! Listen first to what the Greeks themselves have to say of this life, which spreads itself before you with such puzzling serenity. An old legend has it that King Midas hunted a long time in the woods for the wise Silenus, companion of Dionysus, without being able to catch him. When he had finally caught him the king asked him what he considered man's greatest good. The daemon remained sullen and uncommunicative until finally, forced by the king, he broke into a shrill laugh and spoke: "Ephemeral wretch, begotten by accident and toil, why do you force me to tell you what it would be your greatest boon not to hear? What would be best for you is quite beyond your reach: not to have been born, not to be, to be nothing. But the second best is to die soon."

What is the relation of the Olympian gods to this popular wisdom? It is that of the entranced vision of the martyr to his torment.

Now the Olympian magic mountain opens itself before us, showing us its very roots. The Greeks were keenly aware of the terrors and horrors of existence; in order to be able to live at all they had to place before them the shining fantasy of the Olympians. Their tremendous distrust of the titanic forces of nature: Moira, mercilessly enthroned beyond the knowable world; the vulture which fed upon the great philanthropist Prometheus; the terrible lot drawn by wise Oedipus; the curse on the house of Atreus which brought Orestes to the murder of his mother: that whole Panic philosophy, in short, with its mythic examples, by which the gloomy Etruscans perished, the Greeks conquered--or at least hid from view--again and again by means of this artificial Olympus. In order to live at all the Greeks had to construct these deities. The Apollinian need for beauty had to develop the Olympian hierarchy of joy by slow degrees from the original titanic hierarchy of terror, as roses are seen to break from a thorny thicket. How else could life have been borne by a race so hypersensitive, so emotionally intense, so equipped for suffering? The same drive which called art into being as a completion and consummation of existence, and as a guarantee of further existence, gave rise also to that Olympian realm which acted as a transfiguring mirror to the Hellenic will. The gods justified human life by living it themselves--the only satisfactory theodicy ever invented. To exist in the clear sunlight of such deities was now felt to be the highest good, and the only real grief suffered by Homeric man was inspired by the thought of leaving that sunlight, especially when the departure seemed imminent. Now it became possible to stand the wisdom of Silenus on its head and proclaim that it was the worst evil for man to die soon, and second worst for him to die at all. Such laments as arise now arise over short-lived Achilles, over the generations ephemeral as leaves, the decline of the heroic age. It is not unbecoming to even the greatest hero to yearn for an afterlife, though it be as a day laborer. So impetuously, during the Apollinian phase, does man's will desire to remain on earth, so identified does he become with existence, that even his lament turns to a song of praise.

It should have become apparent by now that the harmony with nature which we late comers regard with such nostalgia, and for which Schiller has coined the cant term naive, is by no means a simple and inevitable condition to be found at the gateway to every culture, a kind of paradise. Such a belief could have been endorsed only by a period for which Rousseau's Emile was an artist and Homer just such an artist nurtured in the bosom of nature. Whenever we encounter "naivete" in art, we are face to face with the ripest fruit of Apollinian culture--which must always triumph first over titans, kill monsters, and overcome the somber contemplation of actuality, the intense susceptibility to suffering, by means of illusions strenuously and zestfully entertained. But how rare are the instances of true naivete, of that complete identification with the beauty of appearance! It is this achievement which makes Homer so magnificent--Homer, who, as a single individual, stood to Apollinian popular culture in the same relation as the individual dream artist to the oneiric capacity of a race and of nature generally. The naivete of Homer must be viewed as a complete victory of Apollinian illusion. Nature often uses illusions of this sort in order to accomplish its secret purposes. The true goal is covered over by a phantasm. We stretch out our hands to the latter, while nature, aided by our deception, attains the former. In the case of the Greeks it was the will wishing to behold itself in the work of art, in the transcendence of genius; but in order so to behold itself its creatures had first to view themselves as glorious, to transpose themselves to a higher sphere, without having that sphere of pure contemplation either challenge them or upbraid them with insufficiency. It was in that sphere of beauty that the Greeks saw the Olympians as their mirror images; it was by means of that aesthetic mirror that the Greek will opposed suffering and the somber wisdom of suffering which always accompanies artistic talent. As a monument to its victory stands Homer, the naive artist.

4

We can learn something about that naive artist through the analogy of dream. We can imagine the dreamer as he calls out to himself, still caught in the illusion of his dream and without disturbing it, "This is a dream, and I want to go on dreaming," and we can infer, on the one hand, that he takes deep delight in the contemplation of his dream, and, on the other, that he must have forgotten the day, with its horrible importunity, so to enjoy his dream. Apollo, the interpreter of dreams, will furnish the clue to what is happening here. Although of the two halves of life--the waking and the dreaming--the former is generally considered not only the more important but the only one which is truly lived, I would, at the risk of sounding paradoxical, propose the opposite view. The more I have come to realize in nature those omnipotent formative tendencies and, with them, an intense longing for illusion, the more I feel inclined to the hypothesis that the original Oneness, the ground of Being, ever suffering and contradictory, time and again has need of rapt vision and delightful illusion to redeem itself. Since we ourselves are the very stuff of such illusions, we must view ourselves as the truly non-existent, that is to say, as a perpetual unfolding in time, space, and causality--what we label "empiric reality." But if, for the moment, we abstract from our own reality, viewing our empiric existence, as well as the existence of the world at large, as the idea of the original Oneness, produced anew each instant, then our dreams will appear to us as illusions of illusions, hence as a still higher form of satisfaction of the original desire for illusion. It is for this reason that the very core of nature takes such a deep delight in the naive artist and the naive work of art, which likewise is merely the illusion of an illusion. Raphael, himself one of those immortal "naive" artists, in a symbolic canvas has illustrated that reduction of illusion to further illusion which is the original act of the naive artist and at the same time of all Apollinian culture. In the lower half of his "Transfiguration," through the figures of the possessed boy, the despairing bearers, the helpless, terrified disciples, we see a reflection of original pain, the sole ground of being: "illusion" here is a reflection of eternal contradiction, begetter of all things. From this illusion there rises, like the fragrance of ambrosia, a new illusory world, invisible to those enmeshed in the first: a radiant vision of pure delight, a rapt seeing through wide open eyes. Here we have, in a great symbol of art, both the fair world of Apollo and its substratum, the terrible wisdom of Silenus, and we can comprehend intuitively how they mutually require one another. But Apollo appears to us once again as the apotheosis of the principium individuationis, in whom the eternal goal of the original Oneness, namely its redemption through illusion, accomplishes itself. With august gesture the god shows us how there is need for a whole world of torment in order for the individual to produce the redemptive vision and to sit quietly in his rocking rowboat in mid sea, absorbed in contemplation.

If this apotheosis of individuation is to be read in normative terms, we may infer that there is one norm only: the individual-- or, more precisely, the observance of the limits of the individual: sophrosune. As a moral deity Apollo demands self-control from his people and, in order to observe such self-control, a knowledge of self. And so we find that the aesthetic necessity of beauty is accompanied by the imperatives, "Know thyself," and "Nothing too much." Conversely, excess and hubris come to be regarded as the hostile spirits of the non-Apollinian sphere, hence as properties of the pre-Apollinian era--the age of Titans -- and the extra-Apollinian world, that is to say the world of the barbarians. It was because of his Titanic love of man that Prometheus had to be devoured by vultures; it was because of his extravagant wisdom which succeeded in solving the riddle of the Sphinx that Oedipus had to be cast into a whirlpool of crime: in this fashion does the Delphic god interpret the Greek past.

The effects of the Dionysian spirit struck the Apollinian Greeks as titanic and barbaric; yet they could not disguise from themselves the fact that they were essentially akin to chose deposed Titans and heroes. They felt more than that: their whole existence, with its temperate beauty, rested upon a base of suffering and knowledge which had been hidden from them until the reinstatement of Dionysus uncovered it once more. And lo and behold! Apollo found it impossible to live without Dionysus. The elements of titanism and barbarism fumed out to be quite as fundamental as the Apollinian element. And now let us imagine how the ecstatic sounds of the Dionysian rites penetrated ever more enticingly into that artificially restrained and discreet world of illusion, how this clamor expressed the whole outrageous gamut of nature--delight, grief, knowledge--even to the most piercing cry; and then let us imagine how the Apollinian artist with his thin, monotonous harp music must have sounded beside the demoniac chant of the multitude! The muses presiding over the illusory arts paled before an art which enthusiastically told the truth, and the wisdom of Silenus cried "Woe!" against the serene Olympians. The individual, with his limits and moderations, forgot himself in the Dionysian vortex and became oblivious to the laws of Apollo. Indiscreet extravagance revealed itself as truth, and contradiction, a delight born of pain, spoke out of the bosom of nature. Wherever the Dionysian voice was heard, the Apollinian norm seemed suspended or destroyed. Yet it is equally true that, in those places where the first assault was withstood, the prestige and majesty of the Delphic god appeared more rigid and threatening than before. The only way I am able to view Doric art and the Doric state is as a perpetual military encampment of the Apollinian forces. An art so defiantly austere, so ringed about with fortifications--an education so military and exacting--a polity so ruthlessly cruel--could endure only in a continual state of resistance against the titanic and barbaric menace of Dionysus.

Up to this point I have developed at some length a theme which was sounded at the beginning of this essay: how the Dionysian and Apollinian elements, in a continuous chain of creations, each enhancing the other, dominated the Hellenic mind; how from the Iron Age, with its battles of Titans and its austere popular philosophy, there developed under the aegis of Apollo the Homeric world of beauty; how this "naive" splendor was then absorbed once more by the Dionysian torrent, and how, face to face with this new power, the Apollinian code rigidified into the majesty of Doric art and contemplation. If the earlier phase of Greek history may justly be broken down into four major artistic epochs dramatizing the battle between the two hostile principles, then we must inquire further (lest Doric art appear to us as the acme and final goal of all these striving tendencies) what was the true end toward which that evolution moved. And our eyes will come to rest on the sublime and much lauded achievement of the dramatic dithyramb and Attic tragedy, as the common goal of both urges; whose mysterious marriage, after long discord, ennobled itself with such a child, at once Antigone and Cassandra.

5

minds, from whom a stream of fire flowed onto the entire later Greek world. Homer, the hoary dreamer, caught in utter abstraction, prototype of the Apollinian naive artist, stares in amazement at the passionate head of Archilochus, soldierly servant of the Muses, knocked about by fortune. All that more recent aesthetics has been able to add by way of interpretation is that here the "objective" artist is confronted by the first "subjective" artist. We find this interpretation of little use, since to us the subjective artist is simply the bad artist, and since we demand above all, in every genre and range of art, a triumph over subjectivity, deliverance from the self, the silencing of every personal will and desire; since, in fact, we cannot imagine the smallest genuine art work lacking objectivity and disinterested contemplation. For this reason our aesthetic must first solve the following problem: how is the lyrical poet at all possible as artist--he who, according to the experience of all times, always says "I" and recites to us the entire chromatic scale of his passions and appetites? It is this Archilochus who most disturbs us, placed there beside Homer, with the stridor of his hate and mockery, the drunken outbursts of his desire. Isn't he--the first artist to be called subjective--for that reason the veritable non-artist? How, then, are we to explain the reverence in which he was held as a poet, the honor done him by the Delphic oracle, that seat of "objective" art, in a number of very curious sayings?

Schiller has thrown some light on his own manner of composition by a psychological observation which seems inexplicable to himself without, however, giving him pause. Schiller confessed that, prior to composing, he experienced not a logically connected series of images but rather a musical mood. "With me emotion is at the beginning without clear and definite ideas; those ideas do not arise until later on. A certain musical disposition of mind comes first, and after follows the poetical idea." If we enlarge on this, taking into account the most important phenomenon of ancient poetry, by which I mean that union-- nay identity--everywhere considered natural, between musician and poet (alongside which our modern poetry appears as the statue of a god without a head), then we may, on the basis of the aesthetics adumbrated earlier, explain the lyrical poet in the following manner. He is, first and foremost, a Dionysian artist, become wholly identified with the original Oneness, its pain and contradiction, and producing a replica of that Oneness as music, if music may legitimately be seen as a repetition of the world; however, this music becomes visible to him again, as in a dream similitude, through the Apollinian dream influence. That reflection, without image or idea, of original pain in music, with its redemption through illusion, now produces a second reflection as a single simile or example. The artist had abrogated his subjectivity earlier, during the Dionysian phase: the image which now reveals to him his oneness with the heart of the world is a dream scene showing forth vividly, together with original pain, the original delight of illusion. The "I" thus sounds out of the depth of being; what recent writers on aesthetics speak of as "subjectivity" is a mere figment. When Archilochus, the first lyric poet of the Greeks, hurls both his frantic love and his contempt at the daughters of Lycambes, it is not his own passion that we see dancing before us in an orgiastic frenzy: we see Dionysus and the maenads, we see the drunken reveler Archilochus, sunk down in sleep--as Euripides describes him for us in the Bacchae, asleep on a high mountain meadow, in the midday sun--and now Apollo approaches him and touches him with his laurel. The sleeper's enchantment through Dionysian music now begins to emit sparks of imagery, poems which, at their point of highest evolution, will bear the name of tragedies and dramatic dithyrambs.

The sculptor, as well as his brother, the epic poet, is committed to the pure contemplation of images. The Dionysian musician, himself imageless, is nothing but original pain and reverberation of the image. Out of this mystical process of un-selving, the poet's spirit feels a whole world of images and similitudes arise, which are quite different in hue, causality, and pace from the images of the sculptor or narrative poet. While the last lives in those images, and only in them, with joyful complacence, and never tires of scanning them down to the most minute features, while even the image of angry Achilles is no more for him than an image whose irate countenance he enjoys with a dreamer's delight in appearance--so that this mirror of appearance protects him from complete fusion with his characters--the lyrical poet, on the other hand, himself becomes his images, his images are objectified versions of himself. Being the active center of that world he may boldly speak in the first person, only his "I" is not that of the actual waking man, but the "I" dwelling, truly and eternally, in the ground of being. It is through the reflections of that "I" that the lyric poet beholds the ground of being. Let us imagine, next, how he views himself too among these reflections--as non-genius, that is, as his own subject matter, the whole teeming crowd of his passions and intentions directed toward a definite goal; and when it now appears as though the poet and the nonpoet joined to him were one, and as though the former were using the pronoun "I," we are able to see through this appearance, which has deceived those who have attached the label "subjective" to the lyrical poet. The man Archilochus, with his passionate loves and hates, is really only a vision of genius, a genius who is no longer merely Archilochus but the genius of the universe, expressing its pain through the similitude of Archilochus the man. Archilochus, on the other hand, the subjectively willing and desiring human being, can never be a poet. Nor is it at all necessary for the poet to see only the phenomenon of the man Archilochus before him as a reflection of Eternal Being: the world of tragedy shows us to what extent the vision of the poet can remove itself from the urgent, immediate phenomenon.

Schopenhauer, who was fully aware of the difficulties the lyrical poet creates for the speculative aesthetician, thought that he had found a solution, which, however, I cannot endorse. It is true that he alone possessed the means, in his profound philosophy of music, for solving this problem; and I think I have honored his achievement in these pages, I hope in his own spirit. Yet in the first part of The World as Will and Idea he characterizes the essence of song as follows: "The consciousness of the singer is filled with the subject of will, which is to say with his own willing. That willing may either be a released, satisfied willing (joy), or, as happens more commonly, an inhibited willing (sadness). In either case there is affect here: passion, violent commotion. At the same time, however, the singer is moved by the contemplation of nature surrounding him to experience himself as the subject of pure, unwilling ideation, and the unshakable tranquillity of that ideation becomes contrasted with the urgency of his willing, its limits, and its lacks. It is the experience of this contrast, or tug of war, which he expresses in his song. While we find ourselves in the lyrical condition, pure ideation approaches us, as it were, to deliver us from the urgencies of willing; we obey, yet obey for moments only. Again and again our willing, our memory of personal objectives, distracts us from tranquil contemplation, while, conversely, the next scene of beauty we behold will yield us up once more to pure ideation. For this reason we find in song and in the lyrical mood a curious mixture of willing (our personal interest in purposes) and pure contemplation (whose subject matter is furnished by our surroundings); relations are sought and imagined between these two sets of experiences. Subjective mood--the affection of the will--communicates its color to the purely viewed surroundings, and vice versa. All authentic song reflects a state of mind mixed and divided in this manner."

Who can fail to perceive in this description that lyric poetry is presented as an art never completely realized, indeed a hybrid whose essence is made to consist in an uneasy mixture of will and contemplation, i.e., the aesthetic and the non-aesthetic conditions. We, on our part, maintain that the distinction between subjective and objective, which even Schopenhauer still uses as a sort of measuring stick to distinguish the arts, has no value whatever in aesthetics; the reason being that the subject--the striving individual bent on furthering his egoistic purposes--can be thought of only as an enemy to art, never as its source. But to the extent that the subject is an artist he is already delivered from individual will and has become a medium through which the True Subject celebrates His redemption in illusion. For better or worse, one thing should be quite obvious to all of us: the entire comedy of art is not played for our own sakes--for our betterment or education, say--nor can we consider ourselves the true originators of that art realm; while on the other hand we have every right to view ourselves as aesthetic projections of the veritable creator and derive such dignity as we possess from our status as art works. Only as an aesthetic product can the world be justified to all eternity--although our consciousness of our own significance does scarcely exceed the consciousness a painted soldier might have of the battle in which he takes part. Thus our whole knowledge of art is at bottom illusory, seeing that as mere knowers we can never be fused with that essential spirit, at the same time creator and spectator, who has prepared the comedy of art for his own edification. Only as the genius in the act of creation merges with the primal architect of the cosmos can he truly know something of the eternal essence of art. For in that condition he resembles the uncanny fairy tale image which is able to see itself by turning its eyes. He is at once subject and object, poet, actor, and audience.

6

Scholarship has discovered in respect of Archilochus that he introduced folk song into literature, and that it was this feat which earned him the unique distinction of being placed beside Homer. Yet what does folk song represent in contrast to epic poetry, which is wholly Apollinian? Surely the classical instance of a union between Apollinian and Dionysian intentions. Its tremendous distribution, as well as its constant proliferation wherever we look, attests the strength of that dual generative motive in nature: a motive which leaves its traces in folk song much the way the orgiastic movements of a nation leave their traces in music. Nor should it be difficult to show by historical evidence that every period which abounded in folk songs has, by the same token, been deeply stirred by Dionysian currents. Those currents have long been considered the necessary substratum, or precondition, of folk poetry.

But first of all we must regard folk song as a musical mirror of the cosmos, as primordial melody casting about for an analogue and finding that analogue eventually in poetry. Since melody precedes all else, it may have to undergo any number of objectifications, such as a variety of texts presents. But it is always, according to the naive estimation of the populace, much superior in importance to those texts. Melody gives birth to poetry again and again: this is implied by the atrophic form of folk song. for a long time I wondered at this phenomenon, until finally the following explanation offered itself. If we examine any collection of folk poetry--for example, Des Knaben Wunderhorn--in this light, we shall find countless examples of

melody generating whole series of images, and those images,
in their varicolored hues, abrupt transitions, and headlong
forward rush, stand in the most marked contrast to the equable
movement, the calm illusion, of epic verse. Viewed from the
standpoint of the epic the uneven and irregular imagery of folk
song becomes quite objectionable. Such must have been the
feeling which the solemn rhapsodists of the Apollinian rites,
during the age of Terpander, entertained with regard to popular
lyric effusions.

In folk poetry we find, moreover, the most intense effort of
language to imitate the condition of music. For this reason
Archilochus may be claimed to have ushered in an entirely new
world of poetry, profoundly at variance with the Homeric; and by
this distinction we have hinted at the only possible relation
between poetry and music, word and sound. Word, image, and
idea, in undergoing the power of music, now seek for a kind of
expression that would parallel it. In this sense we may
distinguish two main currents in the history of Greek verse,
according as language is used to imitate the world of appearance
or that of music. To understand more profoundly the significance
of this distinction, let the reader ponder the utter dissimilarity of
verbal color, syntax and phraseology in the works of Homer and
Pindar. He then cannot fail to conjecture that in the interval there
must have sounded the orgiastic flute notes of Olympus, which,
as late as Aristotle's time, in the midst of an infinitely more
complex music, still rouses men to wild enthusiasm, and which
at their inception must have challenged all contemporaries to
imitate them by every available poetic resource. I wish to
instance in this connection a well-known phenomenon of our
own era which our modish aestheticians consider most
exceptionable. We have noticed again and again how a
Beethoven symphony compels the individual hearers to use
pictorial speech--though it must be granted that a collocation of
these various descriptive sequences might appear rather
checkered, fantastic, even contradictory. Small wonder, then, that
our critics have exercised their feeble wit on these musical
images, or else passed over the phenomenon--surely one worthy
of further investigation--in complete silence. Even in cases where
the composer himself has employed pictorial tags in talking

about his work-- calling one symphony "Pastoral," one movement "Brook Scene" and another "Jolly Concourse of Peasants"--these tropes are properly reducible to purely musical elements rather than standing for actual objects expressed through music. It is true that such musical representations can neither instruct us much concerning the Dionysian content of music nor yet lay claim to any distinctive value as images. But once we study this discharge of music through images in a youthful milieu, among a people whose linguistic creativity is unimpaired, we can form some idea of how atrophic folk song must have arisen and how a nation's entire store of verbal resources might be mobilized by means of that novel principle, imitation of the language of music.

If we are right in viewing lyric poetry as an efflorescence of music in images and ideas, then our next question will be, "How does music manifest itself in that mirror of images and ideas?" It manifests itself as will, using the term in Schopenhauer's sense, that is to say as the opposite of the aesthetic, contemplative, unwilling disposition. At this point it becomes necessary to discriminate very clearly between essence and appearance--for it is obviously impossible for music to represent the essential nature of the will; if it did, we would have to banish it from the realm of art altogether, seeing that the will is the non-aesthetic element par excellence. Rather we should say that music appears as the will. In order to express that appearance through images the lyrical poet must employ the whole register of emotions, from the whisper of love to the roar of frenzy; moved by the urge to talk of music in Apollinian similitudes, he must first comprehend the whole range of nature, including himself, as the eternal source of volition, desire, appetite. But to the extent that he interprets music through images he is dwelling on the still sea of Apollinian contemplation, no matter how turbulently all that he beholds through the musical medium may surge about him. And when he looks at himself through that medium he will discover his own image in a state of turmoil: his own willing and desiring, his groans and jubilations, will all appear to him as a similitude by which music is interpreted. Such is the phenomenon of the lyric poet. Being an Apollinian genius, he interprets music through the image of the will, while he is himself turned into the pure, unshadowed eye of the sun, utterly detached from the will and its greed.

Throughout this inquiry I have maintained the position that lyric poetry is dependent on the spirit of music to the same degree that music itself, in its absolute sovereignty, is independent of either image or concept, though it may tolerate both. The poet cannot tell us anything that was not already contained, with a most universal validity, in such music as prompted him to his figurative discourse. The cosmic symbolism of music resists any adequate treatment by language, for the simple reason that music, in referring to primordial contradiction and pain, symbolizes a sphere which is both earlier than appearance and beyond it. Once we set it over against music, all appearance becomes a mere analogy. So it happens that language, the organ and symbol of appearance, can never succeed in bringing the innermost core of music to the surface. Whenever it engages in the imitation of music, language remains in purely superficial contact with it, and no amount of poetic eloquence will carry us a step closer to the essential secret of that art.

7

At this point we need to call upon every aesthetic principle so far discussed, in order to find our way through the labyrinthine origins of Greek tragedy. I believe I am saying nothing extravagant when I claim that the problem of these origins has never even been posed, much less solved, no matter how often the elusive rags of ancient tradition have been speculatively sewn together and ripped apart That tradition tells us in no uncertain terms that tragedy arose out of the tragic chorus and was, to begin with, nothing but chorus. We are thus bound to scan the chorus closely as the archetypal drama, disregarding the current explanations of it as the idealized spectator, or as representing the populace over against the noble realm of the set. The latter interpretation, which sounds so grandly edifying to certain politicians (as though the democratic Athenians had represented in the popular chorus the invariable moral law, always right in face of the passionate misdeeds and extravagances of kings) may have been suggested by a phrase in Aristotle, but this lofty notion can have had no influence whatever on the original formation of tragedy, whose purely religious origins would exclude not only the opposition between the people and their rulers but any kind of political or social context. Likewise we would consider it blasphemous, in the light of the classical form of the chorus as we know it from Aeschylus and Sophocles, to speak of a "foreshadowing' of constitutional democracy, though others have not stuck at such blasphemy. No ancient polity ever embodied constitutional democracy, and one dares to hope that ancient tragedy did not even foreshadow it.

Much more famous than this political explanation of the chorus is the notion of A. W. Schlegel, who advises us to regard the chorus as the quintessence of the audience, as the "ideal spectator." If we hold this view against the historical tradition according to which tragedy was, in the beginning, nothing but chorus, it turns out to be a crude, unscholarly, though dazzling hypothesis--dazzling because of the effective formulation, the typically German bias for anything called "ideal," and our momentary wonder at the notion. For we are indeed amazed when we compare our familiar theater audience with the tragic chorus and ask ourselves whether the former could conceivably be construed into something analogous to the latter. We tacitly deny the possibility, and then are brought to wonder both at the boldness of Schlegel's assertion and at what must have been the totally different complexion of the Greek audience. We had supposed all along that the spectator, whoever he might be, would always have to remain conscious of the fact that he had before him a work of art, not empiric reality, whereas the tragic chorus of the Greeks is constrained to view the characters enacted on the stage as veritably existing. The chorus of the Oceanides think that they behold the actual Titan Prometheus, and believe themselves every bit as real as the god. Are we seriously to assume that the highest and purest type of spectator is he who, like the Oceanides, regards the god as physically present and real? That it is characteristic of the ideal spectator to rush on stage and deliver the god from his fetters? We had put our faith in an artistic audience, believing that the more intelligent the individual spectator was, the more capable he was of viewing the work of art as art; and now Schlegel's theory suggests to us that the perfect spectator viewed the world of the stage not at all as art but as reality. "Oh these Greeks!" we moan. "They upset our entire aesthetic!" But once we have grown accustomed to it, we repeat Schlegel's pronouncement whenever the question of the chorus comes up.

The emphatic tradition I spoke of militates against Schlegel: chorus as such, without stage--the primitive form of tragedy--is incompatible with that chorus of ideal spectators. What sort of artistic genre would it be that derived from the idea of the spectator and crystallized itself in the mode of the "pure" spectator? A spectator with out drama is an absurdity. We suspect that the birth of tragedy can be explained neither by any reverence for the moral intelligence of the multitude nor by the notion of a spectator without drama, and, altogether, we consider the problem much too complex to be touched by such facile interpretations.

An infinitely more valuable insight into the significance of the chorus was furnished by Schiller in the famous preface to his Bride of Messina, where the chorus is seen as a living wall which tragedy draws about itself in order to achieve insulation from the actual world, to preserve its ideal ground and its poetic freedom.

Schiller used this view as his main weapon against commonplace naturalism, against the illusionistic demand made upon dramatic poetry. While the day of the stage was conceded to be artificial, the architecture of the set symbolic, the metrical discourse stylized, a larger misconception still prevailed. Schiller was not content to have what constitutes the very essence of poetry merely tolerated as poetic license. He insisted that the introduction of the chorus was the decisive step by which any naturalism in art was openly challenged. This way of looking at art seems to me the one which our present age, thinking itself so superior, has labeled pseudo idealism. But I very much fear that we, with our idolatry of verisimilitude, have arrived at the opposite pole of all idealism, the realm of the waxworks. This too betrays a kind of art, as do certain popular novels of today. All I ask is that we not be importuned by the pretense that such art has left Goethe's and Schiller's "pseudo-idealism" behind.

It is certainly true, as Schiller saw, that the Greek chorus of satyrs, the chorus of primitive tragedy, moved on ideal ground, a ground raised high above the common path of mortals. The Greek has built for his chow he scaffolding of a fictive chthonic realm and placed thereon fictive nature spirits. Tragedy developed on this foundation, and so has been exempt since its beginning from the embarrassing task of copying actuality. All the same, the world of tragedy is by no means a world arbitrarily projected between heaven and earth; rather it is a world having the same reality and credibility as Olympus possessed for the devout Greek. The satyr, as the Dionysian chorist, dwells in a reality sanctioned by myth and ritual. That tragedy should begin with him, that the Dionysian wisdom of tragedy should speak through him, is as puzzling a phenomenon as, more generally, the origin of tragedy from the chorus. Perhaps we can gain a starting point for this inquiry by claiming that the satyr, that fictive nature sprite, stands to cultured man in the same relation as Dionysian music does to civilization. Richard Wagner has said of the latter that it is absorbed by music as lamplight by daylight. In the same manner, I believe, the cultured Greek felt himself absorbed into the satyr chorus, and in the next development of Greek tragedy state and society, in fact all that separated man from man, gave way before an overwhelming sense of unity which led back into the heart of nature. The metaphysical solace (with which, I wish to say at once, all true tragedy sends us away) that, despite every phenomenal change life is at bottom indestructibly joyful and powerful, was expressed most concretely in the chorus of satyrs, nature beings who dwell behind all civilization and preserve their identity through every change of generations and historical movement.

With this chorus the profound Greek, so uniquely susceptible to the subtlest and deepest suffering, who had penetrated the destructive agencies of both nature and history, solaced himself. Though he had been in danger of craving a Buddhistic denial of the will, he was saved by art, and through art life reclaimed him.

While the transport of the Dionysian state, with its suspension of all the ordinary barriers of existence, lasts, it carries with it a Lethean element in which everything that has been experienced by the individual is drowned. This chasm of oblivion separates the quotidian reality from the Dionysian. But as soon as that quotidian reality enters consciousness once more it is viewed with loathing, and the consequence is an ascetic, abulic state of mind. In this sense Dionysian man might be said to resemble Hamlet: both have looked deeply into the true nature of things, they have gained knowledge and are now loath to act. They realize that no action of theirs can work any change in the eternal condition of things, and they regard the imputation as ludicrous or debasing that they should set right the time which is out of joint. Knowledge kills action, for in order to act we require the veil of illusion; such is Hamlet's doctrine, not to be confounded with the cheap wisdom of Jack the Dreamer, who through too much reflection, as it were a surplus of possibilities, never arrives at action. What, both in the case of Hamlet and of Dionysian man, overbalances any motive leading to action, is not reflection but knowledge, the apprehension of truth and its terror. Now no comfort any longer avails, desire reaches beyond the transcendental world, beyond the gods themselves, and existence, together with its glittering reflection in the gods and an immortal Beyond, is denied. The truth once seen, man is aware everywhere of the ghastly absurdity of existence, comprehends the symbolism of Ophelia's fate and the wisdom of the wood sprite Silenus: nausea invades him.

Then, in this supreme jeopardy of the will, art, that sorceress expert in healing, approaches him; only she can turn his fits of nausea into imaginations with which it is possible to live. These are on the one hand the spirit of the sublime, which subjugates terror by means of art; on the other hand the comic spirit, which releases us, through art, from the tedium of absurdity. The satyr chorus of the dithyramb was the salvation of Greek art; the threatening paroxysms I have mentioned were contained by the intermediary of those Dionysian attendants.

8

The satyr and the idyllic shepherd of later times have both been products of a desire for naturalness and simplicity. But how firmly the Greek shaped his wood sprite, and how self-consciously and mawkishly the modern dallies with his tender, fluting shepherd! For the Greek the satyr expressed nature in a rude, uncultivated state: he did not, for that reason, confound him with the monkey. Quite the contrary, the satyr was man's true prototype, an expression of his highest and strongest aspirations. He was an enthusiastic reveler, filled with transport by the approach of the god; a compassionate companion re enacting the sufferings of the god; a prophet of wisdom born out of nature's womb; a symbol of the sexual omnipotence of nature, which the Greek was accustomed to view with reverent wonder. The satyr was sublime and divine--so he must have looked to the traumatically wounded vision of Dionysian man. Our tricked out, contrived shepherd would have offended him, but his eyes rested with sublime satisfaction on the open, undistorted limnings of nature. Here archetypal man was cleansed of the illusion of culture, and what revealed itself was authentic man, the bearded satyr jubilantly greeting his god. Before him cultured man dwindled to a false cartoon. Schiller is also correct as regards these beginnings of the tragic art: the chorus is a living wall against the onset of reality because it depicts reality more truthfully and more completely than does civilized man, who ordinarily considers himself the only reality. Poetry does not lie outside the world as a fantastic impossibility begotten of the poet's brain; it seeks to be the exact opposite, an unvarnished expression of truth, and for this reason must cast away the trumpery garments worn by the supposed reality of civilized man. The contrast between this truth of nature and the pretentious lie of civilization is quite similar to that between the eternal core of things and the entire phenomenal world. Even as tragedy, with its metaphysical solace, points to the eternity of true being surviving every phenomenal change, so does the symbolism of the satyr chorus express analogically the primordial relation between the thing in itself and appearance. The idyllic shepherd of modern man is but a replica of the sum of cultural illusions which he mistakes for nature. The Dionysian Greek, desiring truth and nature at their highest power, sees himself metamorphosed into the satyr.

Such are the dispositions and insights of the reveling throng of Dionysus; and the power of these dispositions and insights transforms them in their own eyes, until they behold themselves restored to the condition of genii, of satyrs. Later the tragic chorus came to be an aesthetic imitation of that natural phenomenon; which then necessitated a distinction between Dionysian spectators and votaries actually spellbound by the god. What must be kept in mind in all these investigations is that the audience of Attic tragedy discovered itself in the chorus of the orchestra. Audience and chorus were never fundamentally set over against each other: all was one grand chorus of dancing, singing satyrs, and of those who let themselves be represented by them. This granted, Schlegel's dictum assumes a profounder meaning. The chorus is the "ideal spectator" inasmuch as it is the only seer--seer of the visionary world of the proscenium. An audience of spectators, such as we know it, was unknown to the Greeks. Given the terraced structure of the Greek theater, rising in concentric arcs, each spectator could quite literally survey the entire cultural world about him and imagine himself, in the fullness of seeing, as a chorist. Thus we are enabled to view the chorus of primitive proto-tragedy as the projected image of Dionysian man. The clearest illustration of this phenomenon is the experience of the actor, who, if he is truly gifted, has before his eyes the vivid image of the role he is to play. The satyr chorus is, above all, a vision of the Dionysian multitude, just as the world of the stage is a vision of that satyr chorus--a vision so powerful that it blurs the actors' sense of the "reality" of cultured spectators ranged row on row about him. The structure of the Greek theater reminds us of a lonely mountain valley: the architecture of the stage resembles a luminous cloud configuration which the Bacchae behold as they swarm down from the mountaintops; a marvelous frame in the center of which Dionysus manifests himself to them.

Our scholarly ideas of elementary artistic process are likely to be offended by the primitive events which I have adduced here to explain the tragic chorus. And yet nothing can be more evident than the fact that the poet is poet only insofar as he sees himself surrounded by living acting shapes into whose innermost being he penetrates. It is our peculiar modem weakness to see all primitive aesthetic phenomena in too complicated and abstract a way. Metaphor, for the authentic poet, is not a figure of rhetoric a representative image standing concretely before him in lieu of a concept. A character, to him, is not an assemblage of individual traits laboriously pieced together, but a personage beheld as insistently living before his eyes, differing from the image of the painter only in its capacity to continue living and acting. What is it that makes Homer so much more vivid and concrete in his description than any other poet? His lively eye, with which he discerns so much more. We all talk about poetry so abstractly because we all tend to be indifferent poets. At bottom the aesthetic phenomenon is quite simple: all one needs in order to be a poet is the ability to have a lively action going on before one continually, to live surrounded by hosts of spirits. To be a dramatist all one needs is the urge to transform oneself and speak out of strange bodies and souls.

Dionysian excitation is capable of communicating to a whole multitude this artistic power to feel itself surrounded by, and one with, a host of spirits. What happens in the dramatic chorus is the primary dramatic phenomenon: projecting oneself outside oneself and then acting as though one had really entered another body, another character. This constitutes the first step in the evolution of drama. This art is no longer that of the rhapsodist, who does not merge with his images but, like the painter, contemplates them as something outside himself; what we have here is the individual effacing himself through entering a strange being. It should be made clear that this phenomenon is not singular but epidemic: a whole crowd becomes rapt in this manner. It is for this reason that the dithyramb differs essentially from any other kind of chorus. The virgins who, carrying laurel branches and singing a processional chant, move solemnly toward the temple of Apollo, retain their identities and their civic names. The dithyrambic chorus on the other hand is a chorus of the transformed, who have forgotten their civic past and social rank, who have become timeless servants of their god and live outside all social spheres. While all the other types of Greek choric verse are simply the highest intensification of the Apollinian musician, in the dithyramb we see a community of unconscious actors all of whom see one another as enchanted.

Enchantment is the precondition of all dramatic art. In this enchantment the Dionysian reveler sees himself as satyr, and as satyr, in turn, he sees the god. In his transformation he sees a new vision, which is the Apollinian completion of his state. And by the same token this new vision completes the dramatic act.

Thus we have come to interpret Greek tragedy as a Dionysian chorus which again and again discharges itself in Apollinian images. Those choric portions with which the tragedy is interlaced constitute, as it were, the matrix of the dialogue, that is to say, of the entire stage-world of the actual drama. This substratum of tragedy irradiates, in several consecutive discharges, the vision of the drama--a vision on the one hand completely of the nature of Apollinian dream-illusion and therefore epic, but on the other hand, as the objectification of a Dionysian condition, tending toward the shattering of the individual and his fusion with the original Oneness. Tragedy is an Apollinian embodiment of Dionysian insights and powers, and for that reason separated by a tremendous gulf from the epic.

On this view the chorus of Greek tragedy, symbol of an entire multitude agitated by Dionysus, can be fully explained. Whereas we who are accustomed to the role of the chorus in modem theater, especially opera, find it hard to conceive how the chorus of the Greeks should have been older, more central than the dramatic action proper (although we have clear testimony to this effect) and whereas we have never been quite able to reconcile with this position of importance the fact that the chorus was composed of such lowly beings as--originally--goatlike satyrs; and whereas, further, the orchestra in front of the stage has always seemed a riddle to us--we now realize that the stage with its action was originally conceived as pure vision and that the only reality was the chorus, who created that vision out of itself and proclaimed it through the medium of dance, music, and spoken word. Since, in this vision, the chorus beholds its lord and master Dionysus, it remains forever an attending chorus, it sees how the god suffers and transforms himself, and it has, for that reason, no need to act. But, notwithstanding its subordination to the god, the chorus remains the highest expression of nature, and, like nature, utters in its enthusiasm oracular words of wisdom. Being compassionate as well as wise, it proclaims a truth that issues from the heart of the world. Thus we see how that fantastic and at first sight embarrassing figure arises, the wise and enthusiastic satyr who is at the same time the "simpleton" as opposed to the god. The satyr is a replica of nature in its strongest tendencies and at the same time, a herald of its wisdom and art. He combines in his person the roles of musician, poet, dancer and visionary.

It is in keeping both with this insight and with general tradition that in the earliest tragedy Dionysus was not actually present but merely imagined. Original tragedy is only chorus and not drama at all. Later an attempt was made to demonstrate the god as real and to bring the visionary figure, together with the transfiguring frame, vividly before the eyes of every spectator. This marks the beginning of drama in the strict sense of the word. It then became the task of the dithyrambic chorus so to excite the mood of the listeners that when the tragic hero appeared they would behold not the awkwardly masked man but a figure born of their own rapt vision. If we imagine Admetus brooding on the memory of his recently departed wife, consuming himself in a spiritual contemplation of her form, and how a figure of similar shape and gait is led toward him in deep disguise; if we then imagine his tremor of excitement, his impetuous comparisons, his instinctive conviction--then we have an analogue for the excitement of the spectator beholding the god, with whose sufferings he has already identified himself, stride onto the stage. Instinctively he would project the shape of the god that was magically present to his mind onto that masked figure of a man, dissolving the latter's reality into a ghostly unreality. This is the Apollinian dream state, in which the daylight world is veiled and a new world-- clearer, more comprehensible, more affecting than the first, and at the same time more shadowy--falls upon the eye in ever changing shapes. Thus we may recognize a drastic stylistic opposition: language, color, pace, dynamics of speech are polarized into the Dionysian poetry of the chorus, on the one hand, and the Apollinian dream world of the scene on the other. The result is two completely separate spheres of expression. The Apollinian embodiments in which Dionysus assumes objective shape are very different from the continual interplay of shifting forces in the music of the chorus, from those powers deeply felt by the enthusiast, but which he is incapable of condensing into a clear image. The adept no longer obscurely senses the approach of the god: the god now speaks to him from the proscenium with the clarity and firmness of epic, as an epic hero, almost in the language of Homer.

9

Everything that rises to the surface in the Apollinian portion of Greek tragedy (in the dialogue) looks simple, transparent, beautiful. In this sense the dialogue is a mirror of the Greek mind, whose nature manifests itself in dance, since in dance the maximum power is only potentially present, betraying itself in the suppleness and opulence of movement. The language of the Sophoclean heroes surprises us by its Apollinian determinacy and lucidity. It seems to us that we can fathom their innermost being, and we are somewhat surprised that we had such a short way to go. However, once we abstract from the character of the hero as it rises to the surface and becomes visible (a character at bottom no more than a luminous shape projected onto a dark wall, that is to say, appearance through and through) and instead penetrate into the myth which is projected in these luminous reflections, we suddenly come up against a phenomenon which is the exact opposite of a familiar optical one. After an energetic attempt to focus on the sun we have, by way of remedy almost, dark spots before our eyes when we turn away. Conversely, the luminous images of the Sophoclean heroes--those Apollinian masks--are the necessary productions of a deep look into the horror of nature; luminous spots, as it were, designed to cure an eye hurt by the ghastly night. Only in this way can we form an adequate notion of the seriousness of Greek "serenity"; whereas we find that serenity generally misinterpreted nowadays as a condition of undisturbed complacence.

Sophocles conceived doomed Oedipus the greatest sufferer of the Greek stage, as a pattern of nobility, destined to error and misery despite his wisdom, yet exercising a beneficent influence upon his environment in virtue of his boundless grief. The profound poet tells us that a man who is truly noble is incapable of sin;

though every law, every natural order, indeed the entire canon
of ethics, perish by his actions, those very actions will create a
circle of higher consequences able to found a new world on the
ruins of the old. This is the poet's message, insofar as he is at the
same time a religious thinker. In his capacity as poet he presents
us in the beginning with a complicated legal knot in the slow
unraveling of which the judge brings about his own destruction.
The typically Greek delight in this dialectical solution is so great
that it imparts an element of triumphant serenity to the work, and
thus removes the sting lurking in the ghastly premises of the plot.
In Oedipus at Colonus we meet this same serenity, but utterly
transfigured. In contrast to the aged hero, stricken with excess of
grief and passively undergoing his many misfortunes, we have
here a transcendent serenity issuing from above and hinting that
by his passive endurance the hero may yet gain a consummate
energy of action. This activity (so different from his earlier
conscious striving, which had resulted in pure passivity) will
extend far beyond the limited experience of his own life. Thus
the legal knot of the Oedipus fable, which had seemed to mortal
eyes incapable of being disentangled, is slowly loosened. And we
experience the most profound human joy as we witness this
divine counterpart of dialectics. If this explanation has done the
poet justice, it may yet be asked whether it has exhausted the
implications of the myth; and now we see that the poet's entire
conception was nothing more nor less than the luminous
afterimage which kind nature provides our eyes after a look into
the abyss. Oedipus, his father's murderer, his mother's lover,
solver of the Sphinx's riddle! What is the meaning of this triple
fate? An ancient popular belief, especially strong in Persia, holds
that a wise magus must be incestuously begotten. If we examine
Oedipus, the solver of riddles and liberator of his mother, in the
light of this Parsee belief, we may conclude that wherever
soothsaying and magical powers have broken the spell of present
and future, the rigid law of individuation, the magic circle of
nature, extreme unnaturalness--in this case incest--is the
necessary antecedent; for how should man force nature to yield
up her secrets but by successfully resisting her, that is to say, by
unnatural acts? This is the recognition I find expressed in the
terrible triad of Oedipean fates: the same man who solved the
riddle of nature (the ambiguous Sphinx) must also, as murderer

of his father and husband of his mother, break the consecrated tables of the natural order. It is as though the myth whispered to us that wisdom, and especially Dionysian wisdom, is an unnatural crime, and that whoever, in pride of knowledge, hurls nature into the abyss of destruction, must himself experience nature's disintegration. "The edge of wisdom is turned against the wise man; wisdom is a crime committed on nature": such are the terrible words addressed to us by myth. Yet the Greek poet, like a sunbeam, touches the terrible and austere Memnon's Column of myth, which proceeds to give forth Sophoclean melodies. Now I wish to contrast to the glory of passivity the glory of action, as it irradiates the Prometheus of Aeschylus. Young Goethe has revealed to us, in the bold words his Prometheus addresses to Zeus, what the thinker Aeschylus meant to say, but what, as poet, he merely gave us to divine in symbol:

Here l sit, forming men

in my own image,

a race to be like me,

to suffer, to weep,

to delight and to rejoice,

and to defy you,

as I do.

Man, raised to titanic proportions, conquers his own civilization and compels the gods to join forces with him, since by his autonomous wisdom he commands both their existence and the limitations of their sway. What appears most wonderful, however, in the Prometheus poem--ostensibly a hymn in praise of impiety--is its profound Aeschylean longing for justice. The immense suffering of the bold individual, on the one hand, and on the other the extreme jeopardy of the gods, prefiguring a "twilight of the gods"--the two together pointing to a reconciliation, a merger of their universes of suffering--all this reminds one vividly of the central tenet of Aeschylean speculation in which Moira, as eternal justice, is seen enthroned above men and gods alike. In considering the extraordinary boldness with which Aeschylus places the Olympian world on his scales of justice, we must remember that the profound Greek had an absolutely stable basis of metaphysical thought in his mystery cults and that he was free to discharge all his skeptical velleities on the Olympians. The Greek artist, especially, experienced in--respect of these divinities an obscure sense of mutual dependency, a feeling which has been perfectly symbolized in the Prometheus of Aeschylus. The titanic artist was strong in his defiant belief that he could create men and, at the least, destroy Olympian gods; this he was able to do by virtue of his superior wisdom, which, to be sure, he must atone for by eternal suffering. The glorious power to do, which is possessed by great genius, and for which even eternal suffering is not too high a price to pay--the artist's austere pride--is of the very essence of Aeschylean poetry, while Sophocles in his Oedipus intones a paean to the saint. But even Aeschylus' interpretation of the myth fails to exhaust its extraordinary depth of terror. Once again, we may see the artist's buoyancy and creative joy as a luminous cloud shape reflected upon the dark surface of a lake of sorrow. The legend of Prometheus is indigenous to the entire community of Aryan races and attests to their prevailing talent for profound and tragic vision. In fact, it is not improbable that this myth has the same characteristic importance for the Aryan mind as the myth of the Fall has for the Semitic, and that the two myths are related as brother and sister. The presupposition of the Prometheus myth is primitive man's belief in the supreme value of fire as the true palladium of every rising civilization. But for man to dispose of fire freely, and not receive it as a gift from heaven in the kindling thunderbolt and the warming sunlight, seemed a crime to thoughtful primitive man, a despoiling of divine nature. Thus this original philosophical problem poses at once an insoluble conflict between men and the gods, which lies like a huge boulder at the gateway to every culture. Man's highest good must be bought with a crime and paid for by the flood of grief and suffering which the offended divinities visit upon the human race in its noble ambition. An austere notion, this, which by the dignity it confers on crime presents a strange contrast to the Semitic myth of the Fall--a myth that exhibits curiosity, deception, suggestibility, concupiscence, in short a whole series of principally feminine frailties, as the root of all evil. What distinguishes the Aryan conception is an exalted notion of active sin as the properly Promethean virtue; this notion provides us with the ethical substratum of pessimistic tragedy, which comes to be seen as a justification of human ills, that is to say of human guilt as well as the suffering purchased by that guilt. The tragedy at the heart of things, which the thoughtful Aryan is not disposed to quibble away, the contrariety at the center of the universe, is seen by him as an interpenetration of several worlds, as for instance a divine and a human, each individually in the right but each, as it encroaches upon the other, having to suffer for its individuality. The individual, in the course of his heroic striving towards universality, de-individuation, comes up against that primordial contradiction and learns both to sin and to suffer. The Aryan nations assign to crime the male, the Semites to sin the female gender; and it is quite consistent with these notions that the original act of hubris should be attributed to a man, original sin to a woman. For the rest, perhaps not too much should be made of this distinction, cf. the chorus of wizards in Goethe's Faust:

If that is so, we do not mind it:

With a thousand steps the women find it;

But though they rush, we do not care:

With one big jump the men get there.

[Goethe's Faust, lines 3982-85.]

Once we have comprehended the substance of the Prometheus myth--the imperative necessity of hubris for the titanic individual--we must realize the non-Apollinian character of this pessimistic idea. It is Apollo who tranquilizes the individual by drawing boundary lines, and who, by enjoining again and again the practice of self-knowledge, reminds him of the holy, universal norms. But lest the Apollinian tendency freeze all form into Egyptian rigidity, and in attempting to prescribe its orbit to each particular wave inhibit the movement of the lake, the Dionysian flood tide periodically destroys all the little circles in which the Apollinian will would confine Hellenism. The swiftly rising Dionysian tide then shoulders all the small individual wave crests, even as Prometheus' brother, the Titan Atlas, shouldered the world. This titanic urge to be the Atlas of all individuals, to bear them on broad shoulders ever farther and higher, is the common bond between the Promethean and the Dionysian forces. In this respect the Aeschylean Prometheus appears as a Dionysian mask, while in his deep hunger for justice Aeschylus reveals his paternal descent from Apollo, god of individuation and just boundaries. We may express the Janus face, at once Dionysian and Apollinian, of the Aeschylean Prometheus in the following formula: "All that exists is just and unjust and equally justified in both."

That is your world! A world indeed!-- [Goethe's Faust, line 409.]

10

It is an unimpeachable tradition that in its earliest form Greek tragedy records only the sufferings of Dionysus, and that he was the only actor. But it may be claimed with equal justice that, up to Euripides, Dionysus remains the sole dramatic protagonist and that all the famous characters of the Greek stage, Prometheus, Oedipus, etc., are only masks of that original hero. The fact that a god hides behind all these masks accounts for the much-admired "ideal" character of those celebrated figures. Someone, I can't recall who, has claimed that all individuals, as individuals, are comic, and therefore untragic; which seems to suggest that the Greeks did not tolerate individuals at all on the tragic stage. And in fact they must have felt this way. The Platonic distinction between the idea and the eidolon ["idol"] is deemed rooted in the Greek temperament If we wished to use Plato's terminology we might speak of the tragic characters of the Greek stage somewhat as follows: the one true Dionysus appears in a multiplicity of characters, in the mask of warrior hero, and enmeshed in the web of individual will. The god ascends the stage in the likeness of a striving and suffering individual. That he can appear at all with this clarity and precision is due to dream interpreter Apollo, who projects before the chorus its Dionysian condition in this analogical figure. Yet in truth that hero is the suffering Dionysus of the mysteries. He of whom the wonderful myth relates that as a child he was dismembered by Titans now experiences in his own person the pains of individuation, and in this condition is worshipped as Zagreus. We have here an indication that dismemberment--the truly Dionysian suffering--was like a separation into air, water, earth, and fire, and that individuation should be regarded as the source of all suffering, and rejected. The smile of this Dionysus has given birth to the Olympian gods, his tears have given birth to men. In his existence as a dismembered god, Dionysus shows the double nature of a cruel, savage daemon and a mild, gentle ruler. Every hope of the Eleusinian initiates pointed to a rebirth of Dionysus, which we can now interpret as meaning the end of individuation; the thundering paean of the adepts addressed itself to the coming of the third Dionysus. This hope alone sheds a beam of joy on a ravaged and fragmented world--as is shown by the myth of sorrowing Demeter, who rejoiced only when she was told that she might once again bear Dionysus. In these notions we already find all the components of a profound and mystic philosophy and, by the same token, of the mystery doctrine of tragedy; a recognition that whatever exists is of a piece, and that individuation is the root of all evil; a conception of art as the sanguine hope that the spell of individuation may yet be broken. as an augury of eventual reintegration.

I have said earlier that the Homeric epic was the poetic expression of Olympian culture, its victory song over the terrors of the battle with the Titans. Now, under the overmastering influence of tragic poetry, the Homeric myths were once more transformed and by this metempsychosis proved that in the interim Olympian culture too had been superseded by an even deeper philosophy. The contumacious Titan, Prometheus, now announced to his Olympian tormentor that unless the latter promptly joined forces with him, his reign would be in supreme danger. In the work of Aeschylus we recognize the alliance of the Titan with a frightened Zeus in terror of his end. Thus we find the earlier age of Titans brought back from Tartarus and restored to the light of day. A philosophy of wild, naked nature looks with the bold countenance of truth upon the flitting myths of the Homeric world: they pale and tremble before the lightning eye of this goddess, until the mighty fist of the Dionysian artist forces them into the service of a new divinity. The Dionysian truth appropriates the entire realm of myth as symbolic language for its own insights, which it expresses partly in the public rite of tragedy and partly in the secret celebrations of dramatic mysteries, but always under the old mythic veil. What was the power that rescued Prometheus from his vultures and transformed myth into a vehicle of Dionysian wisdom? It was the Heraclean power of music, which reached its highest form in tragedy and endowed myth with a new and profound significance. Such, as we have said earlier, is the mighty prerogative of music. For it is the lot of every myth to creep gradually into the narrows of supposititious historical fact and to be treated by some later time as a unique event of history. And the Greeks at that time were already well on their way to reinterpreting their childhood dream, cleverly and arbitrarily, into pragmatic childhood history. It is the sure sign of the death of a religion when its mythic presuppositions become systematized, under the severe, rational eyes of an orthodox dogmatism, into a ready sum of historical events, and when people begin timidly defending the veracity of myth but at the same time resist its natural continuance--when the feeling for myth withers and its place is taken by a religion claiming historical foundations. This decaying myth was now seized by the newborn genius of Dionysian music, in whose hands it flowered once more, with new colors and a fragrance that aroused a wistful longing for a metaphysical world. After this last florescence myth declined, its leaves withered, and before long all the ironic Lucians of antiquity caught at the faded blossoms whirled away by the wind. It was through tragedy that myth achieved its profoundest content, its most expressive form; it arose once again like a wounded warrior, its eyes alight with unspent power and the calm wisdom of the dying.

What were you thinking of, overweening Euripides, when you hoped to press myth, then in its last agony, into your service? It died under your violent hands; but you could easily put in its place an imitation that, like Heracles' monkey, would trick itself out in the master's robes. And even as myth, music too died under your hands; though you plundered greedily all the gardens of music, you could achieve no more than a counterfeit. And because you had deserted Dionysus. vou were in turn deserted by Apollo. Though you hunted all the passions up from their couch and conjured them into your circle, though you pointed and burnished a sophistic dialectic for the speeches of your heroes, they have only counterfeit passions and speak counterfeit speeches.

11

Greek tragedy perished in a manner quite different from the older sister arts: it died by suicide, in consequence of an insoluble confiict, while the others died serene and natural deaths at advanced ages. If it is the sign of a happy natural condition to die painlessly, leaving behind a fair progeny, then the decease of those older genres exhibits such a condition; they sank slowly, and their children, fairer than they, stood before their dying eyes, lifting up their heads in eagerness. The death of Greek tragedy, on the other hand, created a tremendous vacuum that was felt far and wide. As the Greek sailors in the time of Tiberius heard from a lonely island the agonizing cry "Great Pan is dead!" so could be heard ringing now through the entire Greek world these painful cries: "Tragedy is dead! And poetry has perished with it! Away with you, puny, spiritless imitators! Away with you to Hades, where you may eat your fill of the crumbs thrown you by former masters!"

When after all a new genre sprang into being which honored tragedy as its parent, the child was seen with dismay to bear indeed the features of its mother, but of its mother during her long death struggle. The death struggle of tragedy had been fought by Euripides, while the later art is known as the New Attic comedy. Tragedy lived on there in a degenerate form, a monument to its painful and laborious death.

In this context we can understand the passionate fondness of the writers of the new comedy for Euripides. Now the wish of

52

Philemon--who was willing to be hanged for the pleasure of visiting Euripides in Hades, providing he could be sure that the dead man was still in possession of his senses--no longer seems strange to us. If one were to attempt to say briefly and merely by way of suggestion what Menander and Philemon had in common with Euripides, and what they found so exemplary and exciting in him, one might say that Euripides succeeded in transporting the spectator onto the stage. Once we realize out of what substance the Promethean dramatists before Euripides had formed their heroes and how far it had been from their thoughts to bring onto the stage a true replica of actuality, we shall see clearly how utterly different were Euripides' intentions. Through him the common man found his way from the auditorium onto the stage. That mirror, which previously had shown only the great and bold features, now took on the kind of accuracy that reflects also the paltry traits of nature. Odysseus, the typical Greek of older art, declined under the hands of the new poets to the character of Graeculus, who henceforth held the center of the stage as the good humored, cunning slave. The merit which Euripides, in Aristophanes' Frogs, attributes to himself, of having by his nostrum rid tragic art of its pompous embonpoint, is apparent in every one of his tragic heroes. Now every spectator could behold his exact counterpart on the Euripidean stage and was delighted to find him so eloquent. But that was not the only pleasure. People themselves learned to speak from Euripides-- don't we hear him boast, in his contest with Aeschylus, that through him the populace had learned to observe, make transactions and form conclusions according to all the rules of art, with the utmost cleverness? It was through this revolution in public discourse that the new comedy became possible. From now on the stock phrases to represent everyday affairs were ready to hand. While hitherto the character of dramatic speech had been determined by the demigod in tragedy and the drunken satyr in comedy, that bourgeois mediocrity in which Euripides placed all his political hopes now came to the fore. And so the Aristophanic Euripides could pride himself on having portrayed life "as it really is" and shown men how to attack it: if now all members of the populace were able to philosophize, plead their cases in court and make their business deals with incredible shrewdness, the merit was really his, the result of that wisdom he had inculcated in them.

The new comedy could now address itself to a prepared, enlightened crowd, for whom Euripides had served as choirmaster--only in this case it was the chorus of spectators who had to be trained. As soon as this chorus had acquired a competence in the Euripidean key, the new comedy--that chesslike species of play--with its constant triumphs of cleverness and cunning, arose. Meanwhile choirmaster Euripides was the object of fulsome praise; in fact, people would have killed themselves in order to learn more from him had they not known that the tragic poets were quite as dead as tragedy itself. With tragedy the Greeks had given up the belief in immortality: not only the belief in an ideal past, but also the belief in an ideal future. The words of the famous epitaph "Inconstant and frivolous in old age" apply equally well to the last phase of Hellenism. Its supreme deities are wit, whim, caprice, the pleasure of the moment. The fifth estate, that of the slaves, comes into its own, at least in point of attitude, and if it is possible at all now to speak of Greek serenity, then it must refer to the serenity of the slave, who has no difficult responsibilities, no high aims, and to whom nothing, past or future, is of greater value than the present. It was this semblance of Greek serenity that so outraged the profound and powerful minds of the first four centuries after Christ. This womanish escape from all seriousness and awe, this smug embracing of easy pleasure, seemed to them not only contemptible but the truly antiChristian frame of mind. It was they who handed on to later generations a picture of Greek antiquity painted entirely in the pale rose hues of serenity--as though there had never been a sixth century with its birth of tragedy, its Mysteries, its Pythagoras and Heracleitus, indeed as though the art works of the great period did not exist at all. And yet none of the latter could, of course, have sprung from the soil of such a trivial ignoble cheer, pointing as they do to an entirely different philosophy as their raison d'etre.

When I said earlier that Euripides had brought the spectator on the stage in order to enable him to judge the play, I may have created the impression that the older drama had all along stood in

a false relation to the spectator; and one might then be tempted
to praise Euripides' radical tendency to establish a proper
relationship between art work and audience as an advance upon
Sophocles. But, after all, audience is but a word, not a constant
unchanging value. Why should an author feel obliged to
accommodate himself to a power whose strength is merely in
numbers? If he considers himself superior in his talent and
intentions to every single spectator, why should he show respect
for the collective expression of all those mediocre capacities
rather than for the few members of the audience who seem
relatively the most gifted? The truth of the matter is that no
Greek artist ever treated his audience with greater audacity and
self sulliciency than Euripides; who at a time when the multitude
lay prostrate before him disavowed in noble defiance and
publicly his own tendencies--those very tendencies by which he
had previously conquered the masses. Had this genius had the
slightest reverence for that band of Bedlamites called the public,
he would have been struck down long before the mid point of his
career by the bludgeon blows of his unsuccess. We come to
realize now that our statement, "Euripides brought the spectator
on the stage"--implying that the spectator would be able
henceforth to exercise competent judgment --was merely
provisional and that we must look for a sounder explanation of
his intentions. It is also generally recognized that Aeschylus and
Sophocles enjoyed all through their lives and longer the full
benefit of popular favor, and that for this reason it would be
absurd to speak in either case of a disproportion between art
work and public reception. What was it, then, that drove the
highly talented and incessantly creative Euripides from a path
bathed in the light of those twin luminaries--his great
predecessors--and of popular acclaim as well? What peculiar
consideration for the spectator made him defy that very same
spectator? How did it happen that his great respect for his
audience made him treat that audience with utter disrespect?

Euripides--and this may be the solution of our riddle-- considered
himself quite superior to the crowd as a whole; not, however, to
two of his spectators. He would translate the crowd onto the
stage but insist, all the same, on revering the two members as the
sole judges of his art; on following all their directions and

admonitions, and on instilling in the very hearts of his dramatic characters those emotions, passions and recognitions which had heretofore seconded the stage action, like an invisible chorus, from the serried ranks of the amphitheater. It was in deference to these judges that he gave his new characters a new voice, too, and a new music. Their votes, and no others, determined for him the worth of his efforts. And whenever the public rejected his labors it was their encouragement, their faith in his final triumph, which sustained him.

One of the two spectators I just spoke of was Euripides himself-- the thinker Euripides, not the poet. Of him it may be said that the extraordinary richness of his critical gift had helped to produce, as in the case of Lessing, an authentic creative offshoot. Endowed with such talent, such remarkable intellectual lucidity and versatility, Euripides watched the performances of his predecessors' plays and tried to rediscover in them those fine lineaments which age, as happens in the case of old paintings, had darkened and almost obliterated. And now something occurred which cannot surprise those among us who are familiar with the deeper secrets of Aeschylean tragedy. Euripides perceived in every line, in every trait, something quite incommensurable: a certain deceptive clarity and, together with it, a mysterious depth, an infinite background. The clearest figure trailed after it a comet's tail which seemed to point to something uncertain, something that could not be wholly elucidated. A similar twilight seemed to invest the very structure of drama, especially the function of the chorus. Then again, how ambiguous did the solutions of all moral problems seem! how problematical the way in which the myths were treated! how irregular the distribution of fortune and misfortune! There was also much in the language of older tragedy that he took exception to, or to say the least, found puzzling: why all this pomp in the representation of simple relationships? why all those tropes and hyperboles, where the characters themselves were simple and straightforward? Euripides sat in the theater pondering, a troubled spectator. In the end he had to admit to himself that he did not understand his great predecessors. But since he looked upon reason as the fountainhead of all doing and enjoying, he had to find out whether anybody shared these notions of his, or whether he was alone in facing up to such incommensurable features. But the multitude, including some of the best individuals, gave him only a smile of distrust; none of them would tell him why, notwithstanding his misgivings and reservations, the great masters were right nonetheless. In this tormented state of mind, Euripides discovered his second spectator--one who did not understand tragedy and for that reason spumed it. Allied with him he could risk coming out of his isolation to fight that tremendous battle against the works of Aeschylus and Sophocles; not by means of polemics, but as a tragic poet determined to make his notion of tragedy prevail over the traditional notions.

12

Before giving a name to that other spectator, let us stop a moment and call to mind what we have said earlier of the incommensurable and discrepant elements in Aeschylean tragedy. Let us recollect how strangely we were affected by the chorus and by the tragic hero of a kind of tragedy which refused to conform to either our habits or our tradition--until, that is, we discovered that the discrepancy was closely bound up with the very origin and essence of Greek tragedy, as the expression of two interacting artistic impulses, the Apollinian and the Dionysian. Euripides' basic intention now becomes as clear as day to us: it is to eliminate from tragedy the primitive and pervasive Dionysian element, and to rebuild the drama on a foundation of non-Dionysian art, custom and philosophy.

Euripides himself, towards the end of his life, propounded the question of the value and sign)ficance of this tendency to his contemporaries in a myth. Has the Dionysian spirit any right at all to exist? Should it not, rather, be brutally uprooted from the Hellenic soil? Yes, it should, the poet tells us, if only it were possible, but the god Dionysus is too powerful: even the most intelligent opponent, like Pentheus in the Bacchae, is unexpectedly enchanted by him, and in his enchantment runs headlong to destruction. The opinion of the two old men in the play--Cadmus and Tiresias--seems to echo the opinion of the aged poet himself: that the cleverest individual cannot by his reasoning overturn an ancient popular tradition like the worship of Dionysus, and that it is the proper part of diplomacy in the face of miraculous powers to make at least a prudent show of sympathy; that it is even possible that the god may still take exception to such tepid interest and--as happened in the case of Cadmus--turn the diplomat into a dragon. We are told this by a poet who all his life had resisted Dionysus heroically, only to end his career with a glorification of his opponent and with suicide-- like a man who throws himself from a tower in order to put an end to the unbearable sensation of vertigo. The Bacchae acknowledges the failure of Euripides' dramatic intentions when, in fact, these had already succeeded: Dionysus had already been driven from the tragic stage by a daemonic power speaking through Euripides. For in a certain sense Euripides was but a mask, while the divinity which spoke through him was neither Dionysus nor Apollo but a brand new daemon called Socrates. Thenceforward the real antagonism was to be between Dionysian spirit and the Socratic, and tragedy was to perish in the conflict. Try as he may to comfort us with his recantation, Euripides fails. The marvelous temple lies in ruins; of what avail is the destroyer's lament that it was the most beautiful of all temples? And though, by way of punishment, Euripides has been turned into a dragon by all later critics, who can really regard this as adequate compensation?

Let us now look more closely at the Socratic tendency by means of which Euripides fought and conquered Aeschylean tragedy. What, under the most auspicious conditions, could Euripides have hoped to effect in founding his tragedy on purely un-Dionysian elements? Once it was no longer begotten by music, in the mysterious Dionysian twilight, what form could drama conceivably take? Only that of the dramatized epic, an Apollinian form which precluded tragic effect. It is not a question here of the events represented. I submit that it would have been impossible for Goethe, in the fifth act of his projected Nausicaa, to render tragic the suicide of that idyllic being: the power of the epic Apollinian spirit is such that it transfigures the most horrible deeds before our eyes by the charm of illusion, and redemption through illusion. The poet who writes dramatized narrative can no more become one with his images than can the epic rhapsodist. He too represents serene, wide eyed contemplation gazing upon its images. The actor in such dramatized epic remains essentially a rhapsodist; the consecration of dream lies upon all his actions and prevents him from ever becoming in the full sense an actor.

But what relationship can be said to obtain between such an ideal Apollinian drama and the plays of Euripides? The same as obtains between the early solemn rhapsodist and that more recent variety described in Plato's Ion: "When I say something sad my eyes fill with tears; if, however, what I say is terrible and ghastly, then my hair stands on end and my heart beats loudly." Here there is no longer any trace of epic self forgetfulness, of the true rhapsodist's cool detachment, who at the highest pitch of action, and especially then, becomes wholly illusion and delight in illusion. Euripides is the actor of the beating heart, with hair standing on end. He lays his dramatic plan as Socratic thinker and carries it out as passionate actor. So it happens that the Euripidean drama is at the same time cool and fiery, able alike to freeze and consume us. It cannot possibly achieve the Apollinian effects of the epic, while on the other hand it has severed all connection with the Dionysian mode; so that in order to have any impact at all it must seek out novel stimulants which are to be found neither in the Apollinian nor in the Dionysian realm. Those stimulants are, on the one hand, cold paradoxical ideas put in the place of Apollinian contemplation, and on the other fiery emotions put in the place of Dionysian transports. These last are splendidly realistic counterfeits, but neither ideas nor affects are infused with the spirit of true art.

Having now recognized that Euripides failed in founding the drama solely on Apollinian elements and that, instead, his anti Dionysian tendency led him towards inartistic naturalism, we are ready to deal with the phenomenon of aesthetic Socratism. Its supreme law may be stated as follows: "Whatever is to be beautiful must also be sensible" --a parallel to the Socratic notion that knowledge alone makes men virtuous. Armed with this canon, Euripides examined every aspect of drama--diction, character, dramatic structure, choral music--and made them fit his specifications. What in Euripidean, as compared with

Sophoclean tragedy, has been so frequently censured as poetic lack and retrogression is actually the straight result of the poet's incisive critical gifts, his audacious personality. The Euripidean prologue may seen to illustrate the efficacy of that rationalistic method. Nothing could be more at odds with our dramaturgic notions than the prologue in the drama of Euripides. To have a character appear at the beginning of the play, tell us who he is, what preceded the action, what has happened so far, even what is about to happen in the course of the play--a modern writer for the theater would reject all this as a wanton and unpardonable dismissal of the element of suspense. Now that everyone knows what is going to happen, who will wait to see it happen? Especially since, in this case, the relation is by no means that of a prophetic dream to a later event. But Euripides reasoned quite otherwise. According to him, the effect of tragedy never resided in epic suspense, in a teasing uncertainty as to what was going to happen next. It resided, rather, in those great scenes of lyrical rhetoric in which the passion and dialectic of the protagonist reached heights of eloquence. Everything portended pathos, not action. Whatever did not portend pathos was seen as objectionable. The greatest obstacle to the spectator's most intimate participation in those scenes would be any missing link in the antecedent action: so long as the spectator had to conjecture what this or that figure represented, from whence arose this or that conflict of inclinations and intentions, he could not fully participate in the doings and sufferings of the protagonists, feel with them and fear with them. The tragedy of Aeschylus and Sophocles had used the subtlest devices to furnish the spectator in the early scenes, and as if by chance, with al} the necessary information. They had shown an admirable skill in disguising the necessary structural features and making them seem accidental. All the same, Euripides thought he noticed chat during those early scenes the spectators were in a peculiar state of unrest--so concerned with figuring out the antecedents of the story chat the beauty and pathos of the exposition were lost on them. For this reason he introduced a prologue even before the exposition, and put it into the mouth of a speaker who would command absolute trust. Very often it was a god who had to guarantee to the public the course of the tragedy and so remove any possible doubt as to the reality of the mydh; exactly as

Descartes could only demonstrate the reality of the empirical world by appealing to God's veracity, his inability to tell a lie. At the end of his drama Euripides required the same divine truthfulness to act as security, so to speak, for the future of his protagonists. This was the function of the ill-famed deus ex machina. Between the preview of the prologue and the preview of the epilogue stretched the dramatic lyric present, the drama proper.

As a poet, then, Euripides was principally concerned with rendering his conscious perceptions, and it is this which gives him his position of importance in the history of Greek drama. With regard to his poetic procedure, which was both critical and creative, he must often have felt that he was applying to drama the opening words of Anaxagoras' treatise: "In the beginning all things were mixed together; then reason came and introduced order." And even as Anaxagoras, with his concept of reason, seems like the first sober philosopher in a company of drunkards, so Euripides may have appeared to himself as the first rational maker of tragedy. Everything was mixed together in a chaotic stew so long as reason, the sole principle of universal order, remained excluded from the creative act. Being of this opinion, Euripides had necessarily to reject his less rational peers. Euripides would never have endorsed Sophocles' statement about Aeschylus--that this poet was doing the right thing, but unconsciously; instead he would have claimed that since Aeschylus created unconsciously he couldn't help doing the wrong cling. Even the divine Plato speaks of the creative power of the poet for the most part ironically and as being on a level with the gifts of the soothsayer and interpreter of dreams, since according to the traditional conception the poet is unable to write until reason and conscious control have deserted him. Euripides set out, as Plato was to do, to show the world the opposite of the "irrational" poet; his aesthetic axiom, "whatever is to be beautiful must be conscious" is strictly parallel to the Socratic "whatever is to be good must be conscious." We can hardly go wrong then in calling Euripides the poet of aesthetic Socratism. But Socrates was precisely that second spectator, incapable of understanding the older tragedy and therefore scorning it, and it was in his company that Euripides dared to usher in a new era of poetic activity. If the old tragedy was wrecked' aesthetic Socratism is to blame, and to the extent that the target of the innovators was the Dionysian principle of the older art we may call Socrates the god's chief opponent, the new Orpheus who, though destined to be torn to pieces by the maenads of Athenian judgment, succeeded in putting the overmastering god to flight. The latter, as before, when he fled from Lycurgus, king of the Edoni, took refuge in the depths of the sea; that is to say, in the flood of a mystery cult that was soon to encompass the world.

13

The fact that the aims of Socrates and Euripides were closely allied did not escape the attention of their contemporaries. We have an eloquent illustration of this in the rumotr, current at the time in Athens, that Socrates was helping Euripides with his writing. The two names were bracketed by the partisans of the "good old days'? whenever it was a question of castigating the upstart demagogues of the present. It was they who were blamed for the disappearance of the Marathonian soundness of body and mind in favor of a dubious enlightenment tending toward a progressive atrophy of the traditional virtues. In the comedy of Aristophanes both men are treated in this vein--half indignant, half contemptuous--to the dismay of the rising generation, who, while they were willing enough to sacrifice Euripides, could not forgive the picture of Socrates as the arch Sophist. Their only recourse was to pillory Aristophanes in his turn as a dissolute, Lying Alcibiades of poetry. I won't pause here to defend the pro found instincts of Aristophanes against such attacks but shall proceed to demonstrate the close affinity between Socrates and Euripides, as their contemporaries saw them. It is certainly significant in this connection that Socrates, being a sworn enemy of the tragic art, is said never to have attended the theater except when a new play of Euripides was mounted. The most famous instance of ι conjunction of the two names, however, is found in the Delphic oracle which pronounced Socrates the wisest of men yet allowed that Euripides merited the second place. The third place went to Sophocles, who had boasted that, in contrast to Aeschylus, he not only did the right thing but knew why he did it. Evidently it was the transparency of their knowledge that earned for these three men the reputation of true wisdom in their day.

It was Socrates who expressed most clearly this radically new prestige of knowledge and conscious intelligence when he claimed to be the only one who acknowledged to himself that he knew nothing. He roamed all over Athens, visiting the most distinguished statesmen, orators, poets and artists, and found everywhere merely the presumption of knowledge. He was amazed to discover that all these celebrities lacked true and certain knowledge of their callings and pursued those callings by sheer instinct. The expression "sheer instinct" seems to focus perfectly the Socratic attitude. From this point of view Socrates was forced to condemn both the prevailing art and the prevailing ethics. Wherever his penetrating gaze fell he saw nothing but lack of understanding, fictions rampant, and so was led to deduce a state of affairs wholly discreditable and perverse. Socrates believed it was his mission to correct the situation: a solitary man, arrogantly superior and herald of a radically dissimilar culture, art, and ethics, he stepped into a world whose least hem we should have counted it an honor to have touched. This is the reason why the figure of Socrates disturbs us so profoundly whenever we approach it, and why we are tempted again and again to plumb the meaning and intentions of the most problematical character among the ancients. Who was this man who dared, singlehanded, to challenge the entire world of Hellenism--embodied in Homer, Pindar, and Aeschylus, in Phidias, Pericles, Pythia, and Dionysus--which commands our highest reverence? Who was this daemon daring to pour out the magic philter in the dust? this demigod to whom the noblest spirits of mankind must call out:

Alas!

You have shattered

The beautiful world

With brazen fist;

It falls, it is scattered.

[Goethe's Faust, lines 1607-11.]

We are offered a key to the mind of Socrates in that remarkable phenomenon known as his daimonion. In certain critical situations, when even his massive intellect faltered, he was able to regain his balance through the agency of a divine voice, which he heard only at such moments. The voice always spoke to dissuade. The instinctual wisdom of this anomalous character manifests itself from time to time as a purely inhibitory agent, ready to defy his rational judgment. Whereas in all truly productive men instinct is the strong, affirmative force and reason the dissuader and critic, in the case of Socrates the roles are reversed: instinct is the critic, consciousness the creator. Truly a monstrosity! Because of this lack of every mystical talent Socrates emerges as the perfect pattern of the non-mystic, in whom the logical side has become, through superfetation, as overdeveloped as has the instinctual side in the mystic. Yet it was entirely impossible for Socrates' logical impetus to turn against itself. In its unrestrained onrush it exhibited an elemental power such as is commonly found only in men of violent instincts, where we view it with awed surprise. Whoever in reading Plato has experienced the divine directness and sureness of Socrates' whole way of proceeding must have a sense of the gigantic driving wheel of logical Socratism, turning, as it were, behind Socrates, which we see through Socrates as through a shadow. That he himself was by no means unaware of this relationship appears from the grave dignity with which he stressed, even at the end and before his judges, his divine mission. It is as impossible to controvert him in this as it is to approve of his corrosive influence upon instinctual life. In this dilemma his accusers, when he was brought before the Athenian forum, could think of one appropriate form of punishment only, namely exile: to turn this wholly unclassifiable, mysterious phenomenon out of the state would have given posterity no cause to charge the Athenians with a disgraceful act. When finally death, not banishment, was pronounced against him, it seems to have been Socrates himself who, with complete lucidity of mind and in the absence of every natural fear of death, insisted on it.

He went to his death with the same calm Plato describes when he has him leave the symposium in the early dawn, the last reveler, to begin a new day; while behind him on the benches and on the floor his sleepy companions go on dreaming of Socrates, the true lover. Socrates in his death became the idol of the young Athenian elite. The typical Hellenic youth, Plato, prostrated himself before that image with all the fervent devotion of his enthusiastic mind.

14

Let us now imagine Socrates' great Cyclops' eye--that eye which never glowed with the artist's divine frenzy--turned upon tragedy. Bearing in mind that he was unable to look with any pleasure into the Dionysian abysses, what could Socrates see in that tragic art which to Plato seemed noble and meritorious? Something quite abstruse and irrational, full of causes without effects and effects seemingly without causes, the whole texture so checkered that it must be repugnant to a sober disposition, while it might act as dangerous tinder to a sensitive and impressionable mind. We are told that the only genre of poetry Socrates really appreciated was the Aesopian fable. This he did with the same smiling complaisance with which honest Gellert sings the praise of poetry in his fable of the bee and the hen:

Poems are useful: they can tell

The truth by means of parable

To those who are not very bright.

The fact is that for Socrates tragic art failed even to "convey the truth," although it did address itself to those who were "a bit backward," which is to say to non-philosophers: a double reason for leaving it alone. Like Plato, he reckoned it among the beguiling arts which represent the agreeable, not the useful, and in consequence exhorted his followers to abstain from such unphilosophical stimulants. His success was such that the young tragic poet Plato burned all his writings in order to qualify as a student of Socrates. And while strong native genius might now and again manage to withstand the Socratic injunction, the power of the latter was still great enough to force poetry into entirely new channels.

A good example of this is Plato himself. Although he did not lag behind the naive cynicism of his master in the condemnation of tragedy and of art in general, nevertheless his creative gifts forced him to develop an art form deeply akin to the existing forms which he had repudiated. The main objection raised by Plato to the older art (that it was the imitation of an imitation and hence belonged to an even lower order of empiric reality) must not, at all costs, apply to the new genre; and so we see Plato intent on moving beyond reality and on rendering the idea which underlies it. By a detour Plato the thinker reached the very spot where Plato the poet had all along been at home, and from which Sophocles, and with him the whole poetic tradition of the past, protested such a charge. Tragedy had assimilated to itself all the older poetic genres. In a somewhat eccentric sense the same thing can be claimed for the Platonic dialogue, which was a mixture of all the available styles and forms and hovered between narrative, Iyric, drama, between prose and poetry, once again breaking through the old law of stylistic unity. The Cynic philosophers went even farther in that direction, seeking, by their utterly promiscuous style and constant alternation between verse and prose, to project their image of the "raving Socrates" in literature, as they sought to enact it in life. The Platonic dialogue was the lifeboat in which the shipwrecked older poetry saved itself, together with its numerous offspring. Crowded together in a narrow space, and timidly obeying their helmsman Socrates, they moved forward into a new era which never tired of looking at this fantastic spectacle. Plato has furnished for all posterity the pattern of a new art form, the novel, viewed as the Aesopian fable raised to its highest power; a form in which poetry played the same subordinate role with regard to dialectic philosophy as that same philosophy was to play for many centuries with regard to theology. This, then, was the new status of poetry, and it was Plato who, under the pressure of daemonic Socrates, had brought it about.

It is at this point that philosophical ideas begin to entwine themselves about art, forcing the latter to cling closely to the trunk of dialectic. The Apollinian tendency now appears disguised as logical schematism, just as we found in the case of Euripides a corresponding translation of the Dionysian affect into a naturalistic one. Socrates, the dialectical hero of the Platonic drama, shows a close affinity to the Euripidean hero, who is compelled to justify his actions by proof and counterproof, and for that reason is often in danger of forfeiting our tragic compassion. For who among us can close his eyes to the optimistic element in the nature of dialectics, which sees a triumph in every syllogism and can breathe only in an atmosphere of cool, conscious clarity? Once that optimistic element had entered tragedy, it overgrew its Dionysian regions and brought about their annihilation and, finally, the leap into genteel domestic drama Consider the consequences of the Socratic maxims: virtue is knowledge; all sins arise from ignorance; only the virtuous are happy"--these three basic formulations of optimism spell the death of tragedy. The virtuous hero must henceforth be a dialectician; virtue and knowledge, belief and ethics, be necessarily and demonstrably connected; Aeschylus' transcendental concept of justice be reduced to the brash and shallow principle of poetic justice with its regular deus ex machina.

What is the view taken of the chorus in this new Socratic optimistic stage world, and of the entire musical and Dionysian foundation of tragedy? They are seen as accidental features, as reminders of the origin of tragedy, which can well be dispensed with--while we have in fact come to understand that the chorus is the cause of tragedy and the tragic spirit. Already in Sophocles we find some embarrassment with regard to the chorus, which suggests that the Dionysian floor of tragedy is beginning to give way. Sophocles no longer dares to give the chorus the major role in the tragedy but treats it as almost on the same footing as the actors, as though it had been raised from the orchestra onto the scene. By so doing he necessarily destroyed its meaning, despite Aristotle's endorsement of this conception of the chorus. This shift in attitude, which Sophocles displayed not only in practice but also, we are told, in theory, was the first step toward the total disintegration of the chorus: a process whose rapid phases we can follow in Euripides, Agathon, and the New Comedy. Optimistic dialectics took up the whip of its syllogisms and drove music out of tragedy. It entirely destroyed the meaning of tragedy--which can be interpreted only as a concrete manifestation of Dionysian conditions, music made visible, an ecstatic dream world.

Since we have discovered an anti-Dionysian tendency antedating Socrates, its most brilliant exponent, we must now ask, "Toward what does a figure like Socrates point?" Faced with the evidence of the Platonic dialogues, we are certainly not entitled to see in Socrates merely an agent of disintegration. While it is clear that the immediate result of the Socratic strategy was the destruction of Dionysian drama, we are forced, nevertheless, by the profundity of the Socratic experience to ask ourselves whether, in fact, art and Socratism are diametrically opposed to one another, whether there is really anything inherently impossible in the idea of a Socratic artist?

It appears that this despotic logician had from time to time a sense of void, loss, unfulfilled duty with regard to art. In prison he told his friends how, on several occasions, a voice had spoken to him in a dream, saying "Practice music, Socrates!" Almost to the end he remained confident that his philosophy represented the highest art of the muses, and would not fully believe that a divinity meant to remind him of "common, popular music." Yet in order to unburden his conscience he finally agreed, in prison, to undertake that music which hitherto he had held in low esteem. In this frame of mind he composed a poem on Apollo and rendered several Aesopian fables in verse. What prompted him to these exercises was something very similar to that warning voice of his daimonion: an Apollinian perception that, like a barbarian king, he had failed to comprehend the nature of a divine effigy, and was in danger of offending his own god through ignorance. These words heard by Socrates in his dream are the only indication that he ever experienced any uneasiness about the limits of his logical universe. He may have asked himself: "Have I been too ready to view what was unintelligible to me as being devoid of meaning? Perhaps there is a realm of wisdom, after all, from which the logician is excluded? Perhaps art must be seen as the necessary complement of rational discourse?"

15

In the spirit of these last suggestive questions it must now be said how the influence of Socrates, down to the present moment and even into all future time, has spread over posterity like a shadow that keeps growing in the evening sun, and how it again and again prompts a regeneration of art--of art in the metaphysical, broadest and profoundest sense--and how its own infinity also guarantees the infinity of art.

Before this could be recognized, before the innermost dependence of every art on the Greeks, from Homer to Socrates, was demonstrated conclusively, we had to feel about these Greeks as the Athenians felt about Socrates. Nearly every age and stage of culture has at some time or other sought with profound irritation to free itself from the Greeks, because in their presence everything one has achieved oneself, though apparently quite original and sincerely admired, suddenly seemed to lose life and color and shriveled into a poor copy, even a caricature. And so time after time cordial anger erupts against this presumptuous little people that made bold for all time to designate everything not native as "barbaric." Who are they, one asks, who, though they display only an ephemeral historical splendor, ridiculously restricted institutions, dubious excellence in their mores, and are marked by ugly vices, yet lay claim to that dignity and pre-eminence among peoples which characterize genius among the masses? Unfortunately, no one was lucky enough to find the cup of hemlock with which one could simply dispose of such a character; for all the poison that envy, calumny, and rancor created did not suffice to destroy that self-sufficient splendor. And so one feels ashamed and afraid in the presence of the Greeks, unless one prizes truth above all things and dares acknowledge even this truth: that the Greeks, as charioteers, hold in their hands the reins of our own and every other culture, but that almost always chariot and horses are of inferior quality and not up to the glory of their leaders, who consider it sport to run such a team into an abyss which they themselves clear with the leap of Achilles.

In order to vindicate the dignity of such a leader's position for Socrates, too, it is enough to recognize in him a type of existence unheard of before him: the type of he theoretical man whose significance and aim it is our next task to try to understand. Like the artist, the theoretical man finds an infinite delight in whatever exists, and this satisfaction protects him against the practical ethics of pessimism with its Lyncaeus eyes that shine only in the dark. Whenever the truth is uncovered, the artist will always cling with rapt gaze to what still remains covering even after such uncovering; but the theoretical man enjoys and finds satisfaction in the discarded covering and finds the highest object of his pleasure in the process of an ever happy uncovering that succeeds through his own efforts.

There would be no science if it were concerned only with that one nude goddess and with nothing else. For in that case her devotees would have to feel like men who wanted to dig a hole straight through the earth, assuming that each of them realized that even if he tried his utmost, his whole life long, he would only be able to dig a very small portion of this enormous depth, and even that would be filled in again before his own eyes by the labors of the next in line, so a third person would seem to do well if he picked a new spot for his drilling efforts. Now suppose someone proved convincingly that the goal of the antipodes cannot be reached in this direct manner: who would still wish to go on working in these old depths, unless he had learned meanwhile to be satisfied with finding precious stones or discovering laws of nature?

Therefore Lessing, the most honest theoretical man, dared to announce that he cared more for the search after truth than for truth itself--and thus revealed the fundamental secret of science, to the astonishment, and indeed the anger, of the scientific community. ["If God had locked up all truth in his right hand, and in his left the unique, ever-live striving for truth, albeit with the addition that I should always and eternally err, and he said to me, 'Choose!'--I should humbly clasp his left hand, saying:

'Father, give! Pure truth is after all for thee alone!'"--Gotthold Ephraim Lessing (1729-81), Eine Duplik, 1778.] Beside this isolated insight, born of an excess of honesty if not of exuberance, there is, to be sure, a profound illusion that first saw the light of the world in the person of Socrates: the unshakable faith that thought, using the thread of logic, can penetrate the deepest abysses of being, and that thought is capable not only of knowing being but even of correcting it. This sublime metaphysical illusion accompanies science as an instinct and leads science again and again to its limits at which it must turn into art--which is really the aim of this mechanism.

With the torch of this thought in our hands, let us now look at Socrates: he appears to us as the first who could not only live, guided by the instinct of science, but also--and this is far more-- die that way. Hence the image of the dying Socrates, as the human being whom knowledge and reasons have liberated from the fear of death, is the emblem that, above the entrance gate of science, reminds all of its mission--namely, to make existence appear comprehensible and thus justified; and if reasons do not suffice, myth had to come to their aid in the end--myth which I have just called the necessary consequence, indeed the purpose, of science.

Once we see clearly how after Socrates, the mystagogue of science, one philosophical school succeeds another, wave upon wave; how the hunger for knowledge reached a never-suspected universality in the widest domain of the educated world, became the real task for every person of higher gifts, and led science onto the high seas from which it has never again been driven altogether; how this universality first spread a common net of thought over the whole globe, actually holding out the prospect of the lawfulness of an entire solar system; once we see all this clearly, along with the amazingly high pyramid of knowledge in our own time--we cannot fail to see in Socrates the one turning point and vortex of so-called world history. For if we imagine that the whole incalculable sum of energy used up for this world tendency had been used not in the service of knowledge but for the practical, i.e., egoistic aims of individuals and peoples, then we realize that in that case universal wars of annihilation and continual migrations of peoples would probably have weakened the instinctive lust for life to such an extent that suicide would have become a general custom and individuals might have experienced the final remnant of a sense of duty when, like the inhabitants of the Fiji islands, they had strangled their parents and friends--a practical pessimism that might even have generated a gruesome ethic of genocide [Volkermord.] motivated by pity, and which incidentally is, and was, present in the world wherever art did not appear in some form--especially as religion and science--as a remedy and a preventive for this breath of pestilence.

By contrast with this practical pessimism, Socrates is the prototype of the theoretical optimist who, with his faith that the nature of things can be fathomed, ascribes to knowledge and insight the power of a panacea, while understanding error as the evil par excellence. To fathom the depths and to separate true knowledge from appearance and error, seemed to Socratic man the noblest, even the only truly human vocation. And since Socrates, this mechanism of concepts, judgments, and inferences has been esteemed as the highest occupation and the most admirable gift of nature, above all other capacities. Even the most sublime ethical deeds, the stirrings of pity, self-sacrifice, heroism, and that calm sea of the soul, so difficult to attain, which the Apollinian Greek called sophrosune, were derived from the dialectic knowledge by Socrates and his like-minded successors, down to the present, and accordingly designated as teachable.

Anyone who has ever experienced the pleasure of Socratic insight and felt how, spreading in ever-widening circles, it seeks to embrace the whole world of appearances, will never again find any stimulus toward existence more violent than the craving to complete this conquest and to weave the net impenetrably tight. To one who feels that way, the Platonic Socrates will appear as the teacher of an altogether new form of "Greek cheerfulness" and blissful affirmation of existence that seeks to discharge itself in actions--most often in maieutic and educational influences on noble youths, with a view to eventually producing a genius.

But science, spurred by its powerful illusion, speeds irresistibly towards its limits where its optimism, concealed in the essence of logic, suffers shipwreck. For the periphery of the circle of science has an infinite number of points; and while there is no telling how this circle could ever be surveyed completely, noble and gifted men nevertheless reach, e'er half their time and inevitably, such boundary points on the periphery from which one gazes into what defies illumination. When they see to their horror how logic coils up at these boundaries and finally bites its own tail--suddenly the new form of insight breaks through, tragic insight which, merely to be endured, needs art as a protection and remedy.

Our eyes strengthened and refreshed by our contemplation of the Greeks, let us look at the highest spheres of the world around us; then we shall see how the hunger for insatiable and optimistic knowledge that in Socrates appears exemplary has turned into tragic resignation and destitute need for art--while, to be sure, the same hunger on its lower levels can express itself in hostility to art and must particularly detest Dionysian-tragic art, as was illustrated earlier with the fight of Socratism against Aeschylean tragedy.

Here we knock, deeply moved, at the gates of present and future: will this "turning" lead to ever-new configurations of genius and especially of the Socrates who practices music? Will the net of art, even if it is called religion or science, that is spread over existence be woven even more tightly and delicately, or is it destined to be torn to shreds in the restless, barbarous, chaotic whirl that now calls itself "the present"?

Concerned but not disconsolate, we stand aside a little while, contemplative men to whom it has been granted to be witnesses of these tremendous struggles and transitions. Alas, it is the magic of these struggles that those who behold them must also take part and fight.

By this elaborate historical example we have sought to make
clear how just as tragedy perishes with the evanescence of the
spirit of music, it is only from this spirit that it can be reborn.
Lest this assertion seem too strange, it may be well to disclose
the origin of this insight by considering the analogous
phenomena of our own time; we must enter into the midst of
those struggles, which, as I have just said, are being waged in the
highest spheres of our contemporary world between insatiable
optimistic knowledge and the tragic need of art. In my
examination I shall leave out of account all those other
antagonistic tendencies which at all times oppose art, especially
tragedy, and which now are again extending their triumphant
sway to such an extent that of the theatrical arts only the farce
and the ballet, for example, put forth their blossoms, which
perhaps not everyone cares to smell, in rather rich luxuriance. I
will speak only of the noblest opposition to the tragic world-
conception--and by this I mean science, which is at bottom
optimistic, with its ancestor Socrates at its head. A little later on I
shall also name those forces which seem to me to guarantee a
rebirth of tragedy--and perhaps other blessed hopes for the
German genius!

Before we plunge into the midst of these struggles, let us array
ourselves in the armor of the insights we have acquired. In
contrast to all those who are intent on deriving the arts from one
exclusive principle, as the necessary vital source of every work
of art, I shall keep my eyes fixed on the two artistic deities of the
Greeks, Apollo and Dionysus, and recognize in them the living
and conspicuous representatives of two worlds of art differing in
their intrinsic essence and in their highest aims. I see Apollo as
the transfiguring genius of the principium individuationis
through which alone the redemption in illusion is truly to be
obtained; while by the mystical triumphant cry of Dionysus the
spell of individuation is broken, and the way lies open to the
Mothers of Being, to the innermost heart of things. This
extraordinary contrast, which stretches like a yawning gulf
between plastic art as the Apollinian, and music as the Dionysian
art, has revealed itself to only one of the great thinkers, to such
an extent that, even without this clue to the symbolism of the
Hellenic divinities, he concedes to music a character and an

origin different from all the other arts, because, unlike them, it
is not a copy of the phenomenon, but an immediate copy of the
will itself, and therefore complements everything physical in the
world and every phenomenon by representing what is
metaphysical, the thing in itself. (Schopenhauer, Welt als Wille
und Vorstellung, I, p. 310.)

To this most important insight of aesthetics (with which, in the
most serious sense, aesthetics properly begins), Richard Wagner,
by way of confirmation of its eternal truth, affixed his seal, when
he asserted in his Beethoven that music must be evaluated
according to aesthetic principles quite different form those which
apply to all plastic arts, and not, in general, according to the
category of beauty; although an erroneous aesthetics, inspired by
a mistaken and degenerate art, has, by virtue of the concept of
beauty obtaining in the plastic domain, accustomed itself to
demand of music an effect similar to that produced by works of
plastic art, namely, the arousing of delight in beautiful forms.
Having recognized this extraordinary contrast, I felt a strong
need to approach the essence of Greek tragedy and, with it, the
profoundest revelation of the Hellenic genius; for I at last
thought that I possessed a charm to enable me--far beyond the
phraseology of our usual aesthetics--to represent vividly to my
mind the fundamental problem of tragedy; whereby I was
granted such a surprising and unusual insight into the Hellenic
character that it necessarily seemed to me as if our classical-
Hellenic science that bears itself so proudly had thus far
contrived to subsist mainly on shadow plays and externals.

Perhaps we may touch on this fundamental problem by asking:
what aesthetic effect results when the essentially separate art-
forces, the Apollinian and the Dionysian, enter into simultaneous
activity? Or more briefly: how is music related to image and
concept? Schopenhauer, whom Richard Wagner, with special
reference to this point, praises for an unsurpassable clearness and
clarity of exposition, expresses himself most thoroughly on the
subject in the following passage which I shall cite here at full
length (Welt als Wille und Vorstellung, I, p. 309): "according to
all this, we may regard the phenomenal world, or nature, and
music as two different expressions of the same thing, which is

therefore itself the only medium of their analogy, so that a knowledge of it is demanded in order to understand that analogy. Music, therefore, if regarded as an expression of the world, is in the highest degree a universal language, which is related indeed to the universality of concepts, much as they are related to the particular things. Its, universality, however, is by no means that empty universality of abstraction, but of quite a different kind, and is united with thorough and distinct definiteness. In this respect it resembles geometrical figures and numbers, which are the universal forms of all possible objects of experience and applicable to them all a priori, and yet are not abstract but perceptible and thoroughly determinate. All possible efforts, excitements, and manifestations of will, all that goes on in the heart of man and that reason includes in the wide, negative concept of feeling, may be expressed by the infinite number of possible melodies, but always in the universal, in the mere form, without the material, always according to the thing-in-itself, not the phenomenon, the inmost soul, as it were, of the phenomenon without the body. This deep relation which music has to the true nature of all things also explains the fact that suitable music played to any scene, action, event, or surrounding seems to disclose to us its utmost secret meaning, and appears as the most accurate and distinct commentary upon it. This is so truly the case that whoever gives himself up entirely to the impression of a symphony, seems to see all the possible events of life and the world take place in himself; yet if he reflects, he can find no likeness between the music and the things that passed before his mind. For, as we have said, music is distinguished from all the other arts by the fact that it is not a copy of the phenomenon, or, more accurately, of the adequate objectivity of the will, but an immediate copy of the will itself, and therefore complements everything physical in the world and every phenomenon by representing what is metaphysical, the thing in itself. We might, therefore, just as well call the world embodied music as embodied will; and this is the reason why music makes every painting, and indeed every scene of real life and of the world, at once appear with higher significance, certainly all the more, in proportion as its melody is analogous to the inner spirit of the given phenomenon. Therefore we are able to set a poem to music as a song, or a visible representation as a pantomime, or both as an opera. Such particular pictures of human life, set to the universal language of music, are never bound to it or correspond to it with a stringent necessity; but they stand to it only in the relation of an example chosen at will to a general concept. In the determinateness of the real, they represent that which music expresses in the universality of mere form. For melodies are to a certain extent, like general concepts, an abstraction from the actual. This actual world, then, the world of particular things, affords the object of perception, the special and individual, the particular case, both to the universality of the concepts and to the universality of the melodies. But these two universalities are in a certain respect opposed to each other; for the concepts contain particulars only as the first forms abstracted from perception, as it were, the separated shell of things; thus they are, strictly speaking, abstracta: music, on the other hand, gives the inmost kernel which precedes all forms, or the heart of things. This relation may be very well expressed in the language of the schoolmen, by saying, the concepts are the universalia post rem, but music gives the univesralia ante rem, and the real world the universalia in re. But that in general a relation is possible between a composition and a visible representation rests, as we have said, upon the fact that both are simply different expressions of the same inner being of the world. When now, in the particular case, such a relation is actually given, that is to say, when the composer has been able to express in the universal language of music the stirrings of will which constitute the heart of an event, then the melody of the song, the music of the opera, is expressive. But the analogy discovered by the composer between the two must have proceeded from the direct knowledge of the nature of the world unknown to his reason, and must not be an imitation produced with conscious intention by means of concepts, otherwise the music does not express the inner nature, the will itself, but merely gives an inadequate imitation of its phenomenon. All truly imitative music does this."

According to the doctrine of Schopenhauer, therefore, we understand music as the immediate language of the will, and we feel our fancy stimulated to give form to this invisible and yet so actively stirred spirit-world which speaks to us, and we feel prompted to embody it in an analogous example. On the other hand, image and concept, under the influence of a truly corresponding music, acquires a higher significance. Dionysian art therefore is wont to exercise two kinds of influences on the Apollinian art faculty: music incites to the symbolic intuition of Dionysian universality, and music allows the symbolic image to emerge in its highest significance. From these facts, intelligible in themselves and not inaccessible to a more penetrating examination, I infer the capacity of music to give birth to myth (the most significant example), and particularly the tragic myth: the myth which expresses Dionysian knowledge in symbols. In the phenomenon of the lyrist, I have shown how music strives to express its nature in Apollinian images. If now we reflect that music at its highest stage must seek to attain also to its highest objectification in images, we must deem it possible that it also knows how to find the symbolic expression for its unique Dionysian wisdom; and where shall we seek for this expression if not in tragedy and, in general, in the conception of the tragic?

From the nature of art as it is usually conceived according to the single category of appearance and beauty, the tragic cannot honestly be deduced at all; it is only through the spirit of music that we can understand the joy involved in the annihilation of the individual. For it is only in particular examples of such annihilation that we are clearly the eternal phenomenon of Dionysian art, which gives expression to the will in its omnipotence, as it were, behind the principium individuationis, the eternal life beyond all phenomena, and despite all annihilation. The metaphysical joy in the tragic is a translation of the instinctive unconscious Dionysian wisdom into the language of images: the hero, the highest manifestation of the will, is negated for our pleasure, because he is only phenomenon, and because the eternal life of the will is not affected by his annihilation. "We believe in eternal life," exclaims tragedy; while music is the immediate idea of this life. Plastic art has an altogether different aim: here Apollo overcomes the suffering of the individual by the radiant glorification of the eternity of the phenomenon: here beauty triumphs over the suffering inherent in life; pain is obliterated by lies from the features of nature. In Dionysian art and its tragic symbolism the same nature cries to us with its true, undissembled voice: "Be as I am! Amid the ceaseless flux of phenomena I am the eternally creative primordial mother, eternally impelling to existence, eternally finding satisfaction in this change of phenomena!"

17

Dionysian art, too, wishes to convince us of the eternal joy of existence: only we are to seek this joy not in phenomena, but behind them. We are to recognize that all that comes into being must be ready for a sorrowful end; we are forced to look into the terrors of the individual existence--yet we are not to become rigid with fear: a metaphysical comfort tears us momentarily from the bustle of the changing figures. We are really for a brief moment primordial being itself, feeling its raging desire for existence and joy in existence; the struggle, the pain, the destruction of phenomena, now appear necessary to us, in view of the excess of countless forms of existence which force and push one another into life, in view of the exuberant fertility of the universal will. We are pierced by the maddening stings of these pains just when we have become, as it were, one with the infinite primordial joy in existence, and when we anticipate, in Dionysian ecstasy, the indestructibility and eternity of this joy. In spite of fear and pity, we are the happy living beings, not as individuals, but as the one living being, with whose creative joy we are united.

The history of the rise of Greek tragedy now tells us with luminous precision how the tragic art of the Greeks was really born of the spirit of music. With this conception we believe we have done justice for the first time to the primitive and astonishing significance of the chorus. At the same time, however, we must admit that the meaning of tragic myth set forth above never became clear in transparent concepts to the Greek poets, not to speak of the Greek philosophers: their heroes speak, as it were, more superficially than they act; the myth does not at all obtain adequate objectification in the spoken word. The structure of the scenes and the visual images reveal a deeper wisdom than the poet himself can put into words and concepts: the same is also observable in Shakespeare, whose Hamlet, for instance, similarly, talks more superficially than he acts, so that the previously mentioned lesson of Hamlet is to be deduced, not from his words, but from a profound contemplation and survey of the whole.

With respect to Greek tragedy, which of course presents itself to us only as word-drama, I have even intimated that the lack of congruity between myth and expression might easily lead us to regard it as shallower and less significant than it really is, and accordingly to attribute to it a more superficial effect than it must have had according to the testimony of the ancients: for how easily one forgets that what the word-poet did not succeed in doing, namely, attain the highest spiritualization and ideality of the myth, he might very well succeed in doing every moment as creative musician! To be sure, we are almost forced to construct for ourselves by scholarly research the superior power of the musical effect in order to experience something of the incomparable comfort which must have been characteristic of true tragedy. Even this musical superiority, however, would only have been felt by us had we been Greeks; for in the entire development of Greek music--as compared with the infinitely richer music known and familiar to us--we imagine we hear only the youthful song of the musical genius modestly intoned. The Greeks, as the Egyptian priests say, are eternal children, and in tragic art too they are only children who do not know what a sublime plaything originated in their hands and--was quickly demolished.

The striving of the spirit of music toward visual and mythical objectification, which increases from the beginnings of lyric poetry up to Attic tragedy, suddenly breaks off after attaining a luxuriant development, and disappears, as it were, from the surface of Hellenic art; while the Dionysian world view born of this striving lives on in the mysteries and, in its strangest metamorphoses and debasements, does not cease to attract serious natures. Will it not some day rise once again out of its mystic depths as art?

Here we are detained by the question, whether the power, by virtue of whose opening influence tragedy perished, has for all time sufficient strength to prevent the artistic reawakening of tragedy and the tragic world view. If ancient tragedy was diverted from its course by the dialectical desire for knowledge and the optimism of science, this fact might lead us to believe that there is an eternal conflict between the theoretic and the tragic world view; and only after the spirit of science has been pursued to its limits, and its claim to universal validity destroyed by the evidence of these limits may we hope for a rebirth of tragedy--a form of culture for which we should have to use the symbol of the music-practicing Socrates in the sense spoken of above [See Section 15]. In this contrast, I understand by the spirit of science the faith that first came to light in the person of Socrates--the faith in the explicability of nature and in knowledge as a panacea.

He who recalls the immediate consequences of this restlessly progressing spirit of science will realize at once that myth was annihilated by it, and that, because of this annihilation, poetry was driven like a homeless being from her natural ideal soil. If we have been right in assigning to music the power of again giving birth to myth, we may similarly expect to find the spirit of science on the path where it inimically opposes this mythopoeic power of music. This takes place in the development of the New Attic Dithyramb, the music of which no longer expressed the inner essence, the will itself, but only rendered the phenomenon inadequately, in an imitation by means of concepts. From this intrinsically degenerate music the genuinely musical natures turned away with the same repugnance that they felt for the art-destroying tendency of Socrates. The unerring instinct of Aristophanes was surely right when it included Socrates himself, the tragedy of Euripides, and the music of the New Dithyrambic poets in the same feeling of hatred, recognizing in all three phenomena the signs of a degenerate culture.

In this New Dithyramb, music is outrageously manipulated so as to be the imitative counterfeit of a phenomenon, for instance, of a battle or a storm at sea; and thus, of course, it has been utterly robbed of its mythopoeic power. For if it seeks to arouse pleasure only by impelling us to seek external analogies between a vital or natural process and certain rhythmical figures and characteristic sounds of music; if our understanding is to content itself with the perception of these analogies; we are reduced to a frame of mind which makes impossible any reception of the mythical; for the myth wants to be experienced vividly as a unique example of a universality and truth that gaze into the infinite. The truly Dionysian music presents itself as such a general mirror of the universal will: the vivid event refracted in this mirror expands at once for our consciousness to the copy of an external truth. Conversely, such a vivid event is at once divested of every mythical character by the tone-painting of the New Dithyramb; music now becomes a wretched cop of the phenomenon, and therefore infinitely poorer than the phenomenon itself. And through this poverty it still further reduces the phenomenon for our consciousness, so that now, for example, a musically imitated battle of this sort exhausts itself in marches, signal sounds, etc., and our imagination is arrested precisely by these superficialities. Tone-painting is thus in every respect the opposite of true music with its mythopoeic power: through it the phenomenon, poor in itself, is made still poorer, while through Dionysian music the individual phenomenon is enriched and expanded into an image of the world. It was a great triumph for the un-Dionysian spirit when, by the development of the New Dithyramb, it had estranged music from itself and reduced it to be the slave of phenomena. Euripides, who, though in a higher sense, must be considered a thoroughly unmusical nature, is for this very reason a passionate adherent of the New Dithyrambic Music, and with the liberality of a robber makes use of all its effective tricks and mannerisms.

In another direction also we see at work the power of this un-Dionysian myth-opposing spirit, when we turn our attention to the prevalence of character representation and psychological refinement in tragedy from Sophocles onward. The character must no longer be expanded into an eternal type, but, on the contrary, must develop individually through artistic subordinate traits and shadings, through the nicest precision of all lines, in such a manner that the spectator is in general no longer conscious of the myth, but of the vigorous truth to nature and the artist's imitative power. Here also we observe the victory of the phenomenon over the universal, and the delight in a unique, almost anatomical preparation; we are already in the atmosphere of a theoretical world, where scientific knowledge is valued more highly than the artistic reflection of a universal law.

The movement in the direction of character delineation proceeds rapidly: while Sophocles still portrays complete characters and employs myth for their refined development, Euripides already draws only prominent individual traits of character, which can express themselves in violent bursts of passion. In the New Attic Comedy, however, there are only masks with one expression: frivolous old men, duped panders, and cunning slaves, recurring incessantly. Where now is the mythopoeic spirit of music? What still remains of music is either excitatory or reminiscent music, that is, either a stimulant for dull and faded nerves, or tone-painting. As regards the former, it hardly matters about the text set to it: as soon as his heroes and choruses begin to sing, everything becomes pretty slovenly in Euripides; to what pass must things have come with his impertinent successors?

The new un-Dionysian spirit, however, reveals itself more plainly in the denouements of the new dramas. In the Old Tragedy one could sense at the end that metaphysical comfort without which the delight in tragedy cannot be explained at all. The reconciling tones from another world sound purest, perhaps, in the Oedipus at Colonus. Now that the genius of music has fled from tragedy, tragedy, strictly speaking, is dead: for from what source shall we now draw this metaphysical comfort? The new spirit, therefore, sought for an earthly resolution of the tragic dissonance. The hero, after being sufficiently tortured by fate, earned a well-deserved reward through a splendid marriage or tokens of divine favor. The hero had turned gladiator on whom, after he had been nicely beaten and covered with wounds, freedom was occasionally bestowed. The deus ex machina took the place of metaphysical comfort.

I will not say that the tragic world view was everywhere completely destroyed by this intruding un-Dionysian spirit: we only know that it had to flee from art into the underworld as it were, in the degenerate form of a secret cult. Over the widest extent of the Hellenic character, however, there raged the consuming blast of this spirit, which manifests itself in the form of "Greek cheerfulness," which we have already spoken of as a senile, unproductive love of existence. This cheerfulness stands opposed to the splendid "naivete" of the earlier Greeks, which, according to the characterization given above, must be conceived as the blossom of the Apollinian culture springing from a dark abyss, as the victory which the Hellenic will, through its mirroring of beauty, obtains over suffering and the wisdom of suffering.

The noblest manifestation of that other form of "Greek cheerfulness," the Alexandrian, is the cheerfulness of the theoretical man. It exhibits the same characteristic symptoms that I have just deduced from the spirit of the un-Dionysian: it combats Dionysian wisdom and art, it seeks to dissolve myth, it substitutes for a metaphysical comfort an earthly consonance, in fact, a deus ex machina of its own, the god of machines and crucibles, that is, the powers of the spirits of nature recognized and employed in the service of a higher egoism; it believes that it can correct the world by knowledge, guiding life by science, and actually confine the individual within a limited sphere of solvable problems, from which he can cheerfully say to life: "I desire you; you are worth knowing."

18

It is an eternal phenomenon: the insatiable will always find a way to detain its creatures in life and compel them to live on, by means of an illusion spread over things. One is chained by the Socratic love of knowledge and the delusion of being able thereby to heal the eternal wound of existence; another is ensnared by art's seductive veil of beauty fluttering before his eyes; still another by the metaphysical comfort that beneath the whirl of phenomena eternal life flows on indestructibly--to say nothing of the more vulgar and almost more powerful illusions which the will always has at hand. These three stages of illusion are actually designed only for the more nobly formed natures, who actually feel profoundly the weight and burden of existence, and must be deluded by exquisite stimulants into forgetfulness of their displeasure. All that we call culture is made up of these stimulants; and, according to the proportion of the ingredients, we have either a dominantly Socratic or artistic or tragic culture; or, if historical exemplifications are permitted, there is either an Alexandrian or a Hellenic or a Buddhistic culture.

Our whole modern world is entangled in the net of Alexandrian culture. It proposes as its ideal the theoretical man equipped with the greatest forces of knowledge, and laboring in the service of science, whose archetype and progenitor is Socrates. All our educational methods originally have this ideal in view: every other form of existence must struggle on laboriously beside it, as something tolerated, but not intended. In an almost alarming manner the culture man was for a long time found only in the form of the scholar: even our poetical arts have been forced to evolve from scholarly imitations, and in the main effect, that of rhyme, we still recognize the origin of our poetic form from artificial experiments with a nonindigenous, really scholarly language. How unintelligible must Faust, the modern cultured man, who is in himself intelligible, have appeared to a true Greek--Faust, storming unsatisfied through all the faculties, devoted to magic and the devil from a desire for knowledge; Faust, whom we have but to place beside Socrates for the purpose of comparison, in order to see that modern man is beginning to divine the limits of this Socratic love of knowledge and yearns for a coast in the wide waste of the ocean of knowledge. When Goethe on one occasion said to Eckermann with reference to Napoleon: "Yes, my good friend, there is also a productiveness of deeds," he reminded us in a charmingly naive manner that the nontheorist is something incredible and astounding to modern man; so that we again have need of the wisdom of Goethe to discover that such a surprising form of existence is not only comprehensible, but even pardonable.

Now we must not hide from ourselves what is concealed in the womb of this Socratic culture: optimism, with its delusion of limitless power. We must not be alarmed if the fruits of this optimism ripen--if society, leavened to the very lowest strata by this kind of culture, gradually begins to tremble with wanton agitations and desires, if the belief in the earthly happiness of all, if the belief in the possibility of such a general intellectual culture changes into the threatening demand for such an

Alexandrian earthly happiness, into the conjuring up of a Euripidean deus ex machina.

Let us mark this well: the Alexandrian culture, to be able to exist permanently, requires a slave class, but with its optimistic view of life it denies the necessity of such a class, and consequently, when its beautifully seductive and tranquilizing utterances about the "dignity of man" and the "dignity of labor" are no longer effective, it gradually drifts toward a dreadful destruction. There is nothing more terrible than a class of barbaric slaves who have learned to regard their existence as an injustice, and now prepare to avenge, not only themselves, but all generations. In the face of such threatening storms, who dares to appeal with any confidence to our pale and exhausted religions, the very foundations of which have degenerated into scholarly religions? Myth, the necessary prerequisite of any religion, is already paralyzed everywhere, and even in this domain the optimistic spirit, which we have just designated as the germ of destruction in our society, has attained the mastery.

While the disaster gradually slumbering in the womb of theoretical culture gradually begins to frighten modern man, and he anxiously ransacks the stores of his experience for means to avert the danger, though he has no great faith in these means; while he, therefore, begins to divine the consequences of his situation--great men, universally gifted, have contrived, with an incredible amount of thought, to make use of the paraphernalia of science itself, to point out the limits and the relativity of knowledge generally, and thus to deny decisively the claim of science to universal validity and universal aims. And their demonstration diagnosed for the first time the illusory notion which pretends to be able to fathom the innermost essence of things with the aid of causality. The extraordinary courage and wisdom of Kant and Schopenhauer have succeeded in gaining the most difficult victory, the victory over the optimism concealed in the essence of logic--an optimism that is the basis of our culture. While this optimism, resting on apparently unobjectionable aeternae veritates [Eternal verities.], had believed that all the riddles of the universe could be known and fathomed, and had treated space, time, and causality as entirely unconditional laws of the most universal validity, Kant showed that these really served only to elevate the mere phenomenon, the work of maya, to the position of the sole and highest reality, as if it were the innermost and true essence of things, thus making impossible any knowledge of this essence or, in Schopenhauer's words, lulling the dreamer still more soundly asleep.

With this insight a culture is inaugurated that I venture to call a tragic culture. Its most important characteristic is that wisdom takes the place of science as the highest end--wisdom that, uninfluenced by the seductive distractions of the sciences, turns with unmoved eyes to a comprehensive view of the world, and seeks to grasp, with sympathetic feelings of love, the eternal suffering as its own.

Let us imagine a coming generation with such intrepidity of vision, with such a heroic penchant for the tremendous; let us imagine the bold stride of these dragon-slayers, the proud audacity with which they turn their back on all the weaklings' doctrines of optimism in order to "live resolutely" in wholeness and fullness: would it not be necessary for the tragic man of such a culture, in view of his self-education for seriousness and terror, to desire a new art, the art of metaphysical comfort, to desire tragedy as his own proper Helen, and to exclaim with Faust:

Should not my longing overleap the distance

And draw the fairest form into existence?

[From Goethe's Faust, lines 7438 ff.]

But now that the Socratic culture can only hold the scepter of its infallibility with trembling hands; now that it has been shaken from two directions--once by the fear of its own consequences which it at length begins to surmise, and again because it no longer has its naive confidence in the eternal validity of its foundation--it is a sad spectacle to see how the dance of its thought rushes longingly toward ever-new forms, to embrace them, and then, shuddering, lets them go suddenly as

Mephistopheles does the seductive Lamiae [Faust, lines 7766 ff.]. It is certainly the sign of the "breach" of which everyone speaks as the fundamental malady of modern culture, that the theoretical man, alarmed and dissatisfied at his own consequences, no longer dares entrust himself to the terrible icy current of existence: he runs timidly up and down the bank. So thoroughly has he been pampered by his optimistic views that he no longer wants to have anything whole, with all of nature's cruelty attaching to it.. Besides, he feels that a culture based on the principles of science must be destroyed when it begins to grow illogical, that is, to retreat before its own consequences. Our art reveals this universal distress: in vain does one depend imitatively on all the great productive periods and natures; in vain does one accumulate the entire "world-literature" around modern man for his comfort; in vain does one place oneself in the midst of the art styles and artists of all ages, so that one may give names to them as Adam did to the beasts: one still remains externally hungry, the "critic" without joy and energy, the Alexandrian man, who is at bottom a librarian and corrector of proofs, and wretchedly goes blind from the dust of books and from printers' errors.

19

We cannot indicate the innermost modern content of this Socratic culture more distinctly than by calling it the culture of the opera: for it is in this department that this culture has expressed its aims and perceptions with special naivete, which is surprising when we compare the genesis of the opera and the facts of operatic development with the eternal truths of the Apollinian and Dionysian. I recall first of all the origin of the stilo rappresentativo [Representational style.] and the recitative. Is it credible that this thoroughly externalized operatic music, incapable of devotion, could be received and cherished with enthusiastic favor, as a rebirth, as it were, of all true music, by the very age in which had appeared the ineffably sublime and sacred music of Palestrina? And who, on the other hand, would think of making only the diversion-craving luxuriousness of those Florentine circles and the vanity of their dramatic singers responsible for the love of the opera which spread with such rapidity? That in the same age, even among the same people, this passion for a half-musical mode of speech should awaken alongside of the vaulted structure of Palestrina harmonics which all medieval Christendom had been building up, I can explain to myself only by a cooperating, extra-artistic tendency in the essence of the recitative.

The listener who insists on distinctly hearing the words under the music has his desire fulfilled by the singer in that the latter speaks rather than sings, intensifying the pathetic expression of the words by means of this half-song. By this intensification of the pathos he facilitates the understanding of the words and overcomes the remaining half of the music. The specific danger now threatening him is that in some unguarded moment he may stress the music unduly, which would immediately entail the destruction of the pathos of the speech and the distinctness of the words; while, on the other hand, he feels himself continually impelled to musical discharge and a virtuoso exhibition of his vocal talent. Here the "poet" comes to his aid, who knows how to provide him with abundant opportunities for lyrical interjections, repetitions of words and sentences, etc.--at which places the singer, now in the purely musical element, can rest himself without paying any attention to the words. This alternation of emotionally impressive speech which, however, is only half sung, with interjections which are wholly sung, an alternation characteristic of the stilo rappresentativo, this rapidly changing endeavor to affect now the concepts and imagination of the hearer, now his musical sense, is something so utterly unnatural and likewise so intrinsically contradictory both to the Apollinian and Dionysian artistic impulses, that one has to infer an origin of the recitative lying outside all artistic instincts. According to this description, the recitative must be defined as a mixture of epic and lyric delivery, not by any means as an intrinsically stable mixture, a state not to be attained in the case of such totally disparate elements, but as an entirely superficial mosaic conglutination, such as is totally unprecedented in the domain of nature and experience. But this was not the opinion of the inventors of the recitative: they themselves, together with their age, believed rather that the mystery of antique music has been solved by this stilo rappresentativo, in which, so they thought, was to be found the only explanation of the enormous influence of an Orpheus, an Amphion, and even of Greek tragedy. The new style was looked upon as the reawakening of the most effective music, ancient Greek music: indeed, in accordance with the universal and popular conception of the Homeric as the primitive world, they could abandon themselves to the dream of having descended once more into the paradisiacal beginnings of mankind, where music also must have had that unsurpassed purity, power, and innocence of which the poets, in their pastoral plays, could give such touching accounts. Here we can see into the innermost development of this thoroughly modern variety of art, the opera: art here responds to a powerful need, but it is a nonaesthetic need: the yearning for the idyllic, the faith in the primordial existence of the artistic and good man. The recitative was regarded as the rediscovered language of this primitive man; opera as the rediscovered country of this idyllically or heroically good creature, who simultaneously with every action follows a natural artistic impulse, who accomplishes his speech with a little singing, in order that he may immediately break forth into full song at the slightest emotional excitement.

It is now a matter of indifference to us that the humanists of the time combated the old ecclesiastical conception of man as inherently corrupt and lost, with this newly created picture of the paradisiacal artist: so that opera is to be understood as the opposition dogma of the good man, but may also, at the same time, provide a consolation for that pessimism which, owing to the frightful uncertainty of all conditions of life, attracted precisely the serious-minded men of the time. For us, it is enough to have perceived that the essential charm, and therefore the genesis, of this new art form lies in the gratification of an altogether nonaesthetic need, in the optimistic glorification of man as such, in the conception of the primitive man as the man naturally good and artistic--a principle of the opera that has gradually changed into a threatening and terrible demand which, in face of contemporary socialist movements, we can no longer ignore. The "good primitive man" wants his rights: what paradisiacal prospects!

Besides this I place another equally obvious confirmation of my view that opera is based on the same principles as our Alexandrian culture. Opera is the birth of the theoretical man, the critical layman, not of the artist: one of the most surprising facts in the history of all the arts. It was the demand of thoroughly unmusical hearers that before everything else the words must be understood, so that according to them a rebirth of music is to be expected only when some mode of singing has been discovered in which text-word lords it over counterpoint like master over servant. For the words, it is argued, are a much nobler than the accompanying harmonic system as the soul is nobler than the body.

It was in accordance with the laically unmusical crudeness of these views that the combination of music, image, and words was effected in the beginnings of the opera. In the spirit of this aesthetic the first experiments were made in the leading amateur circles of Florence by the poets and singers patronized there. The man incapable of art creates for himself a kind of art precisely because he is the inartistic man as such. Because he does not sense the Dionysian depth of music, he changes his musical taste into an appreciation of the understandable word-and-tone-rhetoric of the passions in the stilo rappresentativo, and into the voluptuousness of the arts of song. Because he is unable to behold a vision, he forces the machinist and the decorative artist into his service. Because he cannot comprehend the true nature of the artist, he conjures up the "artistic primitive man" to suit his taste, that is, the man who sings and recites verses under the influence of passion. He dreams himself back into a time when passion sufficed to generate songs and poems; as if emotion had ever been able to create anything artistic.

The premise of the opera is a false belief concerning the artistic process: the idyllic belief that every sentient man is an artist. This belief would make opera the expression of the taste of the laity in art, dictating their laws with the cheerful optimism of the theoretical man.

Should we desire to combine the two conceptions that have just been shown to have influenced the origin of opera, it would merely remain for us to speak of an idyllic tendency of the opera. In this connection we need only avail ourselves of the expressions and explanation of Schiller. Nature and the ideal, he says, are either objects of grief, when the former is represented as lost, the latter unattained; or both are objects of joy, in that they are represented as real. The first case furnishes the elegy in its narrower signification, the second the idyll in its widest sense.

Here we must at once call attention to the common characteristic of these two conceptions in the genesis of opera, namely, that in them the ideal is not felt as unattained or nature as lost. This sentiment supposes that there was a primitive age of man when he lay close to the heart of nature, and, owing to this naturalness, had at once attained the ideal of mankind in a paradisiacal goodness and artistry. From this perfect primitive man all of us were supposed to be descended. We were even supposed to be faithful copies of him; only we had to cast off a few things in order to recognize ourselves once more as this primitive man, on the strength of a voluntary renunciation of a superficial learnedness, of superabundant culture. It was to such a concord of nature and the ideal, to an idyllic reality, that the cultured Renaissance man let himself be led back by his operatic imitation of Greek tragedy. He mad use of this tragedy as Dante made use of Vergil, in order to be conducted to the gates of paradise; while from this point he continued unassisted and passed over from an imitation of the highest Greek art-form to a "restoration of all things," to an imitation of man's original art-world. What a cheerful confidence there is about these daring endeavors, in the very heart of theoretical culture!--solely to be explained by the comforting belief, that "man-in-himself" is the eternally virtuous hero of the opera, the eternally piping or singing shepherd, who must always in the end rediscover himself as such, should he ever at any time really lost himself; to be considered solely as the fruit of that optimism, which here rises like a sweetishly seductive column of vapor from the depth of the Socratic world view.

Therefore, the features of the opera do not by any means exhibit the elegiac sorrow of an eternal loss, but rather the cheerfulness of eternal rediscovery, the comfortable delight in an idyllic reality which one can at least always imagine as real. But in this process one may some day grasp the fact that this supposed reality is nothing but a fantastically silly dawdling, at which everyone who could judge it by the terrible seriousness of true nature, and compare it with actual primitive scenes of the beginnings of mankind, would be impelled to call out, nauseated: Away with the phantom!

Nevertheless, it would be a mistake to imagine that it is possible merely by a vigorous shout to frighten away such a playful thing as the opera, as if it were a specter. He who would destroy the opera must take up the struggle against Alexandrian cheerfulness, which expresses itself so naively in opera concerning its favorite idea. Indeed, opera is its specific form of art. But what may art itself expect form the operation of an art form whose beginnings lie entirely outside of the aesthetic province and which has stolen over from a half-moral sphere into the artistic domain, deceiving us only occasionally about its hybrid origin? By what sap is this parasitic opera nourished, if not by that of true art? Must we not suppose that the highest, and, indeed, the truly serious task of art--to save the eye from gazing into the horrors of night and to deliver the suspect by the healing balm of illusion from the spasms of the agitations of the will-- must degenerate under the influence of its idyllic seductions and Alexandrian flatteries to become an empty and merely distracting diversion? What will become of the eternal truths of the Dionysian and Apollinian when the styles are mixed in this fashion, as I have shown to be the essence of the stilo rappresentativo? A style in which music is regarded as the servant, the text as the master, where music is compared with the body, the text with the soul? where at best the highest aim will be directed toward a paraphrastic tone-painting, just as formerly in the New Attic Dithyramb? where music is completely alienated from its true dignity as the Dionysian mirror of the world, so that the only thing left to it, as the slave of phenomena, is to imitate the formal character of phenomena, and to arouse a superficial pleasure in the play of lines and proportions. Closely observed, this fatal influence of the opera on music is seen to coincide exactly with the universal development of modern music; the optimism lurking in the genesis of the opera and in the character of the culture thereby represented, has, with alarming rapidity, succeeded in divesting music of its Dionysian-cosmic mission and impressing on it a playfully formal and pleasurable character: a change comparable to the metamorphosis of the Aeschylean man into the cheerful Alexandrian.

If, however, in the exemplification here indicated, we have rightly associated the disappearance of the Dionysian spirit with a most striking, but hitherto unexplained, transformation and degeneration of the Hellenic man--what hopes must revive in us when the most certain auspices guarantee the reverse process, the gradual awakening of the Dionysian spirit in our modern world! It is impossible that the divine strength of Herakles should languish forever in ample bondage to Omphale [A queen of Lydia by whom Herakles claimed to have been detained for a year of bondage.]. Out of the Dionysian root of the German spirit a power has arisen which, having nothing in common with the primitive conditions of Socratic culture, can neither be explained nor excused by it, but which is rather felt by this culture as something terribly inexplicable and overwhelmingly hostile-- German music as we must understand it, particularly in its vast solar orbit from Bach to Beethoven, from Beethoven to Wagner.

Even under the most favorable circumstances what can the knowledge-craving Socratism of our days do with this demon rising from unfathomable depths? Neither by means of the flourishes and arabesques of operatic melody, nor with the aid of the arithmetical counting board of fugue and contrapuntal dialectic is the formula to be found by whose thrice-powerful light one might subdue this demon and compel it to speak. What a spectacle, when our latter-day aestheticians, with a net of "beauty" peculiar to themselves, pursue and clutch at the genius of music whirling before display activities which are not to be judged by the standard of eternal beauty any more than by the standard of the sublime. Let us but observe these patrons of music at close range, as they really are, indefatigably crying: "Beauty! beauty!" Do they really bear the stamp of nature's darling children who are fostered and nourished at the breast of the beautiful, or are they not rather seeking a mendacious cloak for their own coarseness, an aesthetical pretext for their insensitive sobriety; here I am thinking of Otto Jahn, for example [Professor of classical philology at Bonn.]. But let the liar and the hypocrite beware of German music: for amid all our culture it is really the only genuine, pure, and purifying fire-spirit from which and toward which, as in the teaching of the great Heraclitus of Ephesus, all things move in a double orbit: all that we now call culture, education, civilization, must some day appear before the unerring judge, Dionysus.

Let us recollect further that Kant and Schopenhauer made it possible for the spirit of German philosophy, streaming from similar sources, to destroy scientific Socratism's complacent delight in existence by establishing its boundaries; how through this delimitation was introduced an infinitely profounder and more serious view of ethical problems and of art, which we may designate as Dionysian wisdom comprised in concepts. To what then does the mystery of this oneness of German music and philosophy point if not to a new form of existence, concerning whose character we can only inform ourselves by surmise from Hellenic analogies? For to us who stand on the boundary line between two different forms of existence, the Hellenic prototype retains this immeasurable value, that all these transitions and struggles are imprinted upon it in a classically instructive form; except that we, as it were, pass through the chief epochs of the Hellenic genius, analogically in reverse order, and seem now, for instance, to be passing backward from the Alexandrian age to the period of tragedy. At the same time we have the feeling that the birth of a tragic age simply means a return to itself of the German spirit, a blessed self-rediscovery after powerful intrusive influences had for a long time compelled it, living as it did in a helpless and unchaste barbarism, to servitude under their form. Now at last, upon returning to the primitive source of its being, it may venture to stride along boldly and freely before the eyes of all nations without being attached to the lead strings of a Romanic civilization; if only it can learn constantly from one people--the Greeks, from whom to be able to learn at all itself is a high honor and a rare distinction. And when were we in greater need of these highest of all teachers than at present, when we are experiencing a rebirth of tragedy and are in danger alike of not knowing whence it comes and of being unable to make clear to ourselves whither it tends?

20

Some day, before an impartial judge, it may be decided in what time and in what men the German spirit has s far striven most resolutely to learn from the Greeks; and if we confidently assume that this unique praise must be accorded to the noblest intellectual efforts of Goethe, Schiller, and Winckelmann, we should certainly have to add that since their time and the more immediate consequences of their efforts, the endeavor to attain to culture and to the Greeks on the same path has grown incomprehensibly feebler and feebler. That we may not despair utterly of the German spirit, must we not conclude that, in some essential manner, even these champions did not penetrate into the core of the Hellenic nature, to establish a permanent alliance between German and Greek culture? So an unconscious recognition of this shortcoming may have prompted the disheartening doubt, even in very serious people, whether after such predecessors they could possibly advance further on this path of culture or could reach the goal at all. Accordingly, we see that opinions concerning the value if the Greeks for education have been degenerating in the most alarming manner since that time. Expressions of compassionate condescension may be heard in the most varied camps of the spirit--and of lack of spirit. Elsewhere, ineffectual rhetoric plays with the phrases "Greek harmony," "Greek beauty," "Greek cheerfulness." And those very circles whose dignified task it might be to draw indefatigably from the Greek reservoir for the good of German culture, the teachers of the higher educational institutions, have learned best to come to terms with the Greeks easily and in good time, often by skeptically abandoning the Hellenic ideal and completely perverting the true purpose of antiquarian studies. Whoever in these circles has not completely exhausted himself in his endeavor to be a dependable corrector of old texts or a linguistic microscopist who apes natural history is probably trying to assimilate Greek antiquity "historically," along with other antiquities, at any rate according to the method and with the supercilious airs of our present cultured historiography.

The cultural power of our higher educational institutions has perhaps never been lower or feebler than at present. The "journalist," the paper slave of the day, triumphs over the professor in all matters pertaining to culture; and nothing remains to the latter but the metamorphosis, often experienced by now, of fluttering also like a cheerful cultured butterfly, with the "light elegance" peculiar to this sphere, employing the journalist's style. In what painful confusion must the cultured class of such a period gaze at the phenomenon which perhaps is to be comprehended analogically only by means of the profoundest principle of the hitherto unintelligible Hellenic genius--the phenomenon of the reawakening of the Dionysian spirit and the rebirth of tragedy?

There has never been another period in the history of art in which so-called culture and true art have been so estranged and opposed as we may observe them to be at present. We can understand why so feeble a culture hates true art; it fears destruction from its hands. But has not an entire cultural form, namely, the Socratic-Alexandrian, exhausted itself after culminating in such a daintily tapering point as our present culture? If heroes like Goethe and Schiller could not succeed in breaking open the enchanted gate which leads into the Hellenic magic mountain; if with their most dauntless striving they could not go beyond the longing gaze which Goethe's Iphigenia casts from barbaric Tauris to her home across the ocean, what could the epigones of such heroes hope for--unless, amid the mystic tones of reawakened tragic music, the gate should open for them suddenly of its own accord, from an entirely different side, quite overlooked in all previous cultural endeavors.

Let no one try to blight our faith in a yet-impending rebirth of Hellenic antiquity; for this alone gives us hope for a renovation and purification of the German spirit through the fire magic of music. What else could we name that might awaken any comforting expectations for the future in the midst of the desolation and exhaustion of contemporary culture? In vain we look for a single vigorously developed root, for a spot of fertile and healthy soil: everywhere there is dust and sand; everything has become rigid and languishes. One who is disconsolate and lonely could not choose a better symbol than the knight with death and devil, as Durer has drawn him for us, the armored knight with the iron, hard look, who knows how to pursue his terrible path, undeterred by his gruesome companions, and yet without hope, alone with his horse and dog. Our Schopenhauer was such a Durer knight; he lacked all hope, but he desired truth. He has no peers.

But how suddenly the desert of our exhausted culture, just described in such gloomy terms, is changed when it is touched by the Dionysian magic! A tempest seizes everything that has outlived itself, everything that is decayed, broken, and withered, and, whirling, shrouds it in a cloud of red dust to carry it into the air like a vulture. Confused, our eyes look after what has disappeared; for what they see has been raised as from a depression into golden light, so full and green, so amply alive, immeasurable and full of yearning. Tragedy is seated amid this excess of life, suffering, and pleasure, in sublime ecstasy, listening to a distant melancholy song that tells of the mothers of being whose names are: Delusion, Will, Woe.

Yes, my friends, believe with me in Dionysian life and the rebirth of tragedy. The age of the Socratic man is over; put on wreaths of ivy, put the thyrsus into your hand, and do not be surprised when tigers and panther lie down, fawning, at your feet. Only dare to be tragic men; for you are to be redeemed. You shall accompany the Dionysian pageant from India to Greece. Prepare yourselves for hard strife, but believe in the miracles of your god.

21

Returning from these hortatory tones to the mood befitting contemplation, I repeat that we can learn only from the Greeks what such an almost miraculously sudden awakening of tragedy means for the innermost life ground of a people. It is the people of the tragic mysteries that fights the battles against the Persians; and the people that fought these wars in turn needs tragedy as a necessary potion to recover. Who would have supposed that precisely this people, after it had been deeply agitated through several generations by the strongest spasms of the Dionysian demon, should still have been capable of such a uniformly vigorous effusion of the simplest political feeling, the most natural patriotic instincts, and original manly desire to fight? After all, one feels in every case in which Dionysian excitement gains any significant extent how the Dionysian liberation from the fetters of the individual finds expression first of all in a diminution of, in indifference to, indeed, in hostility to, the political instincts. Just as certainly, Apollo who forms states is also the genius of the principium individuationis, and state and patriotism cannot live without an affirmation of the individual personality. But from orgies a people can take one path only, the path to Indian Buddhism, and in order that this may be endurable at all with its yearning for the nothing, it requires these rare ecstatic states with their elevation above space, time, and the individual. These states in turn demand a philosophy that teaches men how to overcome by the force of an idea the indescribable displeasure of the states that lie between. Where the political drives are taken to be absolutely valid, it is just as necessary that a people should go to the path toward the most extreme secularization whose most magnificent but also most terrifying expression may be found in the Roman imperium.

Placed between India and Rome, and pushed toward a seductive choice, the Greeks succeeded in inventing a third form, in classical purity--to be sure, one they did not long use themselves, but one that precisely for that reason gained immortality. For that the favorites of the gods die early, is true in all things; but it is just as certain that they then live eternally with the gods. After all, one should not demand of what is noblest of all that it should have the durable toughness of leather. That staunch perseverance which characterized, for example, the national instincts of the Romans, probably does not belong among the necessary predicates of perfection. But let us ask by means of what remedy it was possible for the Greeks during their great period, in spite of the extraordinary strength of their Dionysian and political instincts, not to exhaust themselves either in ecstatic brooding or in a consuming chase after worldly power and worldly honor, but rather to attain that splendid mixture which resembles a noble wine in making one feel fiery and contemplative at the same time. Here we must think clearly of the tremendous power that stimulated, purified, and discharged the whole life of the people: tragedy. We cannot begin to sense its highest value until it confronts us, as it did the Greeks, as the quintessence of all prophylactic powers of healing, as the mediator that worked among the strongest and in themselves most fatal qualities of the people.

Tragedy absorbs the highest ecstasies of music, so that it truly brings music, both among the Greeks and among us, to its perfection; but then it places the tragic myth and the tragic hero next to it, and he, like a powerful Titan, takes the whole Dionysian world upon his back and thus relieves us of this burden. On the other hand, by means of the same tragic myth, in the person of the tragic hero; it knows how to redeem us from the greedy thirst for this existence, and with an admonishing gesture it reminds us of another existence and a higher pleasure for which the struggling hero prepares himself by means of his destruction, not by means of his triumphs. Between the universal validity of its music and the listener, receptive in his Dionysian state, tragedy places a sublime parable, the myth, and deceives the listener into feeling that the music is merely the highest means to bring life into the vivid world of myth. Relying on this noble deception, it may now move its limbs in dithyrambic dances and yield unhesitatingly to an ecstatic feeling of freedom in which it could not dare to wallow as pure music without this deception. The myth protects us against the music, while on the other hand it alone gives music the highest freedom. In return, music imparts to the tragic myth an intense and convincing metaphysical significance that word an image without this singular help could never have attained. And above all, it is through music that the tragic spectator is overcome by an assured premonition of a highest pleasure attained through destruction and negation, so he feels as if the innermost abyss of things spoke to him perceptibly.

If these last sentences have perhaps managed to give only a preliminary expression to these difficult ideas and are immediately intelligible only to few, I nevertheless may not desist at this point from trying to stimulate my friends to further efforts and must ask them to use a single example of our common experience in order to prepare themselves for a general insight. In giving this example, I must not appeal to those who use the images of what happens on the stage, the words and emotions of the acting persons, in order to approach with their help the musical feeling; for these people do not speak music as their mother tongue and, in spite of this help, never get beyond the entrance halls of musical perception, without ever being able to as much as touch the inner sanctum. Some of them, like Gervinus [G. G. Gervinus, author of Shakespeare, and Shakespeare Commentaries], do not even reach the entrance halls. I must appeal only to those who, immediately related to music, have in it, as it were, their motherly womb, and are related to things almost exclusively through unconscious musical relations. To these genuine musicians I direct the question whether they can imagine a human being who would be able to perceive the third act of Tristan and Isolde, without any aid of word and image, purely as a tremendous symphonic movement, without expiring in a spasmodic unharnessing of all the wings of the soul?

Suppose a human being has thus put his ear, as it were, to the heart chamber of the world will and felt the roaring desire for existence pouring from there into all the veins of the world, as a thundering current or as the gentlest brook, dissolving into a mist--how could he fail to break suddenly? How could he endure to perceive the echo of innumerable shouts of pleasure and woe in the "wide space of the world night," enclosed in the wretched glass capsule of the human individual, without inexorably fleeing toward his primordial home, as he hears this shepherd's dance of metaphysics? But if such a work could nevertheless be perceived as a whole, without denial of individual existence; if such a creation could be created without smashing its creator--whence do we take the solution of such a contradiction?

Here the tragic myth and the tragic hero intervene between our highest musical emotion and this music--at bottom only as symbols of the most universal facts, of which only music can speak so directly. But if our feelings were those of entirely Dionysian beings, myth as a symbol would remain totally ineffective and unnoticed, and would never for a moment keep us from listening to the re-echo of the universalia ante rem [The universals before the thing.]. Yet here the Apollinian power erupts to restore the almost shattered individual with the healing balm of blissful illusion: suddenly we imagine we see only Tristan, motionless, asking himself dully: "The old tune, why does it wake me?" And what once seemed to us like a hollow sigh from the core of being now merely wants to tell us how "desolate and empty the sea." And where, breathless, we once thought we were being extinguished in a convulsive distention of all feelings, and little remained to tie us to our present existence, we now hear and see only the hero wounded to death, yet not dying, with his despairing cry: "Longing! Longing! In death still longing! for very longing not dying!" And where, formerly after such an excess and superabundance of consuming agonies, the jubilation of the horn cut through our hearts almost like the ultimate agony, the rejoicing Kurwenal now stands between us and this "jubilation in itself," his face turned toward the ship which carries Isolde. However powerfully pity affects us, it nevertheless saves us in a way from the primordial suffering of the world, just as the symbolic image of the myth saves us from the immediate perception of the highest world-idea, just as thought and word save us from the uninhibited effusion of the unconscious will. The glorious Apollinian illusion makes it appear as if even the tone world confronted us as a sculpted world, as if the fate of Tristan and Isolde had been formed and molded in it, too, as in an exceedingly tender and expressive material.

Thus the Apollinian tears us out of the Dionysian universality and lets us find delight in individuals; it attaches our pity to them, and by means of them it satisfies our sense of beauty which longs for great and sublime forms; it presents images of life to us, and incites us to comprehend in thought the core of life they contain. With the immense impact of the image, the concept, the ethical teaching, and the sympathetic emotion, the Apollinian tears man from his orgiastic self-annihilation and blinds him to the universality of the Dionysian process, deluding him into the belief that he is seeing a single image of the world (Tristan and Isolde, for instance), and that, through music, he is merely supposed to see it still better and more profoundly. What can the healing magic of Apollo not accomplish when it can even create the illusion that the Dionysian is really in the service of the Apollinian and capable of enhancing its effects--as if music were essentially the art of presenting an Apollinian content?

By means of the pre-established harmony between perfect drama and its music, the drama attains a superlative vividness unattainable in mere spoken drama. In the independently moving lines of the melody all the living figures of the scene simplify themselves before us to the distinctness of curved lines, and the harmonies of these lines sympathize in a most delicate manner with the events on the stage. These harmonies make the relations of things immediately perceptible to us in a sensuous, by no means abstract manner, and thus we perceive that it is only in these relations that the essence of a character and of a melodic line is revealed clearly. And while music thus compels us to see more and more profoundly than usual, and we see the action on the stage as a delicate web, the world of the stage is expanded infinitely and illuminated for our spiritualized eye. How could a word-poet furnish anything analogous, when he strives to attain this internal expansion and illumination of the visible stage-world by means of a much more imperfect mechanism, indirectly, proceeding from word and concept? Although musical tragedy also avails itself of the word, it can at the same time place beside it the basis and origin of the word, making the development of the word clear to us, from the inside.

Concerning the process just described, however, we may still say with equal assurance that it is merely a glorious appearance, namely, the aforementioned Apollinian illusion whose influence aims to deliver us from the Dionysian flood and excess. For, at bottom, the relation of music to drama is precisely the reverse: music is the real idea of the world, drama is but the reflection of this idea, a single silhouette of it. The identity between the melody and the living figure, between the harmony and the character relations of that figure, is true in a sense opposite to what one would suppose on the contemplation of musical tragedy. Even if we agitate and enliven the figure in the most visible manner, and illuminate it from within, it still remains merely a phenomenon from which no bridge leads us to true reality, into the heart of the world. But music speaks out of this heart; and though countless phenomena of the kind were to accompany this music, they could never exhaust its essence, but would always be nothing more than its externalized copies.

As for the intricate relationship of music and drama, nothing can be explained, while everything may be confused, by the popular and thoroughly false contrast of soul and body; but the unphilosophical crudeness of this contrast seems to have become--who knows for what reasons--a readily accepted article of faith among our aestheticians, while they have learned nothing of the contrast of the phenomenon and the thing-in-itself--or, for equally unknown reasons, have not cared to learn anything about it.

Should our analysis have established that the Apollinian element in tragedy has by means of its illusion gained a complete victory over the primordial Dionysian element of music, making music subservient to its aims, namely, to make the drama as vivid as possible--it would certainly be necessary to add a very important qualification: at the most essential point this Apollinian illusion is broken and annihilated. The drama that, with the aid of music, unfolds itself before us with such inwardly illumined distinctness in all its movements and figures, as if we saw the texture coming into being on the loom as the shuttle flies to and fro--attains as a whole an effect that transcends all Apollinian artistic effects. In the total effect of tragedy, the Dionysian predominates once again. Tragedy closes with a sound which could never come from the realm of Apollinian art. And thus the Apollinian illusion reveals itself as what it really is--the veiling during the performance of the tragedy of the real Dionysian effect; but the latter is so powerful that it ends by forcing the Apollinian drama itself into a sphere where it begins to speak with Dionysian wisdom and even denies itself and its Apollinian visibility. Thus the intricate relation of the Apollinian and the Dionysian in tragedy may really be symbolized by a fraternal union of the two deities: Dionysus speaks the language of Apollo; and Apollo, finally the language of Dionysus and so the highest goal of tragedy and of all art is attained.

22

Let the attentive friend imagine the effect of a true musical tragedy purely and simply, as he knows it from experience. I think I have so portrayed the phenomenon of this effect in both its phases that he can now interpret his own experiences. For he will recollect how with regard to the myth which passed in front of him, he felt himself exalted to a kind of omniscience, as if his visual faculty were no longer merely a surface faculty but capable of penetrating into the interior, and as if he now saw before him, with the aid of music, the waves of the will, the conflict of motives, and the swelling flood of the passions, sensually visible, as it were, like a multitude of vividly moving lines and figures; and he felt he could dip into the most delicate secrets of unconscious emotions. While he thus becomes conscious of the highest exaltation of his instincts for clarity and transfiguration, he nevertheless feels just as definitely that this long series of Apollinian artistic effects still does not generate that blessed continuance in will-less contemplation which the plastic artist and the epic poet, that is to say, the strictly Apollinian artists, evoke in him with their artistic productions: to wit, the justification of the world of the individuatio attained by this contemplation--which is the climax and essence of Apollinian art. He beholds the transfigured world of the stage and nevertheless denies it. He sees the tragic hero before him in epic clearness and beauty, and nevertheless rejoices in his annihilation. He comprehends the action deep down, and yet likes to flee into the incomprehensible. He feels the actions of the hero to be justified, and is nevertheless still more elated when these actions annihilate their agent. He shudders at the sufferings which will befall the hero, and yet anticipates in them a higher, much more overpowering joy. He sees more extensively and profoundly than ever, and yet wishes he were blind.

How must we derive this curious internal bifurcation, this blunting of the Apollinian point, if not from the Dionysian magic that, though apparently exciting the Apollinian emotions to their

highest pitch, still retains the power to force into its service
his excess of Apollinian force?

The tragic myth is to be understood only as a symbolization of
Dionysian wisdom through Apollinian artifices. The myth leads
the world of phenomena to its limits where it denies itself and
seeks to flee back again into the womb of the true and only
reality, where it then seems to commence its metaphysical
swansong, like Isolde:

In the rapture ocean's

billowing roll,

in the fragrance waves'

ringing sound,

in the world breath's

wafting whole--

to drown, to sink--

unconscious--highest joy!

Thus we use the experiences of the truly aesthetic listener to
bring to mind the tragic artist himself as he creates his figures
like a fecund divinity of individuation (so his work can hardly be
understood as an "imitation of nature") and as his vast Dionysian
impulse then devours his entire world of phenomena, in order to
let us sense beyond it, and through its destruction, the highest
artistic primal joy, in the bosom of the primordially One. Of
course our aestheticians have nothing to say about this return to
the primordial home, or the fraternal union of the two art-deities,
nor of the excitement of the hearer which is Apollinian as well as
Dionysian; but they never tire of characterizing the struggle of
the hero with fate, the triumph of the moral world order, or the
purgation of the emotions through tragedy, as the essence of the
tragic. And their indefatigability makes me think that perhaps

they are not aesthetically sensitive at all, but react merely as moral beings when listening to a tragedy.

Never since Aristotle has an explanation of the tragic effect been offered from which aesthetic states or an aesthetic activity of the listener could be inferred. Now the serious events are supposed to prompt pity and fear to discharge themselves in a way that relieves us; now we are supposed to feel elevated and inspired by the triumph of good and noble principles, at the sacrifice of the hero in the interest of a moral vision of the universe. I am sure that for countless men precisely this, and only this, is the effect of tragedy, but it plainly follows that all these men, together with their interpreting aestheticians, have had no experience of tragedy as a supreme art.

The pathological discharge, the catharsis of Aristotle, of which philologists are not sure whether it should be included among medical or moral phenomena, recalls a remarkable notion of Goethe's. "Without a lively pathological interest," he says, "I, too, have never yet succeeded in elaborating a tragic situation of any kind, and hence I have rather avoided than sought it. Can it perhaps have been yet another merit of the ancients that the deepest pathos was with them merely aesthetic play, while with us the truth of nature must cooperate in order to produce such a work?"

We can now answer this profound final question in the affirmative after our glorious experiences, having found to our astonishment that the deepest pathos can indeed be merely aesthetic play in the case of musical tragedy. Therefore we are justified in believing that now for the first time the primal phenomenon of the tragic can be described with some degree of success. Anyone who still persists in talking only of those vicarious effects proceeding from extra-aesthetic spheres, and who does not feel that he is above the pathological-moral process, should despair of his aesthetic nature: should we recommend to him as an innocent equivalent the interpretation of Shakespeare after the manner of Gervinus and the diligent search for poetic justice?

Thus the aesthetic listener is also reborn with the rebirth of tragedy. In his place in the theater, a curious quid pro quo used to sit with half moral and half scholarly pretensions--the "critic." Everything in his sphere so far has been artificial and merely whitewashed with an appearance of life. The performing artist was really at a loss how to deal with a listener who comported himself so critically; so he, as well as the dramatist or operatic composer who inspired him, searched anxiously for the last remains of life in a being so pretentiously barren and incapable of enjoyment. So far, however, such "critics" have constituted the audience: the student, the schoolboy, even the innocuous female had been unwittingly prepared by education and newspapers for this kind of perception of works of art. Confronted with such a public, the nobler natures among the artists counted upon exciting their moral-religious emotions, and the appeal to the moral world-order intervened vicariously where some powerful artistic magic ought to enrapture the genuine listener. Or some more imposing, or at all events exciting, trend of the contemporary political and social world was so vividly presented by the dramatist that the listener could forget his critical exhaustion and abandon himself to emotions similar to those felt in patriotic or warlike moments, or before the tribune of parliament, or at the condemnation of crime and vice--an alienation from the true aims of art that sometimes had to result in an outright cult of tendentiousness. The attempt, for example, to use the theater as an institution for the moral education of the people, still taken seriously in Schiller's time, is already reckoned among the incredible antiques of a dated type of education. While the critic got the upper hand in the theater and concert hall, the journalist in the schools, and the press in society, art degenerated into a particularly lowly topic of conversation, and aesthetic criticism was used as a means of uniting a vain, distracted, selfish, and moreover piteously unoriginal sociability whose character is suggested by Schopenhauer's parable of the porcupines. As a result, art has never been so much talked about and so little esteemed. But is it still possible to have intercourse with a person capable of conversing about Beethoven or Shakespeare? Let each answer this question according to his own feelings: he will at any rate show by his answer his conception of "culture," provided he at least tries to answer the question, and has not already become dumbfounded with astonishment.

On the other hand, many a being more nobly and delicately endowed by nature, though he may have gradually become a critical barbarian in the manner described, might have something to say about the unexpected as well as totally unintelligible effect that a successful performance of Lohengrin, for example, had on him--except that perhaps there was no helpful interpreting hand to guide him; so the incomprehensibly different and altogether incomparable sensation that thrilled him remained isolated and, like a mysterious star, became extinct after a short period of brilliance. But it was then that he had an inkling of what an aesthetic listener is.

23

Whoever wishes to test rigorously to what extent he himself is related to the true aesthetic listener or belongs to the community of the Socratic-critical persons needs only to examine sincerely the feeling with which he accepts miracles represented on the stage: whether he feels his historical sense, which insists on strict psychological causality, insulted by them, whether he makes a benevolent concession and admits the miracle as a phenomenon intelligible to childhood but alien to him, or whether he experiences anything else. For in this way he will be able to determine to what extent he is capable of understanding myth as a concentrated image of the world that, as a condensation of phenomena, cannot dispense with miracles. It is probable, however, that almost everyone, upon close examination, finds that the critical-historical spirit of our culture has so affected him that he can only make the former existence of myth credible to himself by means of scholarship, through intermediary abstractions. But without myth every culture loses the healthy natural power of its creativity: only a horizon defined by myths completes and unifies a whole cultural movement. Myth alone saves all the powers of the imagination and of the Apollinian dream from their aimless wanderings. The images of the myth have to be the unnoticed omnipresent demonic guardians, under whose care the young soul grows to maturity and whose signs help the man to interpret his life and struggles. Even the state knows no more powerful unwritten laws than the mythical foundation that guarantees its connection with religion and its growth from mythical notions.

By way of comparison let us now picture the abstract man, untutored by myth; abstract education; abstract morality; abstract law; abstract state; let us imagine the lawless roving of the artistic imagination, unchecked by any native myth; let us think of a culture that has no fixed and sacred primordial site but is doomed to exhaust all possibilities and to nourish itself wretchedly on all other cultures--there we have the present age, the result of that Socratism which is bent on the destruction of myth. And now the mythless man stands eternally hungry, surrounded by all past ages, and digs and grubs for roots, even if he has to dig for them among the remotest antiquities. The tremendous historical need of our unsatisfied modern culture, the assembling around one of countless other cultures, the consuming desire for knowledge--what does all this point to, if not to the loss of myth, the loss of the mythical home, the mythical maternal womb? Let us ask ourselves whether the feverish and uncanny excitement of this culture is anything but the greedy seizing and snatching at food of a hungry man--and who would care to contribute anything to a culture that cannot be satisfied no matter how much it devours, and at whose contact the most vigorous and wholesome nourishment is changed into "history and criticism"?

We should also have to regard our German character with sorrowful despair, if it had already become inextricably entangled in, or even identical with, its culture, as we may observe to our horror in the case of civilized France. What for a long time was the great advantage of France and the cause of her vast superiority, namely, this very identity of people and culture, might compel us in view of this sight to congratulate ourselves that this so questionable culture of ours has as yet nothing in common with the noble core of our people's character? On the contrary, all our hopes stretch out longingly toward the perception that beneath this restlessly palpitating cultural life and convulsion there is concealed a glorious, intrinsically healthy, primordial power that, to be sure, stirs vigorously only at intervals in stupendous moments, and then continues to dream of a future awakening. It is from this abyss that the German Reformation came forth; and in its chorales the future tune of German music resounded for the first time. So deep, courageous, and spiritual, so exuberantly good and tender did this chorale of Luther sound--as the first Dionysian luring call breaking forth from dense thickets at the approach of spring. And in competing echoes the solemnly exuberant procession of Dionysian revelers responded, to whom we are indebted for German music--and to whom we shall be indebted for the rebirth of German myth.

I know that I must now lead the sympathizing and attentive friend to an elevated position of lonely contemplation, where he will have but a few companions, and I call out encouragingly to him that we must hold fast to our luminous guides, the Greeks. To purify our aesthetic insight, we have previously borrowed from them the two divine figures who rule over separate realms of art, and concerning whose mutual contact and enhancement we have acquired some notion through Greek tragedy. It had to appear to us that the demise of Greek tragedy was brought about through a remarkable and forcible dissociation of these two primordial artistic drives. To this process there corresponded a degeneration and transformation of the character of the Greek people, which calls for serious reflection on how necessary and close the fundamental connections are between art and the people, myth and custom, tragedy and the state. This demise of tragedy was at the same time the demise of myth. Until then the Greeks had felt involuntarily impelled to relate all their experiences immediately to their myths, indeed to understand them only in this relation. Thus even the immediate present had to appear to them right away sub specie aeterni [Under the aspect of the eternal.] and in a certain sense as timeless.

But the state no less than art dipped into this current of the timeless to find rest in it from the burden and the greed of the moment. And any people--just as, incidentally, also any individual--is worth only as much as it is able to press upon its experiences the stamp of the eternal; for thus it is, as it were, desecularized and shows its unconscious inward convictions of the relativity of time and of the true, that is metaphysical, significance of life. The opposite of this happens when a people begins to comprehend itself historically and to smash the mythical works that surround it. At that point we generally find a decisive secularization, a break with the unconscious metaphysics of its previous existence, together with all its ethical consequences. Greek art and pre-eminently Greek tragedy delayed above all the destruction of myth. One had to destroy tragedy, too, in order to be able to live away from the soil of home, uninhibited, in the wilderness of thought, custom, and deed. Even now this metaphysical drive still tries to create for itself a certainly attenuated form of transfiguration, in the Socratism of science that strives for life; but on the lower steps, this same drive led only to a feverish search that gradually lost itself in a pandemonium of myths and superstitions that were collected from all over and piled up in confusion: nevertheless the Greek sat among them with an unstilled heart until he learned to mask this fever with Greek cheerfulness and Greek frivolity, becoming a Graeculus [A contemptuous term for a Greek.], or he numbed his mind completely in some dark Oriental superstition.

Since the reawakening of Alexandrian-Roman antiquity in the fifteenth century we have approximated this state in the most evident manner, after a long interlude that is difficult to describe. On the heights we encounter the same overabundant lust for knowledge, the same unsatisfied delight in discovery, the same tremendous secularization, and beside it a homeless roving, a greedy crowding around foreign tables, a frivolous deification of the present, or a dully dazed retreat--everything sub specie saeculi [Under the aspect of the times, or the spirit of the age.], of the "present age." And these same symptoms allow us to infer the same lack at the heart of this culture, the destruction of myth. It scarcely seems possible to be continuously successful at transplanting a foreign myth without irreparably damaging the tree by this transplantation. In one case it may perhaps be strong and healthy enlugh to eliminate this foreign element in a terrible fight; usually, however, it must consume itself, sick and withered or in diseased superfoetation.

We think so highly of the pure and vigorous core of the German character that we dare to expect of it above all others this elimination of the forcibly implanted foreign elements, and consider it possible that the German spirit will return to itself. Some may suppose that this spirit must begin its fight with the elimination of everything Romanic. If so they may recognize an external preparation and encouragement in the victorious fortitude and bloody glory of the last war; but one must still seek the inner necessity in the ambition to be always worthy of the sublime champions on this way, Luther as well as our great artists and poets. But let him never believe that he could fight similar fights without the gods of his house, or his mythical home, without "bringing back" all German things! And if the German should hesitantly look around for a leader who might bring him back again into his long lost home whose ways and paths he scarcely knows anymore, let him merely listen to the ecstatically luring call of the Dionysian bird that hovers above him and wants to point the way for him.

24

Among the peculiar art effects of musical tragedy we had to emphasize an Apollinian illusion by means of which we were supposed to be saved from the immediate unity with Dionysian music, while our musical excitement could discharge itself in an Apollinian field and in relation to a visible intermediary world that had been interposed. At the same time we thought that we had observed how precisely through this discharge the intermediary world of the action on the stage, and the drama in general, had been made visible and intelligible form the inside to a degree that in all other Apollinian art remains unattained. Where the Apollinian receives wings from the spirit of music and soars, we thus found the highest intensification of its powers, and in this fraternal union of Apollo and Dionysus we had to recognize the apex of the Apollinian as well as the Dionysian aims of art.

To be sure, the Apollinian projection that is thus illuminated from inside by music does not achieve the peculiar effect of the weaker degrees of Apollinian art. What the epic or the animated stone can do, compelling the contemplative eye to find calm delight in the world of individuation, that could not be attained here, in spite of a higher animation and clarity. We looked at the drama and with penetrating eye reached its inner world of motives--and yet we felt as if only a parable passed us by, whose most profound meaning we almost thought we could guess and that we wished to draw away like a curtain in order to behold the primordial image behind it. The brightest clarity of the image did not suffice us, for this seemed to wish just as much to reveal something as to conceal something. Its revelation, being like a parable, seemed to summon us to teat the veil and to uncover the mysterious background; but at the same time this all-illuminated total visibility cast a spell over the eyes and prevented them from penetrating deeper.

Those who have never had the experience of having to see at the same time that they also longed to transcend all seeing will scarcely be able to imagine how definitely and clearly these two processes coexist and are felt at the same time, as one contemplates the tragic myth. But all truly aesthetic spectators will confirm that among the peculiar effects of tragedy this coexistence is the most remarkable. Now transfer this phenomenon of the aesthetic spectator into an analogous process in the tragic artist, and you will have understood the genesis of the tragic myth. With the Apollinian art sphere he shares the complete pleasure in mere appearance and in seeing, yet at the same time he negates this pleasure and finds a still higher satisfaction in the destruction of the visible world of mere appearance.

The content of the tragic myth is , first of all, an epic event and the glorification of the fighting hero. But what is the origin of this enigmatic trait that the suffering and the fate of the hero, the most painful triumphs, the most agonizing oppositions of motives, in short, the exemplification of this wisdom of Silenus, or, to put it aesthetically, that which is ugly and disharmonic, is represented ever anew in such countless forms and with such a distinct preference--and precisely in the most fruitful and youthful period of a people? Surely a higher pleasure must be perceived in all this.

That life really so tragic would least of all explain the origin of an art form--assuming that art is not merely imitation of the reality of nature but rather a metaphysical supplement of the reality of nature, placed beside it for its overcoming. The tragic myth too, insofar as it belongs to art at all, participates fully in this metaphysical intention of art to transfigure. But what does it transfigure when it presents the world of appearance in the image of the suffering hero? Least of all the "reality" of this world of appearance, for it says to us: "Look there! Look closely! This is your life, this is the hand on the clock of your existence."

And the myth should show us this life in order to thus transfigure it? But if not, in what then lies the aesthetic pleasure with which we let these images, too, pass before us? I asked about the aesthetic pleasure, though I know full well that many of these images also produce at times a moral delight, for example, under the form of pity or moral triumph. But those who would derive the effect of the tragic solely from these moral sources--which, to be sure, has been the custom in aesthetics all too long--should least of all believe that they have thus accomplished something for art, which above all must demand purity in its sphere. If you would explain the tragic myth, the first requirement is to seek the pleasure that is peculiar to it in the purely aesthetic sphere, without transgressing into the region of pity, fear, or the morally sublime. How can the ugly and the disharmonic, the content of the tragic myth, stimulate aesthetic pleasure?

Here it becomes necessary to take a bold running start and leap into a metaphysics of art, by repeating the sentence written above [Section 5], that existence and thee world seem justified only as an aesthetic phenomenon. In this sense, it is precisely the tragic myth that has to convince us that even the ugly and disharmonic are part of an artistic game that the will in the eternal amplitude of its pleasure plays with itself. But this primordial phenomenon of Dionysian art is difficult to grasp, and there is only one direct way to make it intelligible and grasp it immediately: through the wonderful significance of musical dissonance. Quite generally, only music, placed beside the world, can give us an idea of what is meant by the justification of the world as an aesthetic phenomenon. The joy aroused by the tragic myth has the same origin as the joyous sensation of dissonance in music. The Dionysian, with its primordial joy experienced even in pain, is the common source of music and tragic myth.

Is it not possible that by calling to our aid the musical relation of dissonance we may meanwhile have made the difficult problem of the tragic effect much easier? For we now understand what it means to wish to see tragedy and at the same time to long to get beyond all seeing: referring to the artistically employed dissonances, we should have to characterize the corresponding state by saying that we desire to hear and at the same time long to get beyond all hearing. The striving for the infinite, the wing-beat of longing that accompanies the highest delight in clearly perceived reality, reminds us that in both states we must recognize a Dionysian phenomenon: again and again it reveals to us the playful construction and destruction of the individual world as the overflow of a primordial delight. Thus the dark Heraclitus compares the world-building force to a playing child that places stones here and there and builds sand hills only to overthrow them again.

In order, then, to form a true estimate of the Dionysian capacity of a people, we must not only think of their music, but also just as necessarily of their tragic myth, as the second witness of this capacity. Considering this extremely close relationship between music and myth, one must suppose that a degeneration and depravation of the one will involve a deterioration of the other, if the weakening of the myth really expresses a weakening of the Dionysian capacity. Concerning both, however, a glance at the development of the German character should not leave us in any doubt. In the opera, just as in the abstract character of our mythless existence, in an art degenerated to mere entertainment as will as in a life guided by concepts, the inartistic as well as life-consuming nature of Socratic optimism had revealed itself to us. Yet we were comforted by indications that nevertheless in some inaccessible abyss the German spirit still rests and dreams, undestroyed, in glorious health, profundity and Dionysian strength, like a knight sunk in slumber; and from this abyss the Dionysian song rises to our ears to let us know that this German knight is still dreaming his primordial Dionysian myth in

blissfully serious visions. Let no one believe that the German
spirit has forever lost its mythical home when it can sill
understand so plainly the voices of the birds that tell of that
home. Some day it will find itself awake in all the morning
freshness following a tremendous sleep: then it will slay dragons,
destroy vicious dwarfs, wake Brunhilde--and even Wotan's spear
will not be able to stop this course!

My friends, you who believe in Dionysian music, you also know
what tragedy means to us. There we have tragic myth reborn
from music--and in this myth we can hope for everything and
forget what is most painful. What is most painful for all of us,
however, is--the prolonged degradation in which the German
genius has lived, estranged from house and home, in the service
of vicious dwarfs. You understand my words--as you will also, in
conclusion, understand my hopes.

25

Music and tragic myth are equally expressions of the Dionysian
capacity of a people, and they are inseparable. Both derive from
a sphere of art that lies beyond the Apollinian; both transfigure a
region in whose joyous chords dissonance as well as the terrible
image of the world fade away charmingly; both play with the
sting of displeasure, trusting in their exceedingly powerful magic
arts; and by means of this play both justify the existence of even
the "worst world." Thus the Dionysian is seen to be, compared to
the Apollinian, the eternal and original artistic power that first
calls the whole world of phenomena into existence--and it is only
in the midst of this world that a new transfiguring illusion
becomes necessary in order to keep the animated world of
individuation alive.

If we could imagine dissonance become man--and what else is
man?--this dissonance, to be able to live, would need a splendid
illusion that would cover dissonance with a veil of beauty. This
is the true artistic aim of Apollo in whose name we comprehend
all those countless illusions of the beauty of mere appearance
that at every moment make life worth living at all and prompt the
desire to live on in order to experience the next moment.

Of this foundation of all existence--the Dionysian basic ground of the world--not one whit more may enter the consciousness of the human individual than can be overcome again by this Apollinian power of transfiguration. Thus these two art drives must unfold their powers in a strict proportion, according to the law of eternal justice. Where the Dionysian powers rise up as impetuously as we experience them now, Apollo, too, must already have descended among us, wrapped in a cloud; and the next generation will probably behold his most ample beautiful effects.

That this effect should be necessary, everybody should be able to feel most assuredly by means of intuition, provided he has ever felt, if only in a dream, that he was carried back into an ancient Greek existence. Walking under lofty Ionic colonnades, looking up toward a horizon that was cut off by pure and noble lines, finding reflections of his transfigured shape in the shining marble at his side, and all around him solemnly striding or delicately moving human beings, speaking with harmonious voices and in a rhythmic language of gestures--in view of this continual influx of beauty, would he not have to exclaim, raising his hand to Apollo: "Blessed people of Hellas! How great must Dionysus be among you if the god of Delos considers such magic necessary to heal your dithyrambic madness!"

To a man in such a mood, however, an old Athenian, looking up at him with the sublime eyes of Aeschylus, might reply: "But say this, too, curious stranger: how much did this people have to suffer to be able to become so beautiful! But now follow me to witness a tragedy, and sacrifice with me in the temple of both deities!"

THE END

SEVENTY-FIVE
APHORISMS
from Five Volumes

CONTENTS

Human, All-Too-Human (1878)

45

Dual prehistory of good and evil.— The concept of good and evil has a dual prehistory; *first,* in the soul of the ruling tribes and castes. Whoever has the power to repay good with good, evil with evil, and also actually repays, thus being grateful and vengeful, is called good; whoever is powerless and unable to repay is considered bad. As one who is good, one belongs to the "good," a community that possesses communal feeling because all individuals are knit together by the sense of repayment. As one who is bad, one belongs to the "bad," a group of subjected, impotent human beings who have no communal feeling. The good are a caste, the bad a mass like dust. Good and bad are for a time the same as noble and low, master and slave. But the *enemy* is not considered evil, he can repay. Trojan and Greek are both good in Homer. Not he that does us harm but he that is contemptible is considered bad. In the community of the good, good is inherited; it is impossible that a bad person should grow out of such good soil. If one of the good nevertheless does something unworthy of the good, then one has recourse to excuses; one blames a god, for example, saying that he struck the good man with delusion and madness.

    Then, in the soul of the oppressed, the powerless. Here all *other* human beings are considered hostile, ruthless, exploiting, cruel, cunning, whether they be noble or low. Evil is the characteristic word for man, indeed for every living being believed in, for example for a god; human or divine means as much as devilish or evil. The signs of graciousness, helpfulness, pity are taken anxiously as wiles, as preludes to a disastrous conclusion, soporifics and craft, in short, as refined malice. As long as individuals have such an attitude, a community can hardly come into being; at best, only its rudiments: hence, wherever this conception of good and evil rules, the ruination of individuals, their tribes and races, is near.

Our current morality has grown on the soil of the *ruling* tribes and castes.

92

Origin of justice.—Justice (fairness)² originates among those who are approximately *equally powerful,* as Thucydides (in the terrible conversation between the Athenian and Melian ambassadors) comprehended correctly: where there is no clearly recognizable predominance and a fight would mean inconclusive mutual damage, there the idea originates that one might come to an understanding and negotiate one's claims: the initial character of justice is the character of a trade. Each satisfies the other inasmuch as each receives what he esteems more than the other does. One gives another what he wants, so that it becomes his, and in return one receives what one wants. Thus justice is repayment and exchange on the assumption of an approximately equal power position; revenge originally belongs in the domain of justice, being an exchange. Gratitude, too.

Justice naturally derives from prudent concern with self-preservation; that means, from the egoism of the consideration: "Why should I harm myself uselessly and perhaps not attain my goal anyway?"

So much on the *origin* of justice. In accordance with their intellectual habits, men have *forgotten* the original purpose of so-called just, fair actions, and for millennia children have been taught to admire and emulate such actions. Hence it has gradually come to appear as if a just action were unegoistic; but the high esteem for it depends on this appearance, and this esteem, moreover, continues to grow all the time, like all esteem; for whatever is highly esteemed becomes the object of striving, emulation, and multiplication, coupled with many sacrifices, and grows further because the value of the effort and zeal is added by every individual to the value of the thing he esteems.

How little the world would look moral without forgetfulness! A poet might say that God made forgetfulness the guard he placed at the threshold of human dignity.

96

Mores and moral. — Being moral or ethical means obeying ancient established law or custom. Whether one submits to it with difficulty or gladly, that is immaterial; it is enough that one does it. *"Good"* is what one calls those who do what is moral as if they did it by nature, after long heredity—in other words, easily and gladly —whatever may be moral in this sense (practicing revenge, for example, when practicing revenge belongs, as it did among the more ancient Greeks, to good mores). He is called good because he is good "for something"; but because benevolence, pity, and that sort of thing have always been felt to be, through many changes in mores, "good for something" and useful, it has come to pass that now the benevolent and helpful are pre-eminently considered "good."

Being evil is being "not *moral"* (immoral), practicing immorality, resisting tradition, however reasonable or stupid tradition may be. Harming the neighbor, however, has been felt to be pre-eminently harmful in all the moral laws of different ages, until now the word "evil" is associated primarily with the deliberate harming of the neighbor.

Not "egoistic" and "unegoistic" is the fundamental pair of contraries that has led men to distinguish moral and immoral, good and evil, but rather: being tied to a tradition and law, and detachment from them. How the tradition *originated* is indifferent; in any case it was without any regard for good and evil or any immanent categorical imperative, but above all in order to preserve a *community, a people*: every superstitious custom that originated on the basis of some misinterpreted accident involves a tradition that it is moral to follow; for detaching oneself from it is dangerous, even more dangerous for the community than for the individual (because the deity punishes the community—and the individual only indirectly—for the sacrilege and the violation of divine privileges). Now every tradition becomes ever more venerable the more remote its origins are and the more they have been forgotten; the veneration shown it is accumulated, generation upon generation; finally, the tradition becomes holy and inspires reverence; and thus the *morality of pious regard for the old* is certainly a much more ancient morality than that which demands unegoistic actions.

136

On Christian asceticism and holiness.—Strongly as individual thinkers have endeavored to present the rare phenomena of morality that are usually called asceticism and holiness as if they were marvels that it would almost be sacrilege and desecration to illuminate by raising the torch of rational explanation up to their face— the temptation to commit this sacrilege is just as strong. A powerful impulse of nature has led men in all ages to protest against these phenomena as such; science, insofar as it is, as mentioned, an imitation of nature, at least takes the liberty to object to their alleged inexplicability and even unapproachability. To be sure, so far it has not succeeded: these phenomena are still unexplained, much to the delight of the said admirers of moral marvels. For, to speak generally: the unexplained should by all means be unexplainable, the unexplainable by all means unnatural, supernatural, miraculous—

thus goes the demand in the souls of all the religious and metaphysicians (of artists, too, if they are at the same time thinkers); while
the scientific person sees in this demand the "evil principle."
The general first probability one encounters as one contemplates holiness and asceticism is this: their nature is *complicated;*
for almost everywhere, in the physical world as well as in the moral
world, one has succeeded in reducing the allegedly miraculous to
the complicated which depends on many conditions. Let us dare
then to begin by isolating single impulses in the souls of holy men
and ascetics, and to conclude by thinking of them as grown together.

137

There is a *defiance of oneself* among whose most sublimated
expressions some forms of asceticism belong. For certain human
beings have such a great need to exercise their force and lust to
rule that, lacking other objects, or because they have always failed
elsewhere, they finally have recourse to tyrannizing certain parts of
their own nature, as it were sections or stages of themselves.

Thus some thinkers profess views that evidently do not serve
to increase or improve their reputations; some practically conjure
up the disrespect of others for them, although it would be easy for
them to remain highly respected, simply by keeping still. Others
recant former opinions and are not afraid of henceforth being
called inconsistent: on the contrary, they exert themselves to that
end and behave like exuberant riders who like their horse best
when it has gone wild, is covered with sweat, and shying.

Thus man ascends the highest mountains on dangerous paths,
to laugh scornfully at his anxiety and his trembling knees; thus the
philosopher professes views of asceticism, humility, and sanctity in
whose splendor his own image is made exceedingly ugly. This
breaking of oneself, this mockery of one's own nature, this *spernere
se sperni* of which religions have made so much, is really a very
high degree of vanity. The whole morality of the Sermon on the
Mount belongs here: man experiences a veritable voluptuousness

in violating himself by means of exaggerated demands and in then deifying this tyrannically demanding force in his soul.

In every ascetic morality man adores part of himself as God and to that end needs to diabolicize the rest.

142

To sum up what has been said here: that state of the soul which the holy man or the man who is becoming holy enjoys is composed of elements which all of us know quite well; they merely take on a different coloring when they are influenced by nonreligious ideas, and then they are usually reproached by men just as much as they can count—or at least could count in former times—on admiration, even worship, when associated with religion and the ultimate meaning of existence.

Sometimes the holy man practices that defiance against himself which is closely related to the lust to rule at any price and which gives even the loneliest the feeling of power; sometimes his swollen feeling changes from the craving to let his passions run their course into the craving to make them collapse like wild horses under the powerful pressure of a proud soul; sometimes he wants the complete cessation of all feelings that disturb, torment, provoke —a wakeful sleep, an enduring rest in the lap of a dumb, animal- or plant-like indolence; sometimes he seeks a fight and inflames it within himself because boredom fixes him with a yawning countenance: he scourges his self-deification with self-contempt and cruelty, he delights in the wild rebellion of his desires, in the sharp pain of sin, even in the idea that he is lost; he knows how to lay a snare for his affects, that of the most extreme lust to rule, for example, so that it changes into the most extreme humiliation and this contrast completely unbalances his hounded soul; and finally: if he should crave visions or conversation with the dead or with divine beings, this is at bottom a rare kind of voluptuousness that he desires, but perhaps that voluptuousness in which all the others are tied up into one knot. Novalis, one of the authorities on questions of holiness, both by experience and by instinct, once expressed the whole secret with a naïve joy: "It is marvelous enough that the association of voluptuousness, religion, and cruelty has not long attracted the attention of men to their close kinship and common tendency."

143

Not what the holy man *is* but what he *signifies* in the eyes of those who are not holy gives him his world-historical value. It was because one was *wrong* about him, because one *misinterpreted* the states of his soul and drew as sharp a line as possible between oneself and him, as if he were something utterly incomparable and strangely superhuman—that he gained that extraordinary power with which he could dominate the imagination of whole peoples and ages. He did not know himself; he understood the writing of his moods, inclinations, and actions according to an art of interpretation which was just as extravagant and artificial as the pneumatic interpretation of the Bible. What was eccentric and sick in his nature, with its fusion of spiritual poverty, faulty knowledge, spoilt health, and overexcited nerves remained concealed from his own eyes and from the eyes of those who looked at him. He was not an especially good person, even less an especially wise person; but he *signified* something that exceeded all human measure of goodness and wisdom. The faith in him supported the faith in the divine and miraculous, in a religious meaning of all existence, in an impending final day of judgment. In the evening splendor of the world-end's sunset that illuminated the Christian peoples, the shadowy figure of the holy man grew into something enormous—indeed, to such a height that even in our time, which no longer believes in God, there are still thinkers who believe in the holy man.

144

It scarcely needs saying that this sketch of the holy man, being drawn after the average of the whole species, can be countered with many sketches that tend to produce a more agreeable feeling. Single exceptions stand out from the species, whether by virtue of great mildness and humanitarianism or by the magic of unusual energy; others are attractive in the highest degree because certain delusions inundate their whole nature with light—as is the case, for example, with the celebrated founder of Christianity who considered himself the inborn son of God and therefore felt he was without sin; thus, by virtue of an illusion—which should not be judged too harshly, for the whole of antiquity was full of sons of gods —he attained the same goal, the feeling of complete freedom from sin, complete lack of responsibility, which is now available to everybody by means of science!

I have also ignored the holy men of India who occupy an intermediate stage between the Christian holy man and the Greek philosopher, and thus do not represent a pure type: knowledge, science—insofar as science existed—raising oneself above other men through the logical discipline and training of thought, were just as much demanded among the Buddhists, as a sign of holiness, as the same qualities were repudiated and pronounced heretical in the Christian world where they were held to be signs of unholiness.

Mixed Opinions
and Maxims (1879)

89

Mores and their victim.— The origin of mores may be found in two thoughts: "society is worth more than the individual," and "enduring advantage is to be preferred to ephemeral advantage"— from which it follows that the enduring advantage of society must be given precedence, unconditionally, over the advantage of the individual, especially over his momentary well-being but also over his enduring advantage and even his continued existence. Whether the individual suffers from an institution that is good for the whole, whether it causes him to atrophy or perish—mores must be preserved, sacrifices must be made. But such an attitude *originates* only in those who are *not* its victims—for they claim in their behalf that the individual may be worth more than many, also that present enjoyment, the moment in paradise, may have to be valued higher than a pallid continuation of painless or complacent states. The philosophy of the sacrificial animal, however, is always sounded too late; and so we retain mores and *morality* —which is no more than the feeling for the whole quintessence of mores under which one lives and has been brought up—brought up not as an individual but as a member of a whole, as a digit of a majority.— Thus it happens constantly that an individual brings to bear upon himself, by means of his morality, the tyranny of the majority.

130

Readers' bad manners.— A reader is doubly guilty of bad manners against the author when he praises his second book at the expense of the first (or vice versa) and then asks the author to be grateful for that.

137

The worst readers.— The worst readers are those who proceed like plundering soldiers: they pick up a few things they can use, soil and confuse the rest, and blaspheme the whole.

145

Value of honest books.— Honest books make the reader honest, at least by luring into the open his hatred and aversion which his sly prudence otherwise knows how to conceal best. But against a book one lets oneself go, even if one is very reserved toward people.

157

Sharpest criticism.— One criticizes a person, a book, most sharply when one pictures their ideal.

168

Praise of aphorisms.— A good aphorism is too hard for the tooth of time and is not consumed by all millennia, although it serves every time for nourishment: thus it is the great paradox of literature, the intransitory amid the changing, the food that always remains esteemed, like salt, and never loses its savor, as even that does.

200

Original.— Not that one is the first to see something new, but that one sees *as new* what is old, long familiar, seen and overlooked by everybody; is what distinguishes truly original minds. The first discoverer is ordinarily that wholly common creature, devoid of spirit and addicted to fantasy—accident.

201

Philosophers' error.— The philosopher supposes that the value of his philosophy lies in the whole, in the structure; but posterity finds its value in the stone which he used for building, and which is used many more times after that for building—better. Thus it finds the value in the fact that the structure can be destroyed and *nevertheless* retains value as building material.

206

Why scholars are nobler than artists.— Science requires *nobler* natures than poetry does: they have to be simpler, less ambitious.

more abstinent, quieter, not so concerned about posthumous fame, and forget themselves over matters that rarely seem worthy in the eyes of many of such a sacrifice of one's personality. To this must be added another loss of which they are conscious: the type of their work, the continual demand for the greatest sobriety, weakens their *will;* the fire is not kept as strong as on the hearth of poetic natures—and therefore they often lose their highest strength and bloom at an earlier age than those men do—and, as mentioned, they *realize* this danger. In any case they *appear* less gifted because they shine less, and they will be considered inferior to what they are.

251

In parting.— Not how one soul comes close to another but how it moves away shows me their kinship and how much they belong together.

298

Virtue has not been invented by the Germans.— Goethe's nobility and lack of envy, Beethoven's noble hermit's resignation, Mozart's charm and grace of the heart, Handel's unbendable manliness and freedom under the law, Bach's confident and transfigured inner life that does not even find it necessary to renounce splendor and success—are these in any way *German* qualities?— But if not, it at least shows for what Germans should strive and what they can attain.

309

Siding against oneself.— Our adherents never forgive us if we take sides against ourselves: for in their eyes this means not only rejecting their love but also exposing their intelligence.

325

Opinions.— Most people are nothing and are considered nothing until they have dressed themselves up in general convictions and public opinions—in accordance with the tailor philosophy: clothes make people. Of the exceptional person, however, it must be said: *only he that wears it makes the costume;* here opinions cease to be public and become something other than masks, finery, and disguises.

341

Loving the master.— Not as apprentices do, loves a master a master.

346

Being misunderstood.— When one is misunderstood as a whole, it is impossible to remove completely a single misunderstanding. One has to realize this lest one waste superfluous energy on one's defense.

404

How duty acquires splendor.— The means for changing your iron duty to gold in everyone's eyes is this: always keep a little more than you promise.

405

Prayer to men.— "Forgive us our virtues"—thus one should pray to men.

408

The journey to Hades.— I, too, have been in the underworld, like Odysseus, and shall be there often yet; and not only rams have I sacrificed to be able to speak with a few of the dead, but I have not spared my own blood. Four pairs it was that did not deny themselves to my sacrifice: Epicurus and Montaigne, Goethe and Spinoza, Plato and Rousseau, Pascal and Schopenhauer. With these I must come to terms when I have long wandered alone; they may call me right and wrong; to them will I listen when in the process they call each other right and wrong. Whatsoever I say, resolve, or think up for myself and others—on these eight I fix my eyes and see their eyes fixed on me.

May the living forgive me that occasionally *they* appear to me as shades, so pale and somber, so restless and, alas, so lusting for life—while those men then seem so alive to me as if now, *after* death, they could never again grow weary of life. But *eternal aliveness* is what counts: what matters "eternal life" or any life!

The Wanderer
and His Shadow (1880)

33

Elements of revenge.— The word "revenge" is said so quickly, it almost seems as if it could not contain more than one root concept and feeling. And so people are still trying to find this root—just as our economists still have not got tired of smelling such a unity in the word "value" and of looking for the original root concept of value. As if all words were not pockets into which now this and now that has been put, and now many things at once! Thus "revenge," too, is now this and now that, and now something very composite.

Let us distinguish, *first,* that return blow of resistance which is almost an involuntary reflex, executed even against lifeless objects that have harmed us (such as moving machines): the sense of this countermove is to stop the harm by bringing the machine to a halt. Occasionally, the strength of the counterblow must be so strong to succeed in this that it smashes the machine; but where that is too strong to be destructible immediately by an individual, he will nevertheless strike as hard as he can—making, as it were, an all-out-attempt. One behaves the same way against persons who harm one, as long as one feels the harm immediately: if you want to call this action an act of revenge, all right; but consider that it is only *self-preservation* that has here put its rational machinery into motion, and that in the last analysis one does not think at all of the harming person in such a case but only of oneself: we act that way *without* any wish to do harm in return, merely in order to *get away* with life and limb.

Time is needed—when instead of concentrating on oneself one begins to think about one's opponent, asking oneself how one can hurt him the most. This happens in the *second* type of revenge: reflection on the other person's vulnerability and capacity for suffering is its presupposition; one wants to hurt. Protecting oneself against further harm, on the other hand, is so little a consideration for the seeker of such vengeance that he almost regularly brings about further harm to himself and quite often anticipates this in cold blood. In the first type of revenge it was fear of a second blow that made the counterblow as strong as possible; here we find almost total indifference to what the opponent *will* do yet; the strength of the counterblow is determined solely by what he *has* done to us. But what has he done? And what use is it to us if he now suffers after we have suffered on his account? What matters is a *restoration,* while the act of revenge of the first type serves only *self-preservation.* Perhaps we have lost through our opponent possessions, rank, friends, children: such losses are not brought back by revenge; the restoration concerns solely a *loss incidental* to all these losses. The revenge of restoration does not protect against further harm; it does not make good the harm suffered—except in one case. If our *honor* has suffered from our opponent, then revenge can *restore* it. But this has suffered damage in every instance in which suffering has been inflicted on us deliberately; for our opponent thus demonstrated that he did not *fear* us. By revenge we demonstrate that we do not fear him either: this constitutes the equalization, the restoration. (The intent of showing one's utter lack of *fear* goes so far in some persons that the danger their revenge involves for them—loss of health or life or other damage—is for them an indispensable condition of all revenge. Therefore they choose the means of a duel although the courts offer them help in obtaining satisfaction for the insult: but they do not accept an undangerous restoration of their honor as sufficient, because it cannot demonstrate their lack of fear.)

In the first type of revenge it is fear that strikes the counterblow; here, on the other hand, it is the absence of fear that, as I have tried to show, *wants to prove* itself by means of the counterblow.

Nothing therefore seems more different than the inner motivation of the two ways of action that are called by one name, "revenge." Nevertheless it happens quite frequently that the person seeking revenge is unclear about what really induced him to act: perhaps he delivered the counterblow from fear and in order to preserve himself, but later, when he has time to think about the point of his injured honor, he convinces himself that he avenged himself for his honor's sake—after all, this motive is *nobler* than the other one. Moreover, it is also important whether he believes his honor to have been injured in the eyes of others (the world) or only in the eyes of the opponent who insulted him: in the latter case he will prefer secret revenge, in the former public revenge.

Depending on whether he projects himself strongly or weakly into the soul of his opponent and the spectators, his revenge will be more embittered or tamer; if he lacks this type of imagination entirely, he will not think of revenge at all, for in that case the feeling for "honor" is not present in him and hence cannot be injured. Just so, he will not think of revenge if he *despises* the doer and the spectators of the deed—because they, being despised, cannot accord him any honor and hence also cannot take it away. Finally, he will forgo revenge in the not unusual case in which he loves the doer: to be sure, he thus loses honor in his opponent's eyes and perhaps thus becomes less worthy of being loved in return. But even forgoing all such counterlove is a sacrifice that love is prepared to make if only it does not *have to hurt* the beloved being: that would mean hurting oneself more than this sacrifice hurts.

Thus: everybody will revenge himself unless he is without honor or full of contempt or full of love for the person who has harmed and insulted him. Even when he has recourse to the courts he wants revenge as a private person—but *besides,* being a member of society who thinks further and considers the future, he also wants society's revenge on one who does not *honor* it. Thus judicial punishment *restores* both private honor and the honor of society—which means, punishment is revenge.

Indubitably, it also contains that other element of revenge which we described first, insofar as society uses punishment for its *self-preservation* and deals a counterblow in *self-defense.* Punishment desires to prevent *further* damage; it desires to *deter.* Thus both of these so different elements of revenge are actually *tied together* in punishment, and perhaps this is the main support of that above-mentioned conceptual confusion by virtue of which the individual who revenges himself usually does not *know what* he really *wants.*

194

Dreams.— On the rare occasions when our dreams succeed and achieve perfection—most dreams are bungled—they are symbolic chains of scenes and images in place of a narrative poetic language; they circumscribe our experiences or expectations or situations with such poetic boldness and decisiveness that in the morning we are always amazed at ourselves when we remember our dreams. We use up too much artistry in our dreams—and therefore often are impoverished during the day.

202

Tourists.— They climb mountains like animals, stupid and sweating; one has forgotten to tell them that there are beautiful views on the way up.

203

Too much and too little.— All men now live through too much and think through too little: they suffer at the same time from extreme hunger and from colic, and therefore become thinner and thinner, no matter how much they eat.— Whoever says now, "I have not lived through anything"—is an ass.

204

End and goal.— Not every end is the goal. The end of a melody is not its goal; and yet: as long as the melody has not reached its end, it also hasn't reached its goal. A parable.

208

How to have all men against you.— If anyone dared to say now, "Whoever is not for me, is against me," — he would immediately have all men against him.— This does our time honor.

249

Positive and negative.— This thinker needs nobody to refute him: for that he suffices himself.

263

Way to equality.— A few hours of mountain climbing turn a villain and a saint into two rather equal creatures. Exhaustion is the shortest way to *equality* and *fraternity*—and *liberty* is added eventually by sleep.

297

Not to wish to see too soon.— As long as one lives through an experience, one must surrender to the experience and shut one's eyes instead of becoming an observer *immediately*. For that would disturb the good digestion of the experience: instead of wisdom one would acquire indigestion.

298

From the practice of wise men.— To become wise, one must *wish* to have certain experiences and run, as it were, into their gaping jaws. This, of course, is very dangerous; many a wise guy has been swallowed.

301

A testimony of love.— Somebody said: "About two persons I have never reflected very thoroughly: that is the testimony of my love for them."

302

How one tries to improve bad arguments.— Some people throw a bit of their personality after their bad arguments, as if that might straighten their paths and turn them into right and good arguments—just as a man in a bowling alley, after he has let go of the ball, still tries to direct it with gestures.

307

When taking leave is needed.— From what you would know and measure, you must take leave, at least for a time. Only after having left town, you see how high its towers rise above the houses.

317

Opinions and fish.— Possessing opinions is like possessing fish, assuming one has a fish pond. One has to go fishing and needs some luck—then one has one's own fish, one's own opinions. I am speaking of live opinions, of live fish. Others are satisfied if they own a cabinet of fossils—and in their heads, "convictions."

322

Death.— The certain prospect of death could sweeten every life with a precious and fragrant drop of levity—and now you strange apothecary souls have turned it into an ill-tasting drop of poison that makes the whole of life repulsive.

323

Remorse.— Never give way to remorse, but immediately say to yourself: that would merely mean adding a second stupidity to the first.— If you have done harm, see how you can do good.— If you are punished for your actions, bear the punishment with the feeling that you *are* doing good—by deterring others from falling prey to the same folly. Every evildoer who is punished may feel that he is a benefactor of humanity.

326

Don't touch!— There are terrible people who, instead of solving a problem, bungle it and make it more difficult for all who come after. Whoever can't hit the nail on the head should, please, not hit it at all.

333

Dying for the "truth."— We should not let ourselves be burnt for our opinions: we are not that sure of them. But perhaps for this: that we may have and change our opinions.

The Dawn (1881)

1

Rationality ex post facto.— Whatever lives long is gradually so saturated with reason that its irrational origins become improbable. Does not almost every accurate history of the origin of something sound paradoxical and sacrilegious to our feelings? Doesn't the good historian *contradict* all the time?

18

The morality of voluntary suffering.— What is the supreme enjoyment for men who live in the state of war of those small, continually endangered communities which are characterized by the strictest mores? In other words, for vigorous, vindictive, vicious, suspicious souls who are prepared for what is most terrible and hardened by deprivations and mores? The enjoyment of *cruelty;* and in these circumstances it is even accounted among the *virtues* of such a soul if it is inventive and insatiable in cruelty. The community feels refreshed by cruel deeds, and casts off for once the gloom of continual anxiety and caution. Cruelty belongs to the most ancient festive joys of mankind. Hence one supposes that the *gods,* too, feel refreshed and festive when one offers them the sight of cruelty; and so the idea creeps into the world that *voluntary suffering,* torture one has chosen oneself, has value and makes good sense.

Gradually, the mores shape a communal practice in accordance with this idea: all extravagant well-being henceforth arouses some mistrust, and all hard and painful states more and more confidence. One supposes that the gods might look upon us ungraciously because of our happiness, and graciously because of our suffering—not by any means with pity. For pity is considered contemptible and unworthy of a strong and terrible soul. Rather, graciously, because it delights them and puts them into good spirits; for those who are cruel enjoy the supreme titillation of the feeling of power.

Thus the concept of the "most moral man" of the community comes to contain the virtue of frequent suffering, deprivation, a hard way of life, and of cruel self-mortification—*not*, to say this again and again, as a means of self-discipline, self-control, and the desire for individual happiness, but as a virtue that makes the community look good to the evil gods, steaming up to them like a continual sacrifice of atonement upon some altar. All those spiritual leaders of peoples who succeeded in stirring something in the inert but fertile mud of their mores, had need not only of madness but also of voluntary torture to engender faith—and most and first of all, as always, their faith in themselves. The more their own spirit moved along novel paths and was therefore tormented by pangs of conscience and anxieties, the more cruelly they raged against their own flesh, their own desires, and their own health—as if they wanted to offer the deity some substitute gratification in case it should perhaps be embittered on account of customs one had neglected and fought against and new goals one had championed.

Let us not believe too quickly that now we have rid ourselves completely of such a logic of feeling. Let the most heroic souls question themselves about this. Every smallest step on the field of free thought and the individually formed life has always been fought for with spiritual and physical torments: not only moving forward, no, above all moving, motion, change have required innumerable martyrs, all through the long path-seeking and basic mil-

168 SEVENTY-FIVE APHORISMS

lennia of which, to be sure, people don't think when they talk, as usual, about "world history," that ridiculously small segment of human existence. And even in this so-called world history, which is at bottom much ado about the latest news, there is no really more important theme than the primordial tragedy of the martyrs *who wanted to move the swamps.*

Nothing has been bought more dearly than that little bit of human reason and of a feeling of freedom that now constitutes our pride. But it is this very pride that now makes it almost impossible for us to feel with those vast spans of time characterized by the "morality of mores" which antedate "world history" as the *real and decisive main history that determined the character of humanity*—when suffering was a virtue, cruelty a virtue, dissimulation a virtue, revenge a virtue, the slander of reason a virtue, while well-being was a danger, the craving for knowledge a danger, peace a danger, pity a danger, being pitied ignominy, work ignominy, madness divine, change immoral and pregnant with disaster.

You think that all this has changed, and that humanity must thus have changed its character? You who think you know men, learn to know yourselves better!

112

On the natural history of duty and right.— Our duties—are the rights others have against us. How did the others acquire these rights? By taking us to be capable of contracts and of repayment, as equal and similar to them; by entrusting us with something on this basis and educating, correcting, and supporting us. We do our duty—that means: we justify this idea of our power on the basis of which we have been treated this way; we give back in the same measure in which one has given to us. Thus it is our pride that bids us do our duty—we want to regain our sovereignty when we balance what others have done for us with something we do for them —for in this way they have intruded into the sphere of our power and would keep their hand in it constantly if we did not repay them with our "duty," which means that we intrude into their power. The rights of others can relate only to what is within our power; it would be unreasonable if they wanted something from us that does not belong to us. To be more precise one should say: only to what they suppose is within our power, assuming that it is the same thing we suppose to be within our power. The same error could easily be made on both sides: the sense of a duty depends on our sharing with the others the same *faith* about the extent of our power: namely, that we promise certain things and are *capable* of incurring these duties ("freedom of the will").

My *rights:* they define that part of my power which the others have not only conceded to me but in which they wish to preserve me. What leads the others to do this? First, their prudence and fear and caution—whether they expect something similar in return from us (protection of their rights), or consider a fight with us dangerous or pointless, or see in every diminution of our strength a disadvantage for themselves because it would render us unfit for an alliance with them against a third and hostile power. Then, deeding or ceding. In this case the others have power enough, more than enough, to be able to give some of it away and to guarantee the piece they give away to the person who receives it—in which case a slight feeling of power is assumed in the person who accepts the present. Thus rights originate: recognized and guaranteed degrees of power. If the proportions of power are changed drastically, rights pass away, and new rights come to be—which is apparent in international law with its constant passing away and coming to be. If our power is decreased drastically, the feelings of those who have so far guaranteed our rights change: they consider whether they can restore us to our old full possession—and if they feel incapable of that, then they deny our "rights" henceforth. Just so, when our power is increased drastically, the feelings of those change who have so far recognized it and whose recognition we now no longer need: they may try to reduce our power to its former measure, they may wish to interfere, invoking their "duty"—but this is just a waste of words. Where right *rules,* a state and degree of power is preserved, and a diminution and increase are resisted. The right of others is the concession of our feeling of power to the feeling of power among these others. When our power is proved to have been profoundly shaken and broken, our rights cease; on the other hand, when we have become a great deal more powerful, the rights of others cease for us, at least in the form in which we have so far conceded them.

The "fair person" constantly needs the fine tact of a scale for the degrees of power and right which, in view of the transitory nature of human affairs, will always be balanced only for a short time, while for the most part they either sink or rise: to be fair is therefore difficult and requires much practice, good will, and a great deal of good *spirit*.—

231

Of German virtue.— How degenerate in taste, how slavish before offices, classes, robes, pomp, and splendor must a people have been when it evaluated the simple [*schlicht*] as the bad [*schlecht*], the simple man as the bad man! One should counter the moral arrogance of the Germans with this one little word, *schlecht*, and nothing more.

232

From a disputation.— A: My friend, you have talked yourself hoarse. B: Then I stand refuted. Let us not discuss the matter any further.

236

Punishment.— A strange thing, our punishment! It does not cleanse the criminal, it is no atonement; on the contrary, it pollutes worse than the crime does.

The Gay Science (1882)

51

Sense of truth.— I think well of all skepticism to which I may reply: "Let us try it." But I no longer want to hear anything of all those things and questions which do not permit experiments. This is the limit of my "sense of truth": for there courage has lost its rights.

108

New struggles.— After Buddha was dead, his shadow was still shown for centuries in a cave—a tremendous, gruesome shadow. God is dead: but given the way men are, there may still be caves for thousands of years in which his shadow will be shown.— And we—we still have to vanquish his shadow, too.

121

Life no argument.— We have fixed up a world for ourselves in which we can live—assuming bodies, lines, planes, causes and effects, motion and rest, form and content: without these articles of faith, nobody now would endure life. But that does not mean that they have been proved. Life is no argument; the conditions of life could include error.

129

The conditions of God.— "God himself cannot exist without wise men"—Luther said, and was right. But "God can exist even less without unwise men"—that good old Luther did not say.

130

A dangerous resolve.— The Christian resolve to find the world ugly and bad has made the world ugly and bad.

142

Incense.— Buddha said: "Do not flatter your benefactor." This saying should be repeated in a Christian church—right away it clears the air of everything Christian.

163

After a great victory.— What is best about a great victory is that it rids the victor of fear of defeat. "Why not also lose for once?" he says to himself; "now I am rich enough for that."

173

Being deep and appearing deep.— Whoever knows he is deep, strives for clarity; whoever would like to appear deep to the crowd, strives for obscurity. For the crowd considers anything deep if only it cannot see to the bottom: the crowd is so timid and afraid of going into the water.

200

Laughter.— Laughter means: being *schadenfroh,* but with a good conscience.

205

Need.— A need is considered the cause of the origin: in truth, it is often merely an effect of what did originate.

228

Against mediators.— Those who wish to be mediators between two resolute thinkers are marked as mediocre: they lack eyes to see the unparalleled; seeing things as similar and making them the same is the mark of weak eyes.

231

"Thorough."— Those slow in knowledge suppose that slowness belongs to knowledge.

232

Dreams.— We have no dreams at all or interesting ones. We should learn to be awake the same way—not at all or in an interesting manner.

258

Those who deny chance.— No victor believes in chance.

273

Whom do you call bad?— Those who always want to put tc shame.

274

What do you consider most humane?— To spare someone shame.

275

What is the seal of attained freedom?— No longer being ashamed in front of oneself.

292

To the preachers of morals.— I have no wish to establish morals, but I have this advice for those who do: if you want to do the best things and states out of all honor and worth, then continue to talk about them as you have been doing. Place them at the head of your morality and talk from morning till night of the happiness of virtue, of peace of soul, of justice and immanent retribution: the way you are carrying on, all these good things finally acquire a popularity and are shouted about in the streets; but at the same time all of their gold will be worn off, and even worse—all the gold that was *in* them will have been changed to lead. Truly, you are masters of inverse alchemy, of the devaluation of the most valuable things. Why don't you reach, experimentally, for another recipe, lest you keep attaining the opposite of what you seek: *deny* these good things, deprive them of the mob's acclaim and their constant currency; restore them to the concealed bashfulness of solitary souls; say that *morality is something forbidden.* Perhaps you will in that way gain the support for these things of the only type of men that matter—those who are *heroic.* But then they must have a quality that inspires fear, and not, as hitherto, nausea. Should we not say of morality today what Master Eckhart said: "I ask God that he rid me of God."

312

My dog.— I have given a name to my pain and call it "dog": it is just as faithful, just as obtrusive and shameless, just as entertaining, just as clever as any other dog—and I can scold it and vent my bad moods on it, as others do with their dogs, servants, and wives.

316

Prophetic men.— You have no feeling for the fact that prophetic men are men who suffer a great deal: you merely suppose that they have been granted a beautiful "gift," and you would even like to have it yourself. But I shall express myself in a parable. How much may animals suffer from the electricity in the air and clouds! We see how some species have a prophetic faculty regarding the weather; monkeys, for example (as may be observed even in Europe, and not only in zoos—namely, on Gibraltar). But we do not heed that it is their *pains* that make them prophets. When a strong positive electrical charge, under the influence of an approaching cloud that is as yet far from visible, suddenly changes into negative electricity, these animals behave as if an enemy were drawing near and prepare for defense or escape; most often they try to hide: they do not understand bad weather as a kind of weather but as an enemy whose hand they already *feel*.

322

Parable.— Those thinkers in whom all stars move in cyclic orbits are not the most profound: whoever looks into himself as into vast space and carries galaxies in himself also knows how irregular all galaxies are; they lead into the chaos and labyrinth of existence.

325

What belongs to greatness.— Who will attain anything great if he does not possess the strength and the will to *inflict* great suffering? Being able to suffer is the least thing: weak women and even slaves often attain mastery in that. But not to perish of inner distress and uncertainty when one inflicts great suffering and hears the cry of this suffering—that is great, that belongs to greatness.

327

Taking seriously.— In the great majority, the intellect is a clumsy, gloomy, creaking machine that is difficult to start. They call it "taking the matter seriously," when they work with this machine and want to think well: how onerous they must find thinking well! The lovely beast, man, seems to lose its good spirits every time it thinks well: it becomes "serious." And "where laughter and gaiety are found, the quality of thought is poor"—that is the prejudice of this serious beast against all "gay science."— Well, then, let us prove that it is a prejudice.

332

The bad hour.— Every philosopher has probably had a bad hour when he thought: what do I matter if one does not accept my bad arguments, too?— And then some mischievous little bird flew past him and twittered: "What do you matter? What do you matter?"

381

On the question of being understandable.— One does not only wish to be understood when one writes; one wishes just as surely *not* to be understood. It is not by any means necessarily an objection to a book when anybody finds it impossible to understand: perhaps that was part of the author's intention—he did not want to be understood by just "anybody." Every more noble spirit and taste selects its audience when it wishes to communicate itself; and choosing them, it at the same time erects barriers against "the others." All the more subtle laws of any style have their origin at this point: they at the same time keep away, create a distance, forbid "entrance," understanding, as said above—while they open the ears of those whose ears are related to ours.

And let me say this among ourselves and about my own case: I don't want either my ignorance or the liveliness of my temperament to keep me from being understandable for *you*, my friends— not the liveliness, however much it compels me to tackle a matter swiftly to tackle it at all. For I approach deep problems like cold baths: quickly into them and quickly out again. That one does not get to the depths that way, not deep enough down, is the superstition of those afraid of the water, the enemies of cold water; they speak without experience. The freezing cold makes one swift.

And to ask this incidentally: does a matter necessarily remain ununderstood and unfathomed merely because it has been touched only in flight, glanced at, in a flash? Is it absolutely imperative that one settles down on it? that one has brooded over it as over an egg? *Diu noctuque incubando*, as Newton said of himself? At least there are truths that are singularly shy and ticklish and cannot be caught except suddenly—that must be *surprised* or left alone.

Finally, my brevity has yet another value: given such questions as concern me, I must say many things briefly in order that they may be heard still more briefly. For, being an immoralist, one has to take steps against corrupting innocents—I mean, asses and old maids of both sexes whom life offers nothing but their innocence. Even more, my writings should inspire, elevate, and encourage them to be virtuous. I cannot imagine anything on earth that would be a merrier sight than inspired old asses and maids who feel excited by the sweet sentiments of virtue; and "this I have seen"— thus spoke Zarathustra.

So much regarding brevity. Matters stand worse with my ignorance which I do not try to conceal from myself. There are hours when I feel ashamed of it—to be sure, also hours when I feel ashamed of feeling ashamed. Perhaps all of us philosophers are in a bad position nowadays regarding knowledge: science keeps growing, and the most scholarly among us are close to discovering that they know too little. But it would be still worse if it were different —and we knew *too much;* our task is and remains above all not to mistake ourselves for others. We *are* something different from scholars, although it is unavoidable for us to be also, among other things, scholarly. We have different needs, grow differently, and also have a different digestion: we need more, we also need less. How much a spirit needs for its nourishment, for this there is no formula; but if its taste is for independence, for quick coming and going, for roaming, perhaps for adventures for which only the swiftest are a match, it is better for such a spirit to live in freedom with little to eat than unfree and stuffed. It is not fat but the greatest possible suppleness and strength that a good dancer desires from his nourishment—and I would not know what the spirit of a philosopher might wish more to be than a good dancer. For the dance is his ideal, also his art, and finally also his only piety, his "service of God."

The Anti-Christ

Friedrich Nietzsche

Contents

Friedrich Nietzsche

Introduction by H. L. Mencken

Save for his raucous, rhapsodical autobiography, "Ecce Homo," "The Antichrist" is the last thing that Nietzsche ever wrote, and so it may be accepted as a statement of some of his most salient ideas in their final form. Notes for it had been accumulating for years and it was to have constituted the first volume of his long-projected magnum opus, "The Will to Power." His full plan for this work, as originally drawn up, was as follows:

Vol. I. The Antichrist: an Attempt at a Criticism of Christianity.

Vol. II. The Free Spirit: a Criticism of Philosophy as a Nihilistic Movement.

Vol. III. The Immoralist: a Criticism of Morality, the Most Fatal Form of Ignorance.

Vol. IV. Dionysus: the Philosophy of Eternal Recurrence.

The first sketches for "The Will to Power" were made in 1884, soon after the publication of the first three parts of "Thus Spake Zarathustra," and thereafter, for four years, Nietzsche piled up notes. They were written at all the places he visited on his endless travels in search of health--at Nice, at Venice, at Sils-Maria in the Engadine (for long his favourite resort), at Cannobio, at Zürich, at Genoa, at Chur, at Leipzig. Several times his work was interrupted by other books, first by "Beyond Good and Evil," then by "The Genealogy of Morals" (written in twenty days), then by his Wagner pamphlets. Almost as often he changed his plan. Once he decided to expand "The Will to Power" to ten volumes, with "An Attempt at a New Interpretation of the World" as a general sub-title. Again he adopted the sub-title of "An Interpretation of All That Happens." Finally, he hit upon "An Attempt at a Transvaluation of All Values," and went back to four volumes, though with a number of changes in their arrangement. In September, 1888, he began actual work upon the first volume, and before the end of the month it was completed. The Summer had been one of almost hysterical creative activity. Since the middle of June he had written two other small books, "The Case of Wagner" and "The Twilight of the Idols," and before the end of the year he was destined to write "Ecce Homo." Some time during December his health began to fail rapidly, and soon after the New Year he was helpless. Thereafter he wrote no more.

The Wagner diatribe and "The Twilight of the Idols" were published immediately, but "The Antichrist" did not get into type until 1895. I suspect that the delay was due to the influence of the philosopher's sister, Elisabeth Förster-Nietzsche, an intelligent and ardent but by no means uniformly judicious propagandist of his ideas. During his dark days of neglect and misunderstanding, when even family and friends kept aloof, Frau Förster-Nietzsche went with him farther than any other, but there were bounds beyond which she, also, hesitated to go, and those bounds were marked by crosses. One notes, in her biography of him--a useful but not always accurate work--an evident desire to purge him of the accusation of mocking at sacred things. He had, she says, great admiration for "the elevating effect of Christianity ... upon the weak and ailing," and "a real liking for sincere, pious Christians," and "a tender love for the Founder of Christianity." All his wrath, she continues, was reserved for "St. Paul and his like," who perverted the Beatitudes, which Christ intended for the lowly only, into a universal religion which made war upon aristocratic values. Here, obviously, one is addressed by an interpreter who cannot forget that she is the daughter of a Lutheran pastor and the grand-daughter of two others; a touch of conscience gets into her reading of "The Antichrist." She even hints that the text may have been garbled, after the author's collapse, by some more sinister heretic. There is not the slightest reason to believe that any such garbling ever took place, nor is there any evidence that their common heritage of piety rested upon the brother as heavily as it rested upon the sister. On the contrary, it must be manifest that Nietzsche, in this book, intended to attack Christianity headlong and with all arms, that for all his rapid writing he put the utmost care into it, and that he wanted it to be printed exactly as it stands. The ideas in it were anything but new to him when he set them down. He had been developing them since the days of his beginning. You will find some of them, clearly recognizable, in the first book he ever wrote, "The Birth of Tragedy." You will find the most important of all of them--the conception of Christianity as ressentiment--set forth at length in the first part of "The Genealogy of Morals," published under his own supervision in 1887. And the rest are scattered through the whole vast mass of his notes, sometimes as mere questionings but often worked out very carefully. Moreover, let it not be forgotten that it was Wagner's yielding to Christian sentimentality in "Parsifal" that transformed Nietzsche from the first among his literary advocates into the most bitter of his opponents. He could forgive every other sort of mountebankery, but not that. "In me," he once said, "the Christianity of my forbears reaches its logical conclusion. In me the stern intellectual conscience that Christianity fosters and makes paramount turns against Christianity. In me Christianity ... devours itself."

In truth, the present philippic is as necessary to the completeness of the whole of Nietzsche's system as the keystone is to the arch. All the curves of his speculation lead up to it. What he flung himself against, from beginning to end of his days of writing, was always, in the last analysis, Christianity in some form or other--Christianity as a system of practical ethics, Christianity as a political code, Christianity as metaphysics, Christianity as a gauge of the truth. It would be difficult to think of any intellectual enterprise on his long list that did not, more or less directly and clearly, relate itself to this master enterprise of them all. It was as if his apostasy from the faith of his fathers, filling him with the fiery zeal of the convert, and particularly of the convert to heresy, had blinded him to every other element in the gigantic self-delusion of civilized man. The will to power was his answer to Christianity's affectation of humility and self-sacrifice; eternal recurrence was his mocking criticism of Christian optimism and millennialism; the superman was his candidate for the place of the Christian ideal of the "good" man, prudently abased before the throne of God. The things he chiefly argued for were anti-Christian things--the abandonment of the purely moral view of life, the rehabilitation of instinct, the dethronement of weakness and timidity as ideals, the renunciation of the whole hocus-pocus of dogmatic religion, the extermination of false aristocracies (of the priest, of the politician, of the plutocrat), the revival of the healthy, lordly "innocence" that was Greek. If he was anything in a word, Nietzsche was a Greek born two thousand years too late. His dreams were thoroughly Hellenic; his whole manner of thinking was Hellenic; his peculiar errors were Hellenic no less. But his Hellenism, I need not add, was anything but the pale neo-Platonism that has run like a thread through the thinking of the Western world since the days of the Christian Fathers. From Plato, to be sure, he got what all of us must get, but his real forefather was Heraclitus. It is in Heraclitus that one finds the germ of his primary view of the universe--a view, to wit, that sees it, not as moral phenomenon, but as mere aesthetic representation. The God that Nietzsche imagined, in the end, was not far from the God that such an artist as Joseph Conrad imagines--a supreme craftsman, ever experimenting, ever coming closer to an ideal balancing of lines and forces, and yet always failing to work out the final harmony.

The late war, awakening all the primitive racial fury of the Western nations, and therewith all their ancient enthusiasm for religious taboos and sanctions, naturally focused attention upon Nietzsche, as upon the most daring and provocative of recent amateur theologians. The Germans, with their characteristic tendency to explain their every act in terms as realistic and unpleasant as possible, appear to have mauled him in a belated and unexpected embrace, to the horror, I daresay, of the Kaiser, and perhaps to the even greater horror of Nietzsche's own ghost. The folks of Anglo-Saxondom, with their equally characteristic tendency to explain all their enterprises romantically, simultaneously set him up as the Antichrist he no doubt secretly longed to be. The result was a great deal of misrepresentation and misunderstanding of him. From the pulpits of the allied countries, and particularly from those of England and the United States, a horde of patriotic ecclesiastics denounced him in extravagant terms as the author of all the horrors of the time, and in the newspapers, until the Kaiser was elected sole bugaboo, he shared the honors of that office with von Hindenburg, the Crown Prince, Capt. Boy-Ed, von Bernstorff and von Tirpitz. Most of this denunciation, of course, was frankly idiotic--the naïve pishposh of suburban Methodists, notoriety-seeking college professors, almost illiterate editorial writers, and other such numskulls. In much of it, including not a few official hymns of hate, Nietzsche was gravely discovered to be the teacher of such spokesmen of the extremest sort of German nationalism as von Bernhardi and von Treitschke--which was just as intelligent as making George Bernard Shaw the mentor of Lloyd-George. In other solemn pronunciamentoes he was credited with being philosophically responsible for various imaginary crimes of the enemy--the wholesale slaughter or mutilation of prisoners of war, the deliberate burning down of Red Cross hospitals, the utilization of the corpses of the slain for soap-making. I amused myself, in those gaudy days, by collecting newspaper clippings to this general effect, and later on I shall probably publish a digest of them, as a contribution to the study of war hysteria. The thing went to unbelievable lengths. On the strength of the fact that I had published a book on Nietzsche in 1906, six years after his death, I was called upon by agents of the Department of Justice, elaborately outfitted with badges, to meet the charge that I was an intimate associate and agent of "the German monster, Nietzsky." I quote the official procès verbal, an

10

The Anti-Christ

indignant but often misspelled document. Alas, poor
Nietzsche! After all his laborious efforts to prove that he was
not a German, but a Pole--even after his heroic readiness, via
anti-anti-Semitism, to meet the deduction that, if a Pole, then
probably also a Jew!

But under all this alarmed and preposterous tosh there was at
least a sound instinct, and that was the instinct which
recognized Nietzsche as the most eloquent, pertinacious and
effective of all the critics of the philosophy to which the Allies
against Germany stood committed, and on the strength of
which, at all events in theory, the United States had engaged
itself in the war. He was not, in point of fact, involved with the
visible enemy, save in remote and transient ways; the German,
officially, remained the most ardent of Christians during the
war and became a democrat at its close. But he was plainly a
foe of democracy in all its forms, political, religious and
epistemological, and what is worse, his opposition was set
forth in terms that were not only extraordinarily penetrating
and devastating, but also uncommonly offensive. It was thus
quite natural that he should have aroused a degree of
indignation verging upon the pathological in the two countries
that had planted themselves upon the democratic platform most
boldly, and that felt it most shaky, one may add, under their
feet. I daresay that Nietzsche, had he been alive, would have
got a lot of satisfaction out of the execration thus heaped upon
him, not only because, being a vain fellow, he enjoyed
execration as a tribute to his general singularity, and hence to
his superiority, but also and more importantly because, being
no mean psychologist, he would have recognized the
disconcerting doubts underlying it. If Nietzsche's criticism of
democracy were as ignorant and empty, say, as the average
evangelical clergyman's criticism of Darwin's hypothesis of

11

natural selection, then the advocates of democracy could afford
to dismiss it as loftily as the Darwinians dismiss the blather of
the holy clerks. And if his attack upon Christianity were mere
sound and fury, signifying nothing, then there would be no call
for anathemas from the sacred desk. But these onslaughts, in
point of fact, have behind them a tremendous learning and a
great deal of point and plausibility--there are, in brief, bullets in
the gun, teeth in the tiger,--and so it is no wonder that they
excite the ire of men who hold, as a primary article of belief,
that their acceptance would destroy civilization, darken the sun,
and bring Jahveh to sobs upon His Throne.

But in all this justifiable fear, of course, there remains a false
assumption, and that is the assumption that Nietzsche proposed
to destroy Christianity altogether, and so rob the plain people
of the world of their virtue, their spiritual consolations, and
their hope of heaven. Nothing could be more untrue. The fact is
that Nietzsche had no interest whatever in the delusions of the
plain people--that is, intrinsically. It seemed to him of small
moment what they believed, so long as it was safely imbecile.
What he stood against was not their beliefs, but the elevation of
those beliefs, by any sort of democratic process, to the dignity
of a state philosophy--what he feared most was the pollution
and crippling of the superior minority by intellectual disease
from below. His plain aim in "The Antichrist" was to combat
that menace by completing the work begun, on the one hand,
by Darwin and the other evolutionist philosophers, and, on the
other hand, by German historians and philologians. The net
effect of this earlier attack, in the eighties, had been the
collapse of Christian theology as a serious concern of educated
men. The mob, it must be obvious, was very little shaken; even
to this day it has not put off its belief in the essential Christian
doctrines. But the intelligentsia, by 1885, had been pretty well

convinced. No man of sound information, at the time Nietzsche
planned "The Antichrist," actually believed that the world was
created in seven days, or that its fauna was once overwhelmed
by a flood as a penalty for the sins of man, or that Noah saved
the boa constrictor, the prairie dog and the pediculus capitis by
taking a pair of each into the ark, or that Lot's wife was turned
into a pillar of salt, or that a fragment of the True Cross could
cure hydrophobia. Such notions, still almost universally
prevalent in Christendom a century before, were now confined
to the great body of ignorant and credulous men--that is, to
ninety-five or ninety-six percent. of the race. For a man of the
superior minority to subscribe to one of them publicly was
already sufficient to set him off as one in imminent need of
psychiatrical attention. Belief in them had become a mark of
inferiority, like the allied belief in madstones, magic and
apparitions.

But though the theology of Christianity had thus sunk to the
lowly estate of a mere delusion of the rabble, propagated on
that level by the ancient caste of sacerdotal parasites, the ethics
of Christianity continued to enjoy the utmost acceptance, and
perhaps even more acceptance than ever before. It seemed to
be generally felt, in fact, that they simply must be saved from
the wreck--that the world would vanish into chaos if they went
the way of the revelations supporting them. In this fear a great
many judicious men joined, and so there arose what was, in
essence, an absolutely new Christian cult--a cult, to wit, purged
of all the supernaturalism superimposed upon the older cult by
generations of theologians, and harking back to what was
conceived to be the pure ethical doctrine of Jesus. This cult still
flourishes; Protestantism tends to become identical with it; it
invades Catholicism as Modernism; it is supported by great
numbers of men whose intelligence is manifest and whose

sincerity is not open to question. Even Nietzsche himself yielded to it in weak moments, as you will discover on examining his somewhat laborious effort to make Paul the villain of Christian theology, and Jesus no more than an innocent bystander. But this sentimental yielding never went far enough to distract his attention for long from his main idea, which was this: that Christian ethics were quite as dubious, at bottom, as Christian theology--that they were founded, just as surely as such childish fables as the story of Jonah and the whale, upon the peculiar prejudices and credulities, the special desires and appetites, of inferior men--that they warred upon the best interests of men of a better sort quite as unmistakably as the most extravagant of objective superstitions. In brief, what he saw in Christian ethics, under all the poetry and all the fine show of altruism and all the theoretical benefits therein, was a democratic effort to curb the egoism of the strong--a conspiracy of the chandala against the free functioning of their superiors, nay, against the free progress of mankind. This theory is the thing he exposes in "The Antichrist," bringing to the business his amazingly chromatic and exigent eloquence at its finest flower. This is the "conspiracy" he sets forth in all the panoply of his characteristic italics, dashes, sforzando interjections and exclamation points.

Well, an idea is an idea. The present one may be right and it may be wrong. One thing is quite certain: that no progress will be made against it by denouncing it as merely immoral. If it is ever laid at all, it must be laid evidentially, logically. The notion to the contrary is thoroughly democratic; the mob is the most ruthless of tyrants; it is always in a democratic society that heresy and felony tend to be most constantly confused. One hears without surprise of a Bismarck philosophizing placidly (at least in his old age) upon the delusion of Socialism

and of a Frederick the Great playing the hose of his cynicism
upon the absolutism that was almost identical with his own
person, but men in the mass never brook the destructive
discussion of their fundamental beliefs, and that impatience is
naturally most evident in those societies in which men in the
mass are most influential. Democracy and free speech are not
facets of one gem; democracy and free speech are eternal
enemies. But in any battle between an institution and an idea,
the idea, in the long run, has the better of it. Here I do not
venture into the absurdity of arguing that, as the world wags
on, the truth always survives. I believe nothing of the sort. As a
matter of fact, it seems to me that an idea that happens to be
true--or, more exactly, as near to truth as any human idea can
be, and yet remain generally intelligible--it seems to me that
such an idea carries a special and often fatal handicap. The
majority of men prefer delusion to truth. It soothes. It is easy to
grasp. Above all, it fits more snugly than the truth into a
universe of false appearances--of complex and irrational
phenomena, defectively grasped. But though an idea that is true
is thus not likely to prevail, an idea that is attacked enjoys a
great advantage. The evidence behind it is now supported by
sympathy, the sporting instinct, sentimentality--and
sentimentality is as powerful as an army with banners. One
never hears of a martyr in history whose notions are seriously
disputed today. The forgotten ideas are those of the men who
put them forward soberly and quietly, hoping fatuously that
they would conquer by the force of their truth; these are the
ideas that we now struggle to rediscover. Had Nietzsche lived
to be burned at the stake by outraged Mississippi Methodists, it
would have been a glorious day for his doctrines. As it is, they
are helped on their way every time they are denounced as
immoral and against God. The war brought down upon them
the maledictions of vast herds of right-thinking men. And now

15

"The Antichrist," after fifteen years of neglect, is being reprinted....

One imagines the author, a sardonic wraith, snickering somewhat sadly over the fact. His shade, wherever it suffers, is favoured in these days by many such consolations, some of them of much greater horsepower. Think of the facts and arguments, even the underlying theories and attitudes, that have been borrowed from him, consciously and unconsciously, by the foes of Bolshevism during these last thrilling years! The face of democracy, suddenly seen hideously close, has scared the guardians of the reigning plutocracy half to death, and they have gone to the devil himself for aid. Southern Senators, almost illiterate men, have mixed his acids with well water and spouted them like affrighted geysers, not knowing what they did. Nor are they the first to borrow from him. Years ago I called attention to the debt incurred with characteristic forgetfulness of obligation by the late Theodore Roosevelt, in "The Strenuous Life" and elsewhere. Roosevelt, a typical apologist for the existing order, adeptly dragging a herring across the trail whenever it was menaced, yet managed to delude the native boobery, at least until toward the end, into accepting him as a fiery exponent of pure democracy. Perhaps he even fooled himself; charlatans usually do so soon or late. A study of Nietzsche reveals the sources of much that was honest in him, and exposes the hollowness of much that was sham. Nietzsche, an infinitely harder and more courageous intellect, was incapable of any such confusion of ideas; he seldom allowed sentimentality to turn him from the glaring fact. What is called Bolshevism today he saw clearly a generation ago and described for what it was and is--democracy in another aspect, the old ressentiment of the lower orders in free function once more. Socialism, Puritanism, Philistinism, Christianity--he saw

16

them all as allotropic forms of democracy, as variations upon the endless struggle of quantity against quality, of the weak and timorous against the strong and enterprising, of the botched against the fit. The world needed a staggering exaggeration to make it see even half of the truth. It trembles today as it trembled during the French Revolution. Perhaps it would tremble less if it could combat the monster with a clearer conscience and less burden of compromising theory--if it could launch its forces frankly at the fundamental doctrine, and not merely employ them to police the transient orgy.

Nietzsche, in the long run, may help it toward that greater honesty. His notions, propagated by cuttings from cuttings from cuttings, may conceivably prepare the way for a sounder, more healthful theory of society and of the state, and so free human progress from the stupidities which now hamper it, and men of true vision from the despairs which now sicken them. I say it is conceivable, but I doubt that it is probable. The soul and the belly of mankind are too evenly balanced; it is not likely that the belly will ever put away its hunger or forget its power. Here, perhaps, there is an example of the eternal recurrence that Nietzsche was fond of mulling over in his blacker moods. We are in the midst of one of the perennial risings of the lower orders. It got under way long before any of the current Bolshevist demons was born; it was given its long, secure start by the intolerable tyranny of the plutocracy--the end product of the Eighteenth Century revolt against the old aristocracy. It found resistance suddenly slackened by civil war within the plutocracy itself--one gang of traders falling upon another gang, to the tune of vast hymn-singing and yells to God. Perhaps it has already passed its apogee; the plutocracy, chastened, shows signs of a new solidarity; the wheel continues to swing 'round. But this combat between proletariat and

plutocracy is, after all, itself a civil war. Two inferiorities
struggle for the privilege of polluting the world. What actual
difference does it make to a civilized man, when there is a steel
strike, whether the workmen win or the mill-owners win? The
conflict can interest him only as spectacle, as the conflict
between Bonaparte and the old order in Europe interested
Goethe and Beethoven. The victory, whichever way it goes,
will simply bring chaos nearer, and so set the stage for a
genuine revolution later on, with (let us hope) a new feudalism
or something better coming out of it, and a new Thirteenth
Century at dawn. This seems to be the slow, costly way of the
worst of habitable worlds.

In the present case my money is laid upon the plutocracy. It
will win because it will be able, in the long run, to enlist the
finer intelligences. The mob and its maudlin causes attract only
sentimentalists and scoundrels, chiefly the latter. Politics, under
a democracy, reduces itself to a mere struggle for office by
flatterers of the proletariat; even when a superior man prevails
at that disgusting game he must prevail at the cost of his self-
respect. Not many superior men make the attempt. The average
great captain of the rabble, when he is not simply a weeper
over irremediable wrongs, is a hypocrite so far gone that he is
unconscious of his own hypocrisy--a slimy fellow, offensive to
the nose. The plutocracy can recruit measurably more
respectable janissaries, if only because it can make self-interest
less obviously costly to amour propre. Its defect and its
weakness lie in the fact that it is still too young to have
acquired dignity. But lately sprung from the mob it now preys
upon, it yet shows some of the habits of mind of that mob: it is
blatant, stupid, ignorant, lacking in all delicate instinct and
governmental finesse. Above all, it remains somewhat heavily
moral. One seldom finds it undertaking one of its characteristic

18

imbecilities without offering a sonorous moral reason; it spends almost as much to support the Y. M. C. A., vice-crusading, Prohibition and other such puerilities as it spends upon Congressmen, strike-breakers, gun-men, kept patriots and newspapers. In England the case is even worse. It is almost impossible to find a wealthy industrial over there who is not also an eminent non-conformist layman, and even among financiers there are praying brothers. On the Continent, the day is saved by the fact that the plutocracy tends to become more and more Jewish. Here the intellectual cynicism of the Jew almost counterbalances his social unpleasantness. If he is destined to lead the plutocracy of the world out of Little Bethel he will fail, of course, to turn it into an aristocracy--i. e., a caste of gentlemen--, but he will at least make it clever, and hence worthy of consideration. The case against the Jews is long and damning; it would justify ten thousand times as many pogroms as now go on in the world. But whenever you find a Davidsbündlerschaft making practise against the Philistines, there you will find a Jew laying on. Maybe it was this fact that caused Nietzsche to speak up for the children of Israel quite as often as he spoke against them. He was not blind to their faults, but when he set them beside Christians he could not deny their general superiority. Perhaps in America and England, as on the Continent, the increasing Jewishness of the plutocracy, while cutting it off from all chance of ever developing into an aristocracy, will yet lift it to such a dignity that it will at least deserve a certain grudging respect.

But even so, it will remain in a sort of half-world, midway between the gutter and the stars. Above it will still stand the small group of men that constitutes the permanent aristocracy of the race--the men of imagination and high purpose, the makers of genuine progress, the brave and ardent spirits, above

19

all petty fears and discontents and above all petty hopes and ideals no less. There were heroes before Agamemnon; there will be Bachs after Johann Sebastian. And beneath the Judaized plutocracy, the sublimated bourgeoisie, there the immemorial proletariat, I venture to guess, will roar on, endlessly tortured by its vain hatreds and envies, stampeded and made to tremble by its ancient superstitions, prodded and made miserable by its sordid and degrading hopes. It seems to me very likely that, in this proletariat, Christianity will continue to survive. It is nonsense, true enough, but it is sweet. Nietzsche, denouncing its dangers as a poison, almost falls into the error of denying it its undoubtedly sugary smack. Of all the religions ever devised by the great practical jokers of the race, this is the one that offers most for the least money, so to speak, to the inferior man. It starts out by denying his inferiority in plain terms: all men are equal in the sight of God. It ends by erecting that inferiority into a sort of actual superiority: it is a merit to be stupid, and miserable, and sorely put upon--of such are the celestial elect. Not all the eloquence of a million Nietzsches, nor all the painful marshalling of evidence of a million Darwins and Harnacks, will ever empty that great consolation of its allure. The most they can ever accomplish is to make the superior orders of men acutely conscious of the exact nature of it, and so give them armament against the contagion. This is going on; this is being done. I think that "The Antichrist" has a useful place in that enterprise. It is strident, it is often extravagant, it is, to many sensitive men, in the worst of possible taste, but at bottom it is enormously apt and effective-- and on the surface it is undoubtedly a good show. One somehow enjoys, with the malice that is native to man, the spectacle of anathemas batted back; it is refreshing to see the pitchfork employed against gentlemen who have doomed such innumerable caravans to hell. In Nietzsche they found, after many long years, a foeman worthy of them--not a mere fancy swordsman like Voltaire, or a mob orator like Tom Paine, or a pedant like the heretics of exegesis, but a gladiator armed with steel and armoured with steel, and showing all the ferocious gusto of a mediaeval bishop. It is a pity that Holy Church has no process for the elevation of demons, like its process for the canonization of saints. There must be a long roll of black miracles to the discredit of the Accursed Friedrich--sinners purged of conscience and made happy in their sinning, clerics shaken in their theology by visions of a new and better holy city, the strong made to exult, the weak robbed of their old sad romance. It would be a pleasure to see the Advocatus Diaboli turn from the table of the prosecution to the table of the defence, and move in solemn form for the damnation of the Naumburg hobgoblin....

Of all Nietzsche's books, "The Antichrist" comes nearest to conventionality in form. It presents a connected argument with very few interludes, and has a beginning, a middle and an end. Most of his works are in the form of collections of apothegms, and sometimes the subject changes on every second page. This fact constitutes one of the counts in the orthodox indictment of him: it is cited as proof that his capacity for consecutive thought was limited, and that he was thus deficient mentally, and perhaps a downright moron. The argument, it must be obvious, is fundamentally nonsensical. What deceives the professors is the traditional prolixity of philosophers. Because the average philosophical writer, when he essays to expose his ideas, makes such inordinate drafts upon the parts of speech that the dictionary is almost emptied these defective observers jump to the conclusion that his intrinsic notions are of corresponding weight. This is not unseldom quite untrue. What makes philosophy so garrulous is not the profundity of philosophers, but their lack of art; they are like physicians who sought to cure a slight hyperacidity by giving the patient a carload of burned oyster-shells to eat. There is, too, the endless poll-parrotting that goes on: each new philosopher must prove his learning by laboriously rehearsing the ideas of all previous philosophers.... Nietzsche avoided both faults. He always assumed that his readers knew the books, and that it was thus unnecessary to rewrite them. And, having an idea that seemed to him to be novel and original, he stated it in as few words as possible, and then shut down. Sometimes he got it into a hundred words; sometimes it took a thousand; now and then, as in the present case, he developed a series of related ideas into a connected book. But he never wrote a word too many. He never pumped up an idea to make it appear bigger than it actually was. The pedagogues, alas, are not accustomed to that sort of writing in serious fields. They resent it, and sometimes they even try to improve it. There exists, in fact, a huge and solemn tome on Nietzsche by a learned man of America in which all of his brilliancy is painfully translated into the windy phrases of the seminaries. The tome is satisfactorily ponderous, but the meat of the cocoanut is left out: there is actually no discussion of the Nietzschean view of Christianity!... Always Nietzsche daunts the pedants. He employed too few words for them--and he had too many ideas.

* * * * *

The present translation of "The Antichrist" is published by agreement with Dr. Oscar Levy, editor of the English edition of Nietzsche. There are two earlier translations, one by Thomas Common and the other by Anthony M. Ludovici. That of Mr. Common follows the text very closely, and thus occasionally shows some essentially German turns of phrase; that of Mr.

Ludovici is more fluent but rather less exact. I do not offer my own version on the plea that either of these is useless; on the contrary, I cheerfully acknowledge that they have much merit, and that they helped me at almost every line. I began this new Englishing of the book, not in any hope of supplanting them, and surely not with any notion of meeting a great public need, but simply as a private amusement in troubled days. But as I got on with it I began to see ways of putting some flavour of Nietzsche's peculiar style into the English, and so amusement turned into a more or less serious labour. The result, of course, is far from satisfactory, but it at least represents a very diligent attempt. Nietzsche, always under the influence of French models, wrote a German that differs materially from any other German that I know. It is more nervous, more varied, more rapid in tempo; it runs to more effective climaxes; it is never stodgy. His marks begin to show upon the writing of the younger Germans of today. They are getting away from the old thunderous manner, with its long sentences and its tedious grammatical complexities. In the course of time, I daresay, they will develop a German almost as clear as French and almost as colourful and resilient as English.

I owe thanks to Dr. Levy for his imprimatur, to Mr. Theodor Hemberger for criticism, and to Messrs. Common and Ludovici for showing me the way around many a difficulty.

H. L. MENCKEN.

Friedrich Nietzsche

Author's Preface

This book belongs to the most rare of men. Perhaps not one of them is yet alive. It is possible that they may be among those who understand my "Zarathustra": how could I confound myself with those who are now sprouting ears?--First the day after tomorrow must come for me. Some men are born posthumously.

The conditions under which any one understands me, and necessarily understands me--I know them only too well. Even to endure my seriousness, my passion, he must carry intellectual integrity to the verge of hardness. He must be accustomed to living on mountain tops--and to looking upon the wretched gabble of politics and nationalism as beneath him. He must have become indifferent; he must never ask of the truth whether it brings profit to him or a fatality to him.... He must have an inclination, born of strength, for questions that no one has the courage for; the courage for the forbidden; predestination for the labyrinth. The experience of seven solitudes. New ears for new music. New eyes for what is most distant. A new conscience for truths that have hitherto remained unheard. And the will to economize in the grand

manner--to hold together his strength, his enthusiasm....
Reverence for self; love of self; absolute freedom of self....

Very well, then! of that sort only are my readers, my true
readers, my readers foreordained: of what account are the rest?-
-The rest are merely humanity.--One must make one's self
superior to humanity, in power, in loftiness of soul,--in
contempt.

FRIEDRICH W. NIETZSCHE.

The Anti-Christ

1.

--Let us look each other in the face. We are Hyperboreans--we
know well enough how remote our place is. "Neither by land
nor by water will you find the road to the Hyperboreans": even
Pindar,[1] in his day, knew that much about us. Beyond the
North, beyond the ice, beyond death--our life, our happiness....
We have discovered that happiness; we know the way; we got
our knowledge of it from thousands of years in the labyrinth.
Who else has found it?--The man of today?--"I don't know
either the way out or the way in; I am whatever doesn't know
either the way out or the way in"--so sighs the man of today....
This is the sort of modernity that made us ill,--we sickened on
lazy peace, cowardly compromise, the whole virtuous dirtiness
of the modern Yea and Nay. This tolerance and largeur of the
heart that "forgives" everything because it "understands"
everything is a sirocco to us. Rather live amid the ice than
among modern virtues and other such south-winds!... We were
brave enough; we spared neither ourselves nor others; but we
were a long time finding out where to direct our courage. We
grew dismal; they called us fatalists. Our fate--it was the

fulness, the tension, the storing up of powers. We thirsted for the lightnings and great deeds; we kept as far as possible from the happiness of the weakling, from "resignation"... There was thunder in our air; nature, as we embodied it, became overcast--for we had not yet found the way. The formula of our happiness: a Yea, a Nay, a straight line, a goal....

[1] Cf. the tenth Pythian ode. See also the fourth book of Herodotus. The Hyperboreans were a mythical people beyond the Rhipaean mountains, in the far North. They enjoyed unbroken happiness and perpetual youth.

2.

What is good?--Whatever augments the feeling of power, the will to power, power itself, in man.

What is evil?--Whatever springs from weakness.

What is happiness?--The feeling that power increases--that resistance is overcome.

Not contentment, but more power; not peace at any price, but war; not virtue, but efficiency (virtue in the Renaissance sense, virtu, virtue free of moral acid).

The weak and the botched shall perish: first principle of our charity. And one should help them to it.

What is more harmful than any vice?--Practical sympathy for the botched and the weak--Christianity....

3.

The problem that I set here is not what shall replace mankind in the order of living creatures (--man is an end--): but what type of man must be bred, must be willed, as being the most valuable, the most worthy of life, the most secure guarantee of the future.

This more valuable type has appeared often enough in the past: but always as a happy accident, as an exception, never as deliberately willed. Very often it has been precisely the most feared; hitherto it has been almost the terror of terrors;--and out of that terror the contrary type has been willed, cultivated and attained: the domestic animal, the herd animal, the sick brute-man--the Christian....

4.

Mankind surely does not represent an evolution toward a better or stronger or higher level, as progress is now understood. This "progress" is merely a modern idea, which is to say, a false idea. The European of today, in his essential worth, falls far below the European of the Renaissance; the process of evolution does not necessarily mean elevation, enhancement, strengthening.

True enough, it succeeds in isolated and individual cases in various parts of the earth and under the most widely different cultures, and in these cases a higher type certainly manifests itself; something which, compared to mankind in the mass, appears as a sort of superman. Such happy strokes of high success have always been possible, and will remain possible, perhaps, for all time to come. Even whole races, tribes and nations may occasionally represent such lucky accidents.

5.

We should not deck out and embellish Christianity: it has waged a war to the death against this higher type of man, it has put all the deepest instincts of this type under its ban, it has developed its concept of evil, of the Evil One himself, out of these instincts--the strong man as the typical reprobate, the "outcast among men." Christianity has taken the part of all the weak, the low, the botched; it has made an ideal out of antagonism to all the self-preservative instincts of sound life; it has corrupted even the faculties of those natures that are intellectually most vigorous, by representing the highest intellectual values as sinful, as misleading, as full of temptation. The most lamentable example: the corruption of Pascal, who believed that his intellect had been destroyed by original sin, whereas it was actually destroyed by Christianity!--

6.

It is a painful and tragic spectacle that rises before me: I have drawn back the curtain from the rottenness of man. This word, in my mouth, is at least free from one suspicion: that it involves a moral accusation against humanity. It is used--and I wish to emphasize the fact again--without any moral significance: and this is so far true that the rottenness I speak of is most apparent to me precisely in those quarters where there has been most aspiration, hitherto, toward "virtue" and "godliness." As you probably surmise, I understand rottenness in the sense of décadence: my argument is that all the values on which mankind now fixes its highest aspirations are décadence-values.

I call an animal, a species, an individual corrupt, when it loses its instincts, when it chooses, when it prefers, what is injurious to it. A history of the "higher feelings," the "ideals of humanity"--and it is possible that I'll have to write it--would almost explain why man is so degenerate. Life itself appears to me as an instinct for growth, for survival, for the accumulation of forces, for power: whenever the will to power fails there is disaster. My contention is that all the highest values of humanity have been emptied of this will--that the values of décadence, of nihilism, now prevail under the holiest names.

7.

Christianity is called the religion of pity.--Pity stands in opposition to all the tonic passions that augment the energy of the feeling of aliveness: it is a depressant. A man loses power when he pities. Through pity that drain upon strength which suffering works is multiplied a thousandfold. Suffering is made contagious by pity; under certain circumstances it may lead to a total sacrifice of life and living energy--a loss out of all proportion to the magnitude of the cause (--the case of the death of the Nazarene). This is the first view of it; there is, however, a still more important one. If one measures the effects of pity by the gravity of the reactions it sets up, its character as a menace to life appears in a much clearer light. Pity thwarts the whole law of evolution, which is the law of natural selection. It preserves whatever is ripe for destruction; it fights on the side of those disinherited and condemned by life; by maintaining life in so many of the botched of all kinds, it gives life itself a gloomy and dubious aspect. Mankind has ventured

31

to call pity a virtue (--in every superior moral system it appears as a weakness--); going still further, it has been called the virtue, the source and foundation of all other virtues--but let us always bear in mind that this was from the standpoint of a philosophy that was nihilistic, and upon whose shield the denial of life was inscribed. Schopenhauer was right in this: that by means of pity life is denied, and made worthy of denial--pity is the technic of nihilism. Let me repeat: this depressing and contagious instinct stands against all those instincts which work for the preservation and enhancement of life: in the rôle of protector of the miserable, it is a prime agent in the promotion of décadence--pity persuades to extinction.... Of course, one doesn't say "extinction": one says "the other world," or "God," or "the true life," or Nirvana, salvation, blessedness.... This innocent rhetoric, from the realm of religious-ethical balderdash, appears a good deal less innocent when one reflects upon the tendency that it conceals beneath sublime words: the tendency to destroy life. Schopenhauer was hostile to life: that is why pity appeared to him as a virtue.... Aristotle, as every one knows, saw in pity a sickly and dangerous state of mind, the remedy for which was an occasional purgative: he regarded tragedy as that purgative. The instinct of life should prompt us to seek some means of puncturing any such pathological and dangerous accumulation of pity as that appearing in Schopenhauer's case (and also, alack, in that of our whole literary décadence, from St. Petersburg to Paris, from Tolstoi to Wagner), that it may burst and be discharged.... Nothing is more unhealthy, amid all our unhealthy modernism, than Christian pity. To be the doctors here, to be unmerciful here, to wield the knife here--all this is our business, all this is our sort of humanity, by this sign we are philosophers, we Hyperboreans!--

8.

It is necessary to say just whom we regard as our antagonists: theologians and all who have any theological blood in their veins--this is our whole philosophy.... One must have faced that menace at close hand, better still, one must have had experience of it directly and almost succumbed to it, to realize that it is not to be taken lightly (--the alleged free-thinking of our naturalists and physiologists seems to me to be a joke--they have no passion about such things; they have not suffered--). This poisoning goes a great deal further than most people think: I find the arrogant habit of the theologian among all who regard themselves as "idealists"--among all who, by virtue of a higher point of departure, claim a right to rise above reality, and to look upon it with suspicion.... The idealist, like the ecclesiastic, carries all sorts of lofty concepts in his hand (--and not only in his hand!); he launches them with benevolent contempt against "understanding," "the senses," "honor," "good living," "science"; he sees such things as beneath him, as pernicious and seductive forces, on which "the soul" soars as a pure thing-in-itself--as if humility, chastity, poverty, in a word, holiness, had not already done much more damage to life than all imaginable horrors and vices.... The pure soul is a pure lie.... So long as the priest, that professional denier, calumniator and poisoner of life, is accepted as a higher variety of man, there can be no answer to the question, What is truth? Truth has already been stood on its head when the obvious attorney of mere emptiness is mistaken for its representative....

9.

Upon this theological instinct I make war: I find the tracks of it everywhere. Whoever has theological blood in his veins is shifty and dishonourable in all things. The pathetic thing that grows out of this condition is called faith: in other words, closing one's eyes upon one's self once for all, to avoid suffering the sight of incurable falsehood. People erect a concept of morality, of virtue, of holiness upon this false view of all things; they ground good conscience upon faulty vision; they argue that no other sort of vision has value any more, once they have made theirs sacrosanct with the names of "God," "salvation" and "eternity." I unearth this theological instinct in all directions: it is the most widespread and the most subterranean form of falsehood to be found on earth. Whatever a theologian regards as true must be false: there you have almost a criterion of truth. His profound instinct of self-preservation stands against truth ever coming into honour in any way, or even getting stated. Wherever the influence of theologians is felt there is a transvaluation of values, and the concepts "true" and "false" are forced to change places: whatever is most damaging to life is there called "true," and whatever exalts it, intensifies it, approves it, justifies it and makes it triumphant is there called "false.".... When theologians, working through the "consciences" of princes (or of peoples--), stretch out their hands for power, there is never any doubt as to the fundamental issue: the will to make an end, the nihilistic will exerts that power....

10.

Among Germans I am immediately understood when I say that theological blood is the ruin of philosophy. The Protestant pastor is the grandfather of German philosophy; Protestantism itself is its peccatum originale. Definition of Protestantism: hemiplegic paralysis of Christianity--and of reason.... One need only utter the words "Tübingen School" to get an understanding of what German philosophy is at bottom--a very artful form of theology.... The Suabians are the best liars in Germany; they lie innocently.... Why all the rejoicing over the appearance of Kant that went through the learned world of Germany, three-fourths of which is made up of the sons of preachers and teachers--why the German conviction still echoing, that with Kant came a change for the better? The theological instinct of German scholars made them see clearly just what had become possible again.... A backstairs leading to the old ideal stood open; the concept of the "true world," the concept of morality as the essence of the world (--the two most vicious errors that ever existed!), were once more, thanks to a subtle and wily scepticism, if not actually demonstrable, then at least no longer refutable.... Reason, the prerogative of reason, does not go so far.... Out of reality there had been made "appearance"; an absolutely false world, that of being, had been turned into reality.... The success of Kant is merely a theological success; he was, like Luther and Leibnitz, but one more impediment to German integrity, already far from steady.--

11.

A word now against Kant as a moralist. A virtue must be our invention; it must spring out of our personal need and defence. In every other case it is a source of danger. That which does not belong to our life menaces it; a virtue which has its roots in mere respect for the concept of "virtue," as Kant would have it, is pernicious. "Virtue," "duty," "good for its own sake," goodness grounded upon impersonality or a notion of universal validity--these are all chimeras, and in them one finds only an expression of the decay, the last collapse of life, the Chinese spirit of Königsberg. Quite the contrary is demanded by the

most profound laws of self-preservation and of growth: to wit,
that every man find his own virtue, his own categorical
imperative. A nation goes to pieces when it confounds its duty
with the general concept of duty. Nothing works a more
complete and penetrating disaster than every "impersonal"
duty, every sacrifice before the Moloch of abstraction.--To
think that no one has thought of Kant's categorical imperative
as dangerous to life!... The theological instinct alone took it
under protection!--An action prompted by the life-instinct
proves that it is a right action by the amount of pleasure that
goes with it: and yet that Nihilist, with his bowels of Christian
dogmatism, regarded pleasure as an objection.... What destroys
a man more quickly than to work, think and feel without inner
necessity, without any deep personal desire, without pleasure--
as a mere automaton of duty? That is the recipe for décadence,
and no less for idiocy.... Kant became an idiot.--And such a
man was the contemporary of Goethe! This calamitous spinner
of cobwebs passed for the German philosopher--still passes
today!... I forbid myself to say what I think of the Germans....
Didn't Kant see in the French Revolution the transformation of
the state from the inorganic form to the organic? Didn't he ask
himself if there was a single event that could be explained save
on the assumption of a moral faculty in man, so that on the
basis of it, "the tendency of mankind toward the good" could
be explained, once and for all time? Kant's answer: "That is
revolution." Instinct at fault in everything and anything,
instinct as a revolt against nature, German décadence as a
philosophy--that is Kant!--

12.

I put aside a few sceptics, the types of decency in the history of
philosophy: the rest haven't the slightest conception of

intellectual integrity. They behave like women, all these great enthusiasts and prodigies--they regard "beautiful feelings" as arguments, the "heaving breast" as the bellows of divine inspiration, conviction as the criterion of truth. In the end, with "German" innocence, Kant tried to give a scientific flavour to this form of corruption, this dearth of intellectual conscience, by calling it "practical reason." He deliberately invented a variety of reasons for use on occasions when it was desirable not to trouble with reason--that is, when morality, when the sublime command "thou shalt," was heard. When one recalls the fact that, among all peoples, the philosopher is no more than a development from the old type of priest, this inheritance from the priest, this fraud upon self, ceases to be remarkable. When a man feels that he has a divine mission, say to lift up, to save or to liberate mankind--when a man feels the divine spark in his heart and believes that he is the mouthpiece of supernatural imperatives--when such a mission inflames him, it is only natural that he should stand beyond all merely reasonable standards of judgment. He feels that he is himself sanctified by this mission, that he is himself a type of a higher order!... What has a priest to do with philosophy! He stands far above it!--And hitherto the priest has ruled!--He has determined the meaning of "true" and "not true"!...

13.

Let us not underestimate this fact: that we ourselves, we free spirits, are already a "transvaluation of all values," a visualized declaration of war and victory against all the old concepts of "true" and "not true." The most valuable intuitions are the last to be attained; the most valuable of all are those which determine methods. All the methods, all the principles of the scientific spirit of today, were the targets for thousands of years

of the most profound contempt; if a man inclined to them he
was excluded from the society of "decent" people--he passed as
"an enemy of God," as a scoffer at the truth, as one
"possessed." As a man of science, he belonged to the
Chandala[2].... We have had the whole pathetic stupidity of
mankind against us--their every notion of what the truth ought
to be, of what the service of the truth ought to be--their every
"thou shalt" was launched against us.... Our objectives, our
methods, our quiet, cautious, distrustful manner--all appeared
to them as absolutely discreditable and contemptible.--Looking
back, one may almost ask one's self with reason if it was not
actually an aesthetic sense that kept men blind so long: what
they demanded of the truth was picturesque effectiveness, and
of the learned a strong appeal to their senses. It was our
modesty that stood out longest against their taste.... How well
they guessed that, these turkey-cocks of God!

[2] The lowest of the Hindu castes.

14.

We have unlearned something. We have become more modest
in every way. We no longer derive man from the "spirit," from
the "godhead"; we have dropped him back among the beasts.
We regard him as the strongest of the beasts because he is the
craftiest; one of the results thereof is his intellectuality. On the
other hand, we guard ourselves against a conceit which would
assert itself even here: that man is the great second thought in
the process of organic evolution. He is, in truth, anything but
the crown of creation: beside him stand many other animals, all
at similar stages of development.... And even when we say that
we say a bit too much, for man, relatively speaking, is the most
botched of all the animals and the sickliest, and he has

wandered the most dangerously from his instincts--though for all that, to be sure, he remains the most interesting!--As regards the lower animals, it was Descartes who first had the really admirable daring to describe them as machina; the whole of our physiology is directed toward proving the truth of this doctrine. Moreover, it is illogical to set man apart, as Descartes did: what we know of man today is limited precisely by the extent to which we have regarded him, too, as a machine. Formerly we accorded to man, as his inheritance from some higher order of beings, what was called "free will"; now we have taken even this will from him, for the term no longer describes anything that we can understand. The old word "will" now connotes only a sort of result, an individual reaction, that follows inevitably upon a series of partly discordant and partly harmonious stimuli--the will no longer "acts," or "moves.".... Formerly it was thought that man's consciousness, his "spirit," offered evidence of his high origin, his divinity. That he might be perfected, he was advised, tortoise-like, to draw his senses in, to have no traffic with earthly things, to shuffle off his mortal coil--then only the important part of him, the "pure spirit," would remain. Here again we have thought out the thing better: to us consciousness, or "the spirit," appears as a symptom of a relative imperfection of the organism, as an experiment, a groping, a misunderstanding, as an affliction which uses up nervous force unnecessarily--we deny that anything can be done perfectly so long as it is done consciously. The "pure spirit" is a piece of pure stupidity: take away the nervous system and the senses, the so-called "mortal shell," and the rest is miscalculation--that is all!....

15.

Under Christianity neither morality nor religion has any point of contact with actuality. It offers purely imaginary causes ("God," "soul," "ego," "spirit," "free will"--or even "unfree"), and purely imaginary effects ("sin," "salvation," "grace," "punishment," "forgiveness of sins"). Intercourse between imaginary beings ("God," "spirits," "souls"); an imaginary natural history (anthropocentric; a total denial of the concept of natural causes); an imaginary psychology (misunderstandings of self, misinterpretations of agreeable or disagreeable general feelings--for example, of the states of the nervus sympathicus with the help of the sign-language of religio-ethical balderdash--, "repentance," "pangs of conscience," "temptation by the devil," "the presence of God"); an imaginary teleology (the "kingdom of God," "the last judgment," "eternal life").--This purely fictitious world, greatly to its disadvantage, is to be differentiated from the world of dreams; the latter at least reflects reality, whereas the former falsifies it, cheapens it and denies it. Once the concept of "nature" had been opposed to the concept of "God," the word "natural" necessarily took on the meaning of "abominable"--the whole of that fictitious world has its sources in hatred of the natural (--the real!--), and is no more than evidence of a profound uneasiness in the presence of reality.... This explains everything. Who alone has any reason for living his way out of reality? The man who suffers under it. But to suffer from reality one must be a botched reality.... The preponderance of pains over pleasures is the cause of this fictitious morality and religion: but such a preponderance also supplies the formula for décadence....

16.

A criticism of the Christian concept of God leads inevitably to the same conclusion.--A nation that still believes in itself holds fast to its own god. In him it does honour to the conditions which enable it to survive, to its virtues--it projects its joy in itself, its feeling of power, into a being to whom one may offer thanks. He who is rich will give of his riches; a proud people need a god to whom they can make sacrifices.... Religion, within these limits, is a form of gratitude. A man is grateful for his own existence: to that end he needs a god.--Such a god must be able to work both benefits and injuries; he must be able to play either friend or foe--he is wondered at for the good he does as well as for the evil he does. But the castration, against all nature, of such a god, making him a god of goodness alone, would be contrary to human inclination. Mankind has just as much need for an evil god as for a good god; it doesn't have to thank mere tolerance and humanitarianism for its own existence.... What would be the value of a god who knew nothing of anger, revenge, envy, scorn, cunning, violence? who had perhaps never experienced the rapturous ardeurs of victory and of destruction? No one would understand such a god: why should any one want him?--True enough, when a nation is on the downward path, when it feels its belief in its own future, its hope of freedom slipping from it, when it begins to see submission as a first necessity and the virtues of submission as measures of self-preservation, then it must overhaul its god. He then becomes a hypocrite, timorous and demure; he counsels "peace of soul," hate-no-more, leniency, "love" of friend and foe. He moralizes endlessly; he creeps into every private virtue; he becomes the god of every man; he becomes a private citizen, a cosmopolitan.... Formerly he represented a people, the strength of a people, everything aggressive and thirsty for

power in the soul of a people; now he is simply the good god....
The truth is that there is no other alternative for gods: either
they are the will to power--in which case they are national
gods--or incapacity for power--in which case they have to be
good....

17.

Wherever the will to power begins to decline, in whatever
form, there is always an accompanying decline physiologically,
a décadence. The divinity of this décadence, shorn of its
masculine virtues and passions, is converted perforce into a
god of the physiologically degraded, of the weak. Of course,
they do not call themselves the weak; they call themselves "the
good."... No hint is needed to indicate the moments in history
at which the dualistic fiction of a good and an evil god first
became possible. The same instinct which prompts the inferior
to reduce their own god to "goodness-in-itself" also prompts
them to eliminate all good qualities from the god of their
superiors; they make revenge on their masters by making a
devil of the latter's god.--The good god, and the devil like him-
-both are abortions of décadence.--How can we be so tolerant
of the naïveté of Christian theologians as to join in their
doctrine that the evolution of the concept of god from "the god
of Israel," the god of a people, to the Christian god, the essence
of all goodness, is to be described as progress?--But even
Renan does this. As if Renan had a right to be naïve! The
contrary actually stares one in the face. When everything
necessary to ascending life; when all that is strong, courageous,
masterful and proud has been eliminated from the concept of a
god; when he has sunk step by step to the level of a staff for the
weary, a sheet-anchor for the drowning; when he becomes the
poor man's god, the sinner's god, the invalid's god par

excellence, and the attribute of "saviour" or "redeemer" remains as the one essential attribute of divinity--just what is the significance of such a metamorphosis? what does such a reduction of the godhead imply?--To be sure, the "kingdom of God" has thus grown larger. Formerly he had only his own people, his "chosen" people. But since then he has gone wandering, like his people themselves, into foreign parts; he has given up settling down quietly anywhere; finally he has come to feel at home everywhere, and is the great cosmopolitan--until now he has the "great majority" on his side, and half the earth. But this god of the "great majority," this democrat among gods, has not become a proud heathen god: on the contrary, he remains a Jew, he remains a god in a corner, a god of all the dark nooks and crevices, of all the noisesome quarters of the world!... His earthly kingdom, now as always, is a kingdom of the underworld, a souterrain kingdom, a ghetto kingdom.... And he himself is so pale, so weak, so décadent.... Even the palest of the pale are able to master him--messieurs the metaphysicians, those albinos of the intellect. They spun their webs around him for so long that finally he was hypnotized, and began to spin himself, and became another metaphysician. Thereafter he resumed once more his old business of spinning the world out of his inmost being sub specie Spinozae; thereafter he became ever thinner and paler--became the "ideal," became "pure spirit," became "the absolute," became "the thing-in-itself."... The collapse of a god: he became a "thing-in-itself."

18.

The Christian concept of a god--the god as the patron of the sick, the god as a spinner of cobwebs, the god as a spirit--is one of the most corrupt concepts that has ever been set up in the world: it probably touches low-water mark in the ebbing evolution of the god-type. God degenerated into the contradiction of life. Instead of being its transfiguration and eternal Yea! In him war is declared on life, on nature, on the will to live! God becomes the formula for every slander upon the "here and now," and for every lie about the "beyond"! In him nothingness is deified, and the will to nothingness is made holy!...

19.

The fact that the strong races of northern Europe did not repudiate this Christian god does little credit to their gift for religion--and not much more to their taste. They ought to have been able to make an end of such a moribund and worn-out product of the décadence. A curse lies upon them because they were not equal to it; they made illness, decrepitude and contradiction a part of their instincts--and since then they have not managed to create any more gods. Two thousand years have come and gone--and not a single new god! Instead, there still exists, and as if by some intrinsic right,--as if he were the ultimatum and maximum of the power to create gods, of the creator spiritus in mankind--this pitiful god of Christian monotono-theism! This hybrid image of decay, conjured up out of emptiness, contradiction and vain imagining, in which all the instincts of décadence, all the cowardices and wearinesses of the soul find their sanction!--

20.

In my condemnation of Christianity I surely hope I do no injustice to a related religion with an even larger number of believers: I allude to Buddhism. Both are to be reckoned

among the nihilistic religions--they are both décadence
religions--but they are separated from each other in a very
remarkable way. For the fact that he is able to compare them at
all the critic of Christianity is indebted to the scholars of India.-
-Buddhism is a hundred times as realistic as Christianity--it is
part of its living heritage that it is able to face problems
objectively and coolly; it is the product of long centuries of
philosophical speculation. The concept, "god," was already
disposed of before it appeared. Buddhism is the only genuinely
positive religion to be encountered in history, and this applies
even to its epistemology (which is a strict phenomenalism). It
does not speak of a "struggle with sin," but, yielding to reality,
of the "struggle with suffering." Sharply differentiating itself
from Christianity, it puts the self-deception that lies in moral
concepts behind it; it is, in my phrase, beyond good and evil.--
The two physiological facts upon which it grounds itself and
upon which it bestows its chief attention are: first, an excessive
sensitiveness to sensation, which manifests itself as a refined
susceptibility to pain, and secondly, an extraordinary
spirituality, a too protracted concern with concepts and logical
procedures, under the influence of which the instinct of
personality has yielded to a notion of the "impersonal." (--Both
of these states will be familiar to a few of my readers, the
objectivists, by experience, as they are to me). These
physiological states produced a depression, and Buddha tried to
combat it by hygienic measures. Against it he prescribed a life
in the open, a life of travel; moderation in eating and a careful
selection of foods; caution in the use of intoxicants; the same
caution in arousing any of the passions that foster a bilious
habit and heat the blood; finally, no worry, either on one's own
account or on account of others. He encourages ideas that make
for either quiet contentment or good cheer--he finds means to
combat ideas of other sorts. He understands good, the state of

goodness, as something which promotes health. Prayer is not included, and neither is asceticism. There is no categorical imperative nor any disciplines, even within the walls of a monastery (--it is always possible to leave--). These things would have been simply means of increasing the excessive sensitiveness above mentioned. For the same reason he does not advocate any conflict with unbelievers; his teaching is antagonistic to nothing so much as to revenge, aversion, ressentiment (--"enmity never brings an end to enmity": the moving refrain of all Buddhism....) And in all this he was right, for it is precisely these passions which, in view of his main regiminal purpose, are unhealthful. The mental fatigue that he observes, already plainly displayed in too much "objectivity" (that is, in the individual's loss of interest in himself, in loss of balance and of "egoism"), he combats by strong efforts to lead even the spiritual interests back to the ego. In Buddha's teaching egoism is a duty. The "one thing needful," the question "how can you be delivered from suffering," regulates and determines the whole spiritual diet. (--Perhaps one will here recall that Athenian who also declared war upon pure "scientificality," to wit, Socrates, who also elevated egoism to the estate of a morality).

21.

The things necessary to Buddhism are a very mild climate, customs of great gentleness and liberality, and no militarism; moreover, it must get its start among the higher and better educated classes. Cheerfulness, quiet and the absence of desire are the chief desiderata, and they are attained. Buddhism is not a religion in which perfection is merely an object of aspiration: perfection is actually normal.--

Under Christianity the instincts of the subjugated and the oppressed come to the fore: it is only those who are at the bottom who seek their salvation in it. Here the prevailing pastime, the favourite remedy for boredom is the discussion of sin, self-criticism, the inquisition of conscience; here the emotion produced by power (called "God") is pumped up (by prayer); here the highest good is regarded as unattainable, as a gift, as "grace." Here, too, open dealing is lacking; concealment and the darkened room are Christian. Here body is despised and hygiene is denounced as sensual; the church even ranges itself against cleanliness (--the first Christian order after the banishment of the Moors closed the public baths, of which there were 270 in Cordova alone). Christian, too, is a certain cruelty toward one's self and toward others; hatred of unbelievers; the will to persecute. Sombre and disquieting ideas are in the foreground; the most esteemed states of mind, bearing the most respectable names, are epileptoid; the diet is so regulated as to engender morbid symptoms and over-stimulate the nerves. Christian, again, is all deadly enmity to the rulers of the earth, to the "aristocratic"--along with a sort of secret rivalry with them (--one resigns one's "body" to them; one wants only one's "soul"...). And Christian is all hatred of the intellect, of pride, of courage, of freedom, of intellectual libertinage; Christian is all hatred of the senses, of joy in the senses, of joy in general....

22.

When Christianity departed from its native soil, that of the lowest orders, the underworld of the ancient world, and began seeking power among barbarian peoples, it no longer had to deal with exhausted men, but with men still inwardly savage and capable of self-torture--in brief, strong men, but bungled men. Here, unlike in the case of the Buddhists, the cause of discontent with self, suffering through self, is not merely a general sensitiveness and susceptibility to pain, but, on the contrary, an inordinate thirst for inflicting pain on others, a tendency to obtain subjective satisfaction in hostile deeds and ideas. Christianity had to embrace barbaric concepts and valuations in order to obtain mastery over barbarians: of such sort, for example, are the sacrifices of the first-born, the drinking of blood as a sacrament, the disdain of the intellect and of culture; torture in all its forms, whether bodily or not; the whole pomp of the cult. Buddhism is a religion for peoples in a further state of development, for races that have become kind, gentle and over-spiritualized (--Europe is not yet ripe for it--): it is a summons that takes them back to peace and cheerfulness, to a careful rationing of the spirit, to a certain hardening of the body. Christianity aims at mastering beasts of prey; its modus operandi is to make them ill--to make feeble is the Christian recipe for taming, for "civilizing." Buddhism is a religion for the closing, over-wearied stages of civilization. Christianity appears before civilization has so much as begun-- under certain circumstances it lays the very foundations thereof.

23.

Buddhism, I repeat, is a hundred times more austere, more honest, more objective. It no longer has to justify its pains, its susceptibility to suffering, by interpreting these things in terms of sin--it simply says, as it simply thinks, "I suffer." To the barbarian, however, suffering in itself is scarcely understandable: what he needs, first of all, is an explanation as to why he suffers. (His mere instinct prompts him to deny his suffering altogether, or to endure it in silence.) Here the word "devil" was a blessing: man had to have an omnipotent and terrible enemy--there was no need to be ashamed of suffering at the hands of such an enemy.--

At the bottom of Christianity there are several subtleties that belong to the Orient. In the first place, it knows that it is of very little consequence whether a thing be true or not, so long as it is believed to be true. Truth and faith: here we have two wholly distinct worlds of ideas, almost two diametrically opposite worlds--the road to the one and the road to the other lie miles apart. To understand that fact thoroughly--this is almost enough, in the Orient, to make one a sage. The Brahmins knew it, Plato knew it, every student of the esoteric knows it. When, for example, a man gets any pleasure out of the notion that he has been saved from sin, it is not necessary for him to be actually sinful, but merely to feel sinful. But when faith is thus exalted above everything else, it necessarily follows that reason, knowledge and patient inquiry have to be discredited: the road to the truth becomes a forbidden road.-- Hope, in its stronger forms, is a great deal more powerful stimulans to life than any sort of realized joy can ever be. Mar. must be sustained in suffering by a hope so high that no conflict with actuality can dash it--so high, indeed, that no fulfilment can satisfy it: a hope reaching out beyond this world. (Precisely because of this power that hope has of making the suffering hold out, the Greeks regarded it as the evil of evils, as the most malign of evils; it remained behind at the source of all evil.)[3]--In order that love may be possible, God must become a person; in order that the lower instincts may take a hand in the matter God must be young. To satisfy the ardor of the woman a beautiful saint must appear on the scene, and to satisfy that of the men there must be a virgin. These things are necessary if Christianity is to assume lordship over a soil on which some aphrodisiacal or Adonis cult has already established a notion as to what a cult ought to be. To insist upon chastity greatly strengthens the vehemence and subjectivity of the religious instinct--it makes the cult warmer, more enthusiastic, more soulful.--Love is the state in which man sees things most decidedly as they are not. The force of illusion reaches its highest here, and so does the capacity for sweetening, for transfiguring. When a man is in love he endures more than at any other time; he submits to anything. The problem was to devise a religion which would allow one to love: by this means the worst that life has to offer is overcome--it is scarcely even noticed.--So much for the three Christian virtues: faith, hope and charity: I call them the three Christian ingenuities.--Buddhism is in too late a stage of development, too full of positivism, to be shrewd in any such way.--

[3] That is, in Pandora's box.

24.

Here I barely touch upon the problem of the origin of Christianity. The first thing necessary to its solution is this: that Christianity is to be understood only by examining the soil from which it sprung--it is not a reaction against Jewish instincts; it is their inevitable product; it is simply one more step in the awe-inspiring logic of the Jews. In the words of the Saviour, "salvation is of the Jews."[4]--The second thing to remember is this: that the psychological type of the Galilean is still to be recognized, but it was only in its most degenerate form (which is at once maimed and overladen with foreign features) that it could serve in the manner in which it has been used: as a type of the Saviour of mankind.--

[4] John iv, 22.

The Jews are the most remarkable people in the history of the world, for when they were confronted with the question, to be or not to be, they chose, with perfectly unearthly deliberation, to be at any price: this price involved a radical falsification of all nature, of all naturalness, of all reality, of the whole inner world, as well as of the outer. They put themselves against all those conditions under which, hitherto, a people had been able to live, or had even been permitted to live; out of themselves they evolved an idea which stood in direct opposition to natural conditions--one by one they distorted religion, civilization, morality, history and psychology until each became a contradiction of its natural significance. We meet with the same phenomenon later on, in an incalculably exaggerated form, but only as a copy: the Christian church, put beside the "people of God," shows a complete lack of any claim to originality. Precisely for this reason the Jews are the most fateful people in the history of the world: their influence has so falsified the reasoning of mankind in this matter that today the Christian can cherish anti-Semitism without realizing that it is no more than the final consequence of Judaism.

In my "Genealogy of Morals" I give the first psychological explanation of the concepts underlying those two antithetical things, a noble morality and a ressentiment morality, the second of which is a mere product of the denial of the former. The Judaeo-Christian moral system belongs to the second division, and in every detail. In order to be able to say Nay to everything representing an ascending evolution of life--that is, to well-being, to power, to beauty, to self-approval--the instincts of ressentiment, here become downright genius, had to invent an other world in which the acceptance of life appeared as the most evil and abominable thing imaginable.

51

Psychologically, the Jews are a people gifted with the very
strongest vitality, so much so that when they found themselves
facing impossible conditions of life they chose voluntarily, and
with a profound talent for self-preservation, the side of all
those instincts which make for décadence--not as if mastered
by them, but as if detecting in them a power by which "the
world" could be defied. The Jews are the very opposite of
décadents: they have simply been forced into appearing in that
guise, and with a degree of skill approaching the non plus ultra
of histrionic genius they have managed to put themselves at the
head of all décadent movements (--for example, the
Christianity of Paul--), and so make of them something
stronger than any party frankly saying Yes to life. To the sort
of men who reach out for power under Judaism and
Christianity,--that is to say, to the priestly class--décadence is
no more than a means to an end. Men of this sort have a vital
interest in making mankind sick, and in confusing the values of
"good" and "bad," "true" and "false" in a manner that is not
only dangerous to life, but also slanders it.

25.

The history of Israel is invaluable as a typical history of an
attempt to denaturize all natural values: I point to five facts
which bear this out. Originally, and above all in the time of the
monarchy, Israel maintained the right attitude of things, which
is to say, the natural attitude. Its Jahveh was an expression of
its consciousness of power, its joy in itself, its hopes for itself:
to him the Jews looked for victory and salvation and through
him they expected nature to give them whatever was necessary
to their existence--above all, rain. Jahveh is the god of Israel,
and consequently the god of justice: this is the logic of every
race that has power in its hands and a good conscience in the

use of it. In the religious ceremonial of the Jews both aspects of this self-approval stand revealed. The nation is grateful for the high destiny that has enabled it to obtain dominion; it is grateful for the benign procession of the seasons, and for the good fortune attending its herds and its crops.--This view of things remained an ideal for a long while, even after it had been robbed of validity by tragic blows: anarchy within and the Assyrian without. But the people still retained, as a projection of their highest yearnings, that vision of a king who was at once a gallant warrior and an upright judge--a vision best visualized in the typical prophet (i. e., critic and satirist of the moment), Isaiah.--But every hope remained unfulfilled. The old god no longer could do what he used to do. He ought to have been abandoned. But what actually happened? Simply this: the conception of him was changed--the conception of him was denaturized; this was the price that had to be paid for keeping him.--Jahveh, the god of "justice"--he is in accord with Israel no more, he no longer vizualizes the national egoism; he is now a god only conditionally.... The public notion of this god now becomes merely a weapon in the hands of clerical agitators, who interpret all happiness as a reward and all unhappiness as a punishment for obedience or disobedience to him, for "sin": that most fraudulent of all imaginable interpretations, whereby a "moral order of the world" is set up, and the fundamental concepts, "cause" and "effect," are stood on their heads. Once natural causation has been swept out of the world by doctrines of reward and punishment some sort of un-natural causation becomes necessary: and all other varieties of the denial of nature follow it. A god who demands--in place of a god who helps, who gives counsel, who is at bottom merely a name for every happy inspiration of courage and self-reliance.... Morality is no longer a reflection of the conditions which make for the sound life and development of the people;

53

it is no longer the primary life-instinct; instead it has become abstract and in opposition to life--a fundamental perversion of the fancy, an "evil eye" on all things. What is Jewish, what is Christian morality? Chance robbed of its innocence; unhappiness polluted with the idea of "sin"; well-being represented as a danger, as a "temptation"; a physiological disorder produced by the canker worm of conscience....

26.

The concept of god falsified; the concept of morality falsified;--but even here Jewish priest-craft did not stop. The whole history of Israel ceased to be of any value: out with it!--These priests accomplished that miracle of falsification of which a great part of the Bible is the documentary evidence; with a degree of contempt unparalleled, and in the face of all tradition and all historical reality, they translated the past of their people into religious terms, which is to say, they converted it into an idiotic mechanism of salvation, whereby all offences against Jahveh were punished and all devotion to him was rewarded. We would regard this act of historical falsification as something far more shameful if familiarity with the ecclesiastical interpretation of history for thousands of years had not blunted our inclinations for uprightness in historicis. And the philosophers support the church: the lie about a "moral order of the world" runs through the whole of philosophy, even the newest. What is the meaning of a "moral order of the world"? That there is a thing called the will of God which, once and for all time, determines what man ought to do and what he ought not to do; that the worth of a people, or of an individual thereof, is to be measured by the extent to which they or he obey this will of God; that the destinies of a people or of an individual are controlled by this will of God, which rewards or punishes according to the degree of obedience manifested.--In place of all that pitiable lie reality has this to say: the priest, a parasitical variety of man who can exist only at the cost of every sound view of life, takes the name of God in vain: he calls that state of human society in which he himself determines the value of all things "the kingdom of God"; he calls the means whereby that state of affairs is attained "the will of God"; with cold-blooded cynicism he estimates all peoples, all ages and all individuals by the extent of their subservience or opposition to the power of the priestly order. One observes him at work: under the hand of the Jewish priesthood the great age of Israel became an age of decline; the Exile, with its long series of misfortunes, was transformed into a punishment for that great age--during which priests had not yet come into existence. Out of the powerful and wholly free heroes of Israel's history they fashioned, according to their changing needs, either wretched bigots and hypocrites or men entirely "godless." They reduced every great event to the idiotic formula: "obedient or disobedient to God."--They went a step further: the "will of God" (in other words some means necessary for preserving the power of the priests) had to be determined--and to this end they had to have a "revelation." In plain English, a gigantic literary fraud had to be perpetrated, and "holy scriptures" had to be concocted--and so, with the utmost hierarchical pomp, and days of penance and much lamentation over the long days of "sin" now ended, they were duly published. The "will of God," it appears, had long stood like a rock; the trouble was that mankind had neglected the "holy scriptures".... But the "will of God" had already been revealed to Moses.... What happened? Simply this: the priest had formulated, once and for all time and with the strictest meticulousness, what tithes were to be paid to him, from the largest to the smallest (--not forgetting the most appetizing cuts of meat, for the priest is a great consumer of beefsteaks); in brief, he let it be known just what he wanted, what "the will of God" was.... From this time forward things were so arranged that the priest became indispensable everywhere; at all the great natural events of life, at birth, at marriage, in sickness, at death, not to say at the "sacrifice" (that is, at meal-times), the holy parasite put in his appearance, and proceeded to denaturize it--in his own phrase, to "sanctify" it.... For this should be noted: that every natural habit, every natural institution (the state, the administration of justice, marriage, the care of the sick and of the poor), everything demanded by the life-instinct, in short, everything that has any value in itself, is reduced to absolute worthlessness and even made the reverse of valuable by the parasitism of priests (or, if you chose, by the "moral order of the world"). The fact requires a sanction--a power to grant values becomes necessary, and the only way it can create such values is by denying nature.... The priest depreciates and desecrates nature: it is only at this price that he can exist at all.--Disobedience to God, which actually means to the priest, to "the law," now gets the name of "sin"; the means prescribed for "reconciliation with God" are, of course, precisely the means which bring one most effectively under the thumb of the priest; he alone can "save".... Psychologically considered, "sins" are indispensable to every society organized on an ecclesiastical basis; they are the only reliable weapons of power; the priest lives upon sins; it is necessary to him that there be "sinning".... Prime axiom: "God forgiveth him that repenteth"--in plain English, him that submitteth to the priest.

27.

Christianity sprang from a soil so corrupt that on it everything natural, every natural value, every reality was opposed by the deepest instincts of the ruling class--it grew up as a sort of war to the death upon reality, and as such it has never been surpassed. The "holy people," who had adopted priestly values and priestly names for all things, and who, with a terrible logical consistency, had rejected everything of the earth as "unholy," "worldly," "sinful"--this people put its instinct into a final formula that was logical to the point of self-annihilation: as Christianity it actually denied even the last form of reality, the "holy people," the "chosen people," Jewish reality itself. The phenomenon is of the first order of importance: the small insurrectionary movement which took the name of Jesus of Nazareth is simply the Jewish instinct redivivus--in other words, it is the priestly instinct come to such a pass that it can no longer endure the priest as a fact; it is the discovery of a state of existence even more fantastic than any before it, of a vision of life even more unreal than that necessary to an ecclesiastical organization. Christianity actually denies the church....

I am unable to determine what was the target of the insurrection said to have been led (whether rightly or wrongly) by Jesus, if it was not the Jewish church--"church" being here used in exactly the same sense that the word has today. It was an insurrection against the "good and just," against the "prophets of Israel," against the whole hierarchy of society--not against corruption, but against caste, privilege, order, formalism. It was unbelief in "superior men," a Nay flung at everything that priests and theologians stood for. But the hierarchy that was called into question, if only for an instant, by this movement was the structure of piles which, above everything, was necessary to the safety of the Jewish people in the midst of the "waters"--it represented their last possibility of survival; it was the final residuum of their independent political

existence; an attack upon it was an attack upon the most
profound national instinct, the most powerful national will to
live, that has ever appeared on earth. This saintly anarchist,
who aroused the people of the abyss, the outcasts and
"sinners," the Chandala of Judaism, to rise in revolt against the
established order of things--and in language which, if the
Gospels are to be credited, would get him sent to Siberia today-
-this man was certainly a political criminal, at least in so far as
it was possible to be one in so absurdly unpolitical a
community. This is what brought him to the cross: the proof
thereof is to be found in the inscription that was put upon the
cross. He died for his own sins--there is not the slightest
ground for believing, no matter how often it is asserted, that he
died for the sins of others.--

28.

As to whether he himself was conscious of this contradiction--
whether, in fact, this was the only contradiction he was
cognizant of--that is quite another question. Here, for the first
time, I touch upon the problem of the psychology of the
Saviour.--I confess, to begin with, that there are very few
books which offer me harder reading than the Gospels. My
difficulties are quite different from those which enabled the
learned curiosity of the German mind to achieve one of its
most unforgettable triumphs. It is a long while since I, like all
other young scholars, enjoyed with all the sapient
laboriousness of a fastidious philologist the work of the
incomparable Strauss.[5] At that time I was twenty years old:
now I am too serious for that sort of thing. What do I care for
the contradictions of "tradition"? How can any one call pious
legends "traditions"? The histories of saints present the most
dubious variety of literature in existence; to examine them by

the scientific method, in the entire absence of corroborative documents, seems to me to condemn the whole inquiry from the start--it is simply learned idling....

[5] David Friedrich Strauss (1808-74), author of "Das Leben Jesu" (1835-6), a very famous work in its day. Nietzsche here refers to it.

29.

What concerns me is the psychological type of the Saviour. This type might be depicted in the Gospels, in however mutilated a form and however much overladen with extraneous characters--that is, in spite of the Gospels; just as the figure of Francis of Assisi shows itself in his legends in spite of his legends. It is not a question of mere truthful evidence as to what he did, what he said and how he actually died; the question is, whether his type is still conceivable, whether it has been handed down to us.--All the attempts that I know of to read the history of a "soul" in the Gospels seem to me to reveal only a lamentable psychological levity. M. Renan, that mountebank in psychologicus, has contributed the two most unseemly notions to this business of explaining the type of Jesus: the notion of the genius and that of the hero ("héros"). But if there is anything essentially unevangelical, it is surely the concept of the hero. What the Gospels make instinctive is precisely the reverse of all heroic struggle, of all taste for conflict: the very incapacity for resistance is here converted into something moral: ("resist not evil!"--the most profound sentence in the Gospels, perhaps the true key to them), to wit, the blessedness of peace, of gentleness, the inability to be an enemy. What is the meaning of "glad tidings"?--The true life, the life eternal has been found--it is not merely promised, it is here, it is in you; it is the life that lies in love free from all retreats and exclusions, from all keeping of distances. Every one is the child of God--Jesus claims nothing for himself alone--as the child of God each man is the equal of every other man.... Imagine making Jesus a hero!--And what a tremendous misunderstanding appears in the word "genius"! Our whole conception of the "spiritual," the whole conception of our civilization, could have had no meaning in the world that Jesus lived in. In the strict sense of the physiologist, a quite different word ought to be used here.... We all know that there is a morbid sensibility of the tactile nerves which causes those suffering from it to recoil from every touch, and from every effort to grasp a solid object. Brought to its logical conclusion, such a physiological habitus becomes an instinctive hatred of all reality, a flight into the "intangible," into the "incomprehensible"; a distaste for all formulae, for all conceptions of time and space, for everything established--customs, institutions, the church--; a feeling of being at home in a world in which no sort of reality survives, a merely "inner" world, a "true" world, an "eternal" world.... "The Kingdom of God is within you"....

30.

The instinctive hatred of reality: the consequence of an extreme susceptibility to pain and irritation--so great that merely to be "touched" becomes unendurable, for every sensation is too profound.

The instinctive exclusion of all aversion, all hostility, all bounds and distances in feeling: the consequence of an extreme susceptibility to pain and irritation--so great that it senses all resistance, all compulsion to resistance, as unbearable anguish (--that is to say, as harmful, as prohibited by the instinct of self-preservation), and regards blessedness (joy) as possible only when it is no longer necessary to offer resistance to anybody or anything, however evil or dangerous--love, as the only, as the ultimate possibility of life....

These are the two physiological realities upon and out of which the doctrine of salvation has sprung. I call them a sublime super-development of hedonism upon a thoroughly unsalubrious soil. What stands most closely related to them, though with a large admixture of Greek vitality and nerve-force, is epicureanism, the theory of salvation of paganism. Epicurus was a typical décadent: I was the first to recognize him.--The fear of pain, even of infinitely slight pain--the end of this can be nothing save a religion of love....

31.

I have already given my answer to the problem. The prerequisite to it is the assumption that the type of the Saviour has reached us only in a greatly distorted form. This distortion is very probable: there are many reasons why a type of that sort should not be handed down in a pure form, complete and free of additions. The milieu in which this strange figure moved must have left marks upon him, and more must have been imprinted by the history, the destiny, of the early Christian communities; the latter indeed, must have embellished the type retrospectively with characters which can be understood only as serving the purposes of war and of propaganda. That strange and sickly world into which the Gospels lead us--a world apparently out of a Russian novel, in which the scum of society, nervous maladies and "childish" idiocy keep a tryst--must, in any case, have coarsened the type: the first disciples, in particular, must have been forced to translate an existence visible only in symbols and incomprehensibilities into their

61

own crudity, in order to understand it at all--in their sight the type could take on reality only after it had been recast in a familiar mould.... The prophet, the messiah, the future judge, the teacher of morals, the worker of wonders, John the Baptist--all these merely presented chances to misunderstand it.... Finally, let us not underrate the proprium of all great, and especially all sectarian veneration: it tends to erase from the venerated objects all its original traits and idiosyncrasies, often so painfully strange--it does not even see them. It is greatly to be regretted that no Dostoyevsky lived in the neighbourhood of this most interesting décadent--I mean some one who would have felt the poignant charm of such a compound of the sublime, the morbid and the childish. In the last analysis, the type, as a type of the décadence, may actually have been peculiarly complex and contradictory: such a possibility is not to be lost sight of. Nevertheless, the probabilities seem to be against it, for in that case tradition would have been particularly accurate and objective, whereas we have reasons for assuming the contrary. Meanwhile, there is a contradiction between the peaceful preacher of the mount, the sea-shore and the fields, who appears like a new Buddha on a soil very unlike India's, and the aggressive fanatic, the mortal enemy of theologians and ecclesiastics, who stands glorified by Renan's malice as "le grand maître en ironie." I myself haven't any doubt that the greater part of this venom (and no less of esprit) got itself into the concept of the Master only as a result of the excited nature of Christian propaganda: we all know the unscrupulousness of sectarians when they set out to turn their leader into an apologia for themselves. When the early Christians had need of an adroit, contentious, pugnacious and maliciously subtle theologian to tackle other theologians, they created a "god" that met that need, just as they put into his mouth without hesitation certain ideas that were necessary to them but that were utterly at odds with the Gospels--"the second coming," "the last judgment," all sorts of expectations and promises, current at the time.--

32.

I can only repeat that I set myself against all efforts to intrude the fanatic into the figure of the Saviour: the very word impérieux, used by Renan, is alone enough to annul the type. What the "glad tidings" tell us is simply that there are no more contradictions; the kingdom of heaven belongs to children; the faith that is voiced here is no more an embattled faith--it is at hand, it has been from the beginning, it is a sort of recrudescent childishness of the spirit. The physiologists, at all events, are familiar with such a delayed and incomplete puberty in the living organism, the result of degeneration. A faith of this sort is not furious, it does not denounce, it does not defend itself: it does not come with "the sword"--it does not realize how it will one day set man against man. It does not manifest itself either by miracles, or by rewards and promises, or by "scriptures": it is itself, first and last, its own miracle, its own reward, its own promise, its own "kingdom of God." This faith does not formulate itself--it simply lives, and so guards itself against formulae. To be sure, the accident of environment, of educational background gives prominence to concepts of a certain sort: in primitive Christianity one finds only concepts of a Judaeo-Semitic character (--that of eating and drinking at the last supper belongs to this category--an idea which, like everything else Jewish, has been badly mauled by the church). But let us be careful not to see in all this anything more than symbolical language, semantics[6] an opportunity to speak in parables. It is only on the theory that no work is to be taken literally that this anti-realist is able to speak at all. Set down

among Hindus he would have made use of the concepts of
Sankhya,[7] and among Chinese he would have employed
those of Lao-tse[8]--and in neither case would it have made
any difference to him.--With a little freedom in the use of
words, one might actually call Jesus a "free spirit"[9]--he cares
nothing for what is established: the word killeth,[10] whatever
is established killeth. The idea of "life" as an experience, as he
alone conceives it, stands opposed to his mind to every sort of
word, formula, law, belief and dogma. He speaks only of inner
things: "life" or "truth" or "light" is his word for the innermost-
-in his sight everything else, the whole of reality, all nature,
even language, has significance only as sign, as allegory.--Here
it is of paramount importance to be led into no error by the
temptations lying in Christian, or rather ecclesiastical
prejudices: such a symbolism par excellence stands outside all
religion, all notions of worship, all history, all natural science,
all worldly experience, all knowledge, all politics, all
psychology, all books, all art--his "wisdom" is precisely a pure
ignorance[11] of all such things. He has never heard of culture;
he doesn't have to make war on it--he doesn't even deny it....
The same thing may be said of the state, of the whole
bourgeoise social order, of labour, of war--he has no ground for
denying "the world," for he knows nothing of the ecclesiastical
concept of "the world".... Denial is precisely the thing that is
impossible to him.--In the same way he lacks argumentative
capacity, and has no belief that an article of faith, a "truth,"
may be established by proofs (--his proofs are inner "lights,"
subjective sensations of happiness and self-approval, simple
"proofs of power"--). Such a doctrine cannot contradict: it
doesn't know that other doctrines exist, or can exist, and is
wholly incapable of imagining anything opposed to it.... If
anything of the sort is ever encountered, it laments the

"blindness" with sincere sympathy--for it alone has "light"--but it does not offer objections....

[6] The word Semiotik is in the text, but it is probable that Semantik is what Nietzsche had in mind.

[7] One of the six great systems of Hindu philosophy.

[8] The reputed founder of Taoism.

[9] Nietzsche's name for one accepting his own philosophy.

[10] That is, the strict letter of the law--the chief target of Jesus's early preaching.

[11] A reference to the "pure ignorance" (reine Thorheit) of Parsifal.

33.

In the whole psychology of the "Gospels" the concepts of guilt and punishment are lacking, and so is that of reward. "Sin," which means anything that puts a distance between God and man, is abolished--this is precisely the "glad tidings." Eternal bliss is not merely promised, nor is it bound up with conditions: it is conceived as the only reality--what remains consists merely of signs useful in speaking of it.

The results of such a point of view project themselves into a new way of life, the special evangelical way of life. It is not a "belief" that marks off the Christian; he is distinguished by a different mode of action; he acts differently. He offers no resistance, either by word or in his heart, to those who stand against him. He draws no distinction between strangers and countrymen, Jews and Gentiles ("neighbour," of course, means

fellow-believer, Jew). He is angry with no one, and he despises
no one. He neither appeals to the courts of justice nor heeds
their mandates ("Swear not at all").[12] He never under any
circumstances divorces his wife, even when he has proofs of
her infidelity.--And under all of this is one principle; all of it
arises from one instinct.--

[12] Matthew v, 34.

The life of the Saviour was simply a carrying out of this way of
life--and so was his death.... He no longer needed any formula
or ritual in his relations with God--not even prayer. He had
rejected the whole of the Jewish doctrine of repentance and
atonement; he knew that it was only by a way of life that one
could feel one's self "divine," "blessed," "evangelical," a "child
of God." Not by "repentance," not by "prayer and forgiveness"
is the way to God: only the Gospel way leads to God--it is
itself "God!"--What the Gospels abolished was the Judaism in
the concepts of "sin," "forgiveness of sin," "faith," "salvation
through faith"--the whole ecclesiastical dogma of the Jews was
denied by the "glad tidings."

The deep instinct which prompts the Christian how to live so
that he will feel that he is "in heaven" and is "immortal,"
despite many reasons for feeling that he is not "in heaven": this
is the only psychological reality in "salvation."--A new way of
life, not a new faith....

34.

If I understand anything at all about this great symbolist, it is
this: that he regarded only subjective realities as realities, as
"truths"--that he saw everything else, everything natural,

temporal, spatial and historical, merely as signs, as materials for parables. The concept of "the Son of God" does not connote a concrete person in history, an isolated and definite individual, but an "eternal" fact, a psychological symbol set free from the concept of time. The same thing is true, and in the highest sense, of the God of this typical symbolist, of the "kingdom of God," and of the "sonship of God." Nothing could be more un-Christian than the crude ecclesiastical notions of God as a person, of a "kingdom of God" that is to come, of a "kingdom of heaven" beyond, and of a "son of God" as the second person of the Trinity. All this--if I may be forgiven the phrase--is like thrusting one's fist into the eye (and what an eye!) of the Gospels: a disrespect for symbols amounting to world-historical cynicism.... But it is nevertheless obvious enough what is meant by the symbols "Father" and "Son"--not, of course, to every one--: the word "Son" expresses entrance into the feeling that there is a general transformation of all things (beatitude), and "Father" expresses that feeling itself--the sensation of eternity and of perfection.--I am ashamed to remind you of what the church has made of this symbolism: has it not set an Amphitryon story[13] at the threshold of the Christian "faith"? And a dogma of "immaculate conception" for good measure?... And thereby it has robbed conception of its immaculateness--

[13] Amphitryon was the son of Alcaeus, King of Tiryns. His wife was Alcmene. During his absence she was visited by Zeus, and bore Heracles.

The "kingdom of heaven" is a state of the heart--not something to come "beyond the world" or "after death." The whole idea of natural death is absent from the Gospels: death is not a bridge, not a passing; it is absent because it belongs to a quite different, a merely apparent world, useful only as a symbol.

The "hour of death" is not a Christian idea--"hours," time, the physical life and its crises have no existence for the bearer of "glad tidings."... The "kingdom of God" is not something that men wait for: it had no yesterday and no day after tomorrow, it is not going to come at a "millennium"--it is an experience of the heart, it is everywhere and it is nowhere....

35.

This "bearer of glad tidings" died as he lived and taught--not to "save mankind," but to show mankind how to live. It was a way of life that he bequeathed to man: his demeanour before the judges, before the officers, before his accusers--his demeanour on the cross. He does not resist; he does not defend his rights; he makes no effort to ward off the most extreme penalty--more, he invites it.... And he prays, suffers and loves with those, in those, who do him evil.... Not to defend one's self, not to show anger, not to lay blames.... On the contrary, to submit even to the Evil One--to love him....

36.

--We free spirits--we are the first to have the necessary prerequisite to understanding what nineteen centuries have misunderstood--that instinct and passion for integrity which makes war upon the "holy lie" even more than upon all other lies.... Mankind was unspeakably far from our benevolent and cautious neutrality, from that discipline of the spirit which alone makes possible the solution of such strange and subtle things: what men always sought, with shameless egoism, was their own advantage therein; they created the church out of denial of the Gospels....

Whoever sought for signs of an ironical divinity's hand in the great drama of existence would find no small indication thereof in the stupendous question-mark that is called Christianity. That mankind should be on its knees before the very antithesis of what was the origin, the meaning and the law of the Gospels--that in the concept of the "church" the very things should be pronounced holy that the "bearer of glad tidings" regards as beneath him and behind him--it would be impossible to surpass this as a grand example of world-historical irony--

37.

--Our age is proud of its historical sense: how, then, could it delude itself into believing that the crude fable of the wonder-worker and Saviour constituted the beginnings of Christianity-- and that everything spiritual and symbolical in it only came later? Quite to the contrary, the whole history of Christianity-- from the death on the cross onward--is the history of a progressively clumsier misunderstanding of an original symbolism. With every extension of Christianity among larger and ruder masses, even less capable of grasping the principles that gave birth to it, the need arose to make it more and more vulgar and barbarous--it absorbed the teachings and rites of all the subterranean cults of the imperium Romanum, and the absurdities engendered by all sorts of sickly reasoning. It was the fate of Christianity that its faith had to become as sickly, as low and as vulgar as the needs were sickly, low and vulgar to which it had to administer. A sickly barbarism finally lifts itself to power as the church--the church, that incarnation of deadly hostility to all honesty, to all loftiness of soul, to all discipline of the spirit, to all spontaneous and kindly humanity.--Christian values--noble values: it is only we, we free spirits, who have re-established this greatest of all antitheses in values!...

Friedrich Nietzsche

38.

--I cannot, at this place, avoid a sigh. There are days when I am
visited by a feeling blacker than the blackest melancholy--
contempt of man. Let me leave no doubt as to what I despise,
whom I despise: it is the man of today, the man with whom I
am unhappily contemporaneous. The man of today--I am
suffocated by his foul breath!... Toward the past, like all who
understand, I am full of tolerance, which is to say, generous
self-control: with gloomy caution I pass through whole
millenniums of this madhouse of a world, call it "Christianity,"
"Christian faith" or the "Christian church," as you will--I take
care not to hold mankind responsible for its lunacies. But my
feeling changes and breaks out irresistibly the moment I enter
modern times, our times. Our age knows better.... What was
formerly merely sickly now becomes indecent--it is indecent to
be a Christian today. And here my disgust begins.--I look about
me: not a word survives of what was once called "truth"; we
can no longer bear to hear a priest pronounce the word. Even a
man who makes the most modest pretensions to integrity must
know that a theologian, a priest, a pope of today not only errs
when he speaks, but actually lies--and that he no longer
escapes blame for his lie through "innocence" or "ignorance."
The priest knows, as every one knows, that there is no longer
any "God," or any "sinner," or any "Saviour"--that "free will"
and the "moral order of the world" are lies--: serious reflection,
the profound self-conquest of the spirit, allow no man to
pretend that he does not know it.... All the ideas of the church
are now recognized for what they are--as the worst counterfeits
in existence, invented to debase nature and all natural values;
the priest himself is seen as he actually is--as the most
dangerous form of parasite, as the venomous spider of

70

creation.... We know, our conscience now knows--just what the real value of all those sinister inventions of priest and church has been and what ends they have served, with their debasement of humanity to a state of self-pollution, the very sight of which excites loathing,--the concepts "the other world," "the last judgment," "the immortality of the soul," the "soul" itself: they are all merely so many instruments of torture, systems of cruelty, whereby the priest becomes master and remains master.... Every one knows this, but nevertheless things remain as before. What has become of the last trace of decent feeling, of self-respect, when our statesmen, otherwise an unconventional class of men and thoroughly anti-Christian in their acts, now call themselves Christians and go to the communion-table?... A prince at the head of his armies, magnificent as the expression of the egoism and arrogance of his people--and yet acknowledging, without any shame, that he is a Christian!... Whom, then, does Christianity deny? what does it call "the world"? To be a soldier, to be a judge, to be a patriot; to defend one's self; to be careful of one's honour; to desire one's own advantage; to be proud ... every act of everyday, every instinct, every valuation that shows itself in a deed, is now anti-Christian: what a monster of falsehood the modern man must be to call himself nevertheless, and without shame, a Christian!--

39.

--I shall go back a bit, and tell you the authentic history of Christianity.--The very word "Christianity" is a misunderstanding--at bottom there was only one Christian, and he died on the cross. The "Gospels" died on the cross. What, from that moment onward, was called the "Gospels" was the very reverse of what he had lived: "bad tidings," a

Dysangelium.[14] It is an error amounting to nonsensicality to see in "faith," and particularly in faith in salvation through Christ, the distinguishing mark of the Christian: only the Christian way of life, the life lived by him who died on the cross, is Christian.... To this day such a life is still possible, and for certain men even necessary: genuine, primitive Christianity will remain possible in all ages.... Not faith, but acts; above all, an avoidance of acts, a different state of being.... States of consciousness, faith of a sort, the acceptance, for example, of anything as true--as every psychologist knows, the value of these things is perfectly indifferent and fifth-rate compared to that of the instincts: strictly speaking, the whole concept of intellectual causality is false. To reduce being a Christian, the state of Christianity, to an acceptance of truth, to a mere phenomenon of consciousness, is to formulate the negation of Christianity. In fact, there are no Christians. The "Christian"-- he who for two thousand years has passed as a Christian--is simply a psychological self-delusion. Closely examined, it appears that, despite all his "faith," he has been ruled only by his instincts--and what instincts!--In all ages--for example, in the case of Luther--"faith" has been no more than a cloak, a pretense, a curtain behind which the instincts have played their game--a shrewd blindness to the domination of certain of the instincts.... I have already called "faith" the specially Christian form of shrewdness--people always talk of their "faith" and act according to their instincts.... In the world of ideas of the Christian there is nothing that so much as touches reality: on the contrary, one recognizes an instinctive hatred of reality as the motive power, the only motive power at the bottom of Christianity. What follows therefrom? That even here, in psychologicis, there is a radical error, which is to say one conditioning fundamentals, which is to say, one in substance. Take away one idea and put a genuine reality in its place--and the whole of Christianity crumbles to nothingness!--Viewed calmly, this strangest of all phenomena, a religion not only depending on errors, but inventive and ingenious only in devising injurious errors, poisonous to life and to the heart--this remains a spectacle for the gods--for those gods who are also philosophers, and whom I have encountered, for example, in the celebrated dialogues at Naxos. At the moment when their disgust leaves them (--and us!) they will be thankful for the spectacle afforded by the Christians: perhaps because of this curious exhibition alone the wretched little planet called the earth deserves a glance from omnipotence, a show of divine interest.... Therefore, let us not underestimate the Christians: the Christian, false to the point of innocence, is far above the ape--in its application to the Christians a well-known theory of descent becomes a mere piece of politeness....

[14] So in the text. One of Nietzsche's numerous coinages, obviously suggested by Evangelium, the German for gospel.

40.

--The fate of the Gospels was decided by death--it hung on the "cross."... It was only death, that unexpected and shameful death; it was only the cross, which was usually reserved for the canaille only--it was only this appalling paradox which brought the disciples face to face with the real riddle: "Who was it? what was it?"--The feeling of dismay, of profound affront and injury; the suspicion that such a death might involve a refutation of their cause; the terrible question, "Why just in this way?"--this state of mind is only too easy to understand. Here everything must be accounted for as necessary; everything must have a meaning, a reason, the highest sort of reason; the love of a disciple excludes all chance. Only then did the chasm of doubt yawn: "Who put him to death? who was his natural enemy?"--this question flashed like a lightning-stroke. Answer: dominant Judaism, its ruling class. From that moment, one found one's self in revolt against the established order, and began to understand Jesus as in revolt against the established order. Until then this militant, this nay-saying, nay-doing element in his character had been lacking; what is more, he had appeared to present its opposite. Obviously, the little community had not understood what was precisely the most important thing of all: the example offered by this way of dying, the freedom from and superiority to every feeling of ressentiment--a plain indication of how little he was understood at all! All that Jesus could hope to accomplish by his death, in itself, was to offer the strongest possible proof, or example, of his teachings in the most public manner.... But his disciples were very far from forgiving his death--though to have done so would have accorded with the Gospels in the highest degree; and neither were they prepared to offer themselves, with gentle and serene calmness of heart, for a similar death.... On the contrary, it was precisely the most unevangelical of feelings, revenge, that now possessed them. It seemed impossible that the cause should perish with his death: "recompense" and "judgment" became necessary (--yet what could be less evangelical than "recompense," "punishment," and "sitting in judgment"!). Once more the popular belief in the coming of a messiah appeared in the foreground; attention was rivetted upon an historical moment: the "kingdom of God" is to come, with judgment upon his enemies.... But in all this there was a wholesale misunderstanding: imagine the "kingdom of God" as a last act, as a mere promise! The Gospels had been, in fact, the incarnation, the fulfilment, the realization of this "kingdom of God." It was only now that all the familiar contempt for and bitterness against Pharisees and theologians began to appear in the character of the Master--he was thereby turned into a

Pharisee and theologian himself! On the other hand, the savage veneration of these completely unbalanced souls could no longer endure the Gospel doctrine, taught by Jesus, of the equal right of all men to be children of God: their revenge took the form of elevating Jesus in an extravagant fashion, and thus separating him from themselves: just as, in earlier times, the Jews, to revenge themselves upon their enemies, separated themselves from their God, and placed him on a great height. The One God and the Only Son of God: both were products of ressentiment....

41.

--And from that time onward an absurd problem offered itself: "how could God allow it!" To which the deranged reason of the little community formulated an answer that was terrifying in its absurdity: God gave his son as a sacrifice for the forgiveness of sins. At once there was an end of the gospels! Sacrifice for sin, and in its most obnoxious and barbarous form: sacrifice of the innocent for the sins of the guilty! What appalling paganism!-- Jesus himself had done away with the very concept of "guilt," he denied that there was any gulf fixed between God and man; he lived this unity between God and man, and that was precisely his "glad tidings".... And not as a mere privilege!-- From this time forward the type of the Saviour was corrupted, bit by bit, by the doctrine of judgment and of the second coming, the doctrine of death as a sacrifice, the doctrine of the resurrection, by means of which the entire concept of "blessedness," the whole and only reality of the gospels, is juggled away--in favour of a state of existence after death!... St. Paul, with that rabbinical impudence which shows itself in all his doings, gave a logical quality to that conception, that indecent conception, in this way: "If Christ did not rise from the dead, then all our faith is in vain!"--And at once there sprang from the Gospels the most contemptible of all unfulfillable promises, the shameless doctrine of personal immortality.... Paul even preached it as a reward....

42.

One now begins to see just what it was that came to an end with the death on the cross: a new and thoroughly original effort to found a Buddhistic peace movement, and so establish happiness on earth--real, not merely promised. For this remains--as I have already pointed out--the essential difference between the two religions of décadence: Buddhism promises nothing, but actually fulfils; Christianity promises everything, but fulfils nothing.--Hard upon the heels of the "glad tidings" came the worst imaginable: those of Paul. In Paul is incarnated the very opposite of the "bearer of glad tidings"; he represents the genius for hatred, the vision of hatred, the relentless logic of hatred. What, indeed, has not this dysangelist sacrificed to hatred! Above all, the Saviour: he nailed him to his own cross. The life, the example, the teaching, the death of Christ, the meaning and the law of the whole gospels--nothing was left of all this after that counterfeiter in hatred had reduced it to his uses. Surely not reality; surely not historical truth!... Once more the priestly instinct of the Jew perpetrated the same old master crime against history--he simply struck out the yesterday and the day before yesterday of Christianity, and invented his own history of Christian beginnings. Going further, he treated the history of Israel to another falsification, so that it became a mere prologue to his achievement: all the prophets, it now appeared, had referred to his "Saviour."... Later on the church even falsified the history of man in order to make it a prologue to Christianity.... The figure of the Saviour, his teaching, his way of life, his death, the meaning of his death, even the consequences of his death--nothing remained untouched, nothing remained in even remote contact with reality. Paul simply shifted the centre of gravity of that whole life to a place behind this existence--in the lie of the "risen" Jesus. At bottom, he had no use for the life of the Saviour-- what he needed was the death on the cross, and something more. To see anything honest in such a man as Paul, whose home was at the centre of the Stoical enlightenment, when he converts an hallucination into a proof of the resurrection of the Saviour, or even to believe his tale that he suffered from this hallucination himself--this would be a genuine niaiserie in a psychologist. Paul willed the end; therefore he also willed the means.... What he himself didn't believe was swallowed readily enough by the idiots among whom he spread his teaching.-- What he wanted was power; in Paul the priest once more reached out for power--he had use only for such concepts, teachings and symbols as served the purpose of tyrannizing over the masses and organizing mobs. What was the only part of Christianity that Mohammed borrowed later on? Paul's invention, his device for establishing priestly tyranny and organizing the mob: the belief in the immortality of the soul-- that is to say, the doctrine of "judgment"....

43.

When the centre of gravity of life is placed, not in life itself, but in "the beyond"--in nothingness--then one has taken away its centre of gravity altogether. The vast lie of personal immortality destroys all reason, all natural instinct--henceforth, everything in the instincts that is beneficial, that fosters life and that safeguards the future is a cause of suspicion. So to live that life no longer has any meaning: this is now the "meaning" of

life.... Why be public-spirited? Why take any pride in descent
and forefathers? Why labour together, trust one another, or
concern one's self about the common welfare, and try to serve
it?... Merely so many "temptations," so many strayings from
the "straight path."--"One thing only is necessary".... That
every man, because he has an "immortal soul," is as good as
every other man; that in an infinite universe of things the
"salvation" of every individual may lay claim to eternal
importance; that insignificant bigots and the three-fourths
insane may assume that the laws of nature are constantly
suspended in their behalf--it is impossible to lavish too much
contempt upon such a magnification of every sort of
selfishness to infinity, to insolence. And yet Christianity has to
thank precisely this miserable flattery of personal vanity for its
triumph--it was thus that it lured all the botched, the
dissatisfied, the fallen upon evil days, the whole refuse and off-
scouring of humanity to its side. The "salvation of the soul"--in
plain English: "the world revolves around me."... The
poisonous doctrine, "equal rights for all," has been propagated
as a Christian principle: out of the secret nooks and crannies of
bad instinct Christianity has waged a deadly war upon all
feelings of reverence and distance between man and man,
which is to say, upon the first prerequisite to every step
upward, to every development of civilization--out of the
ressentiment of the masses it has forged its chief weapons
against us, against everything noble, joyous and high-spirited
on earth, against our happiness on earth.... To allow
"immortality" to every Peter and Paul was the greatest, the
most vicious outrage upon noble humanity ever perpetrated.--
And let us not underestimate the fatal influence that
Christianity has had, even upon politics! Nowadays no one has
courage any more for special rights, for the right of dominion,
for feelings of honourable pride in himself and his equals--for

the pathos of distance.... Our politics is sick with this lack of courage!--The aristocratic attitude of mind has been undermined by the lie of the equality of souls; and if belief in the "privileges of the majority" makes and will continue to make revolutions--it is Christianity, let us not doubt, and Christian valuations, which convert every revolution into a carnival of blood and crime! Christianity is a revolt of all creatures that creep on the ground against everything that is lofty: the gospel of the "lowly" lowers....

44.

--The gospels are invaluable as evidence of the corruption that was already persistent within the primitive community. That which Paul, with the cynical logic of a rabbi, later developed to a conclusion was at bottom merely a process of decay that had begun with the death of the Saviour.--These gospels cannot be read too carefully; difficulties lurk behind every word. I confess--I hope it will not be held against me--that it is precisely for this reason that they offer first-rate joy to a psychologist--as the opposite of all merely naïve corruption, as refinement par excellence, as an artistic triumph in psychological corruption. The gospels, in fact, stand alone. The Bible as a whole is not to be compared to them. Here we are among Jews: this is the first thing to be borne in mind if we are not to lose the thread of the matter. This positive genius for conjuring up a delusion of personal "holiness" unmatched anywhere else, either in books or by men; this elevation of fraud in word and attitude to the level of an art--all this is not an accident due to the chance talents of an individual, or to any violation of nature. The thing responsible is race. The whole of Judaism appears in Christianity as the art of concocting holy lies, and there, after many centuries of earnest Jewish training and hard practice of Jewish technic, the business comes to the stage of mastery. The Christian, that ultima ratio of lying, is the Jew all over again--he is threefold the Jew.... The underlying will to make use only of such concepts, symbols and attitudes as fit into priestly practice, the instinctive repudiation of every other mode of thought, and every other method of estimating values and utilities--this is not only tradition, it is inheritance: only as an inheritance is it able to operate with the force of nature. The whole of mankind, even the best minds of the best ages (with one exception, perhaps hardly human--), have permitted themselves to be deceived. The gospels have been read as a book of innocence ... surely no small indication of the high skill with which the trick has been done.--Of course, if we could actually see these astounding bigots and bogus saints, even if only for an instant, the farce would come to an end,-- and it is precisely because I cannot read a word of theirs without seeing their attitudinizing that I have made an end of them.... I simply cannot endure the way they have of rolling up their eyes.--For the majority, happily enough, books are mere literature.--Let us not be led astray: they say "judge not," and yet they condemn to hell whoever stands in their way. In letting God sit in judgment they judge themselves; in glorifying God they glorify themselves; in demanding that every one show the virtues which they themselves happen to be capable of--still more, which they must have in order to remain on top--they assume the grand air of men struggling for virtue, of men engaging in a war that virtue may prevail. "We live, we die, we sacrifice ourselves for the good" (--"the truth," "the light," "the kingdom of God"): in point of fact, they simply do what they cannot help doing. Forced, like hypocrites, to be sneaky, to hide in corners, to slink along in the shadows, they convert their necessity into a duty: it is on grounds of duty that they account for their lives of humility, and that humility becomes merely one more proof of their piety.... Ah, that humble, chaste, charitable brand of fraud! "Virtue itself shall bear witness for us."... One may read the gospels as books of moral seduction: these petty folks fasten themselves to morality--they know the uses of morality! Morality is the best of all devices for leading mankind by the nose!--The fact is that the conscious conceit of the chosen here disguises itself as modesty: it is in this way that they, the "community," the "good and just," range themselves, once and for always, on one side, the side of "the truth"--and the rest of mankind, "the world," on the other.... In that we observe the most fatal sort of megalomania that the earth has ever seen: little abortions of bigots and liars began to claim exclusive rights in the concepts of "God," "the truth," "the light," "the spirit," "love," "wisdom" and "life," as if these things were synonyms of themselves and thereby they sought to fence themselves off from the "world"; little super-Jews, ripe for some sort of madhouse, turned values upside down in order to meet their notions, just as if the Christian were the meaning, the salt, the standard and even the last judgment of all the rest.... The whole disaster was only made possible by the fact that there already existed in the world a similar megalomania, allied to this one in race, to wit, the Jewish: once a chasm began to yawn between Jews and Judaeo-Christians, the latter had no choice but to employ the self-preservative measures that the Jewish instinct had devised, even against the Jews themselves, whereas the Jews had employed them only against non-Jews. The Christian is simply a Jew of the "reformed" confession.--

45.

--I offer a few examples of the sort of thing these petty people have got into their heads--what they have put into the mouth of the Master: the unalloyed creed of "beautiful souls."--

"And whosoever shall not receive you, nor hear you, when ye depart thence, shake off the dust under your feet for a testimony against them. Verily I say unto you, it shall be more tolerable for Sodom and Gomorrha in the day of judgment, than for that city" (Mark vi, 11)--How evangelical!...

"And whosoever shall offend one of these little ones that believe in me, it is better for him that a millstone were hanged about his neck, and he were cast into the sea" (Mark ix, 42).--How evangelical!...

"And if thine eye offend thee, pluck it out: it is better for thee to enter into the kingdom of God with one eye, than having two eyes to be cast into hell fire; Where the worm dieth not, and the fire is not quenched." (Mark ix, 47.[15])--It is not exactly the eye that is meant....

[15] To which, without mentioning it, Nietzsche adds verse 48.

"Verily I say unto you, That there be some of them that stand here, which shall not taste of death, till they have seen the kingdom of God come with power." (Mark ix, 1.)--Well lied, lion![16]...

[16] A paraphrase of Demetrius' "Well roar'd, Lion!" in act v, scene 1 of "A Midsummer Night's Dream." The lion, of course, is the familiar Christian symbol for Mark.

"Whosoever will come after me, let him deny himself, and take up his cross, and follow me. For..." (Note of a psychologist. Christian morality is refuted by its fors: its reasons are against it,--this makes it Christian.) Mark viii, 34.--

"Judge not, that ye be not judged. With what measure ye mete, it shall be measured to you again." (Matthew vii, 1.[17])--What a notion of justice, of a "just" judge!...

[17] Nietzsche also quotes part of verse 2.

"For if ye love them which love you, what reward have ye? do not even the publicans the same? And if ye salute your brethren only, what do ye more than others? do not even the publicans so?" (Matthew v, 46.[18])--Principle of "Christian love": it insists upon being well paid in the end....

[18] The quotation also includes verse 47.

"But if ye forgive not men their trespasses, neither will your Father forgive your trespasses." (Matthew vi, 15.)--Very compromising for the said "father."...

"But seek ye first the kingdom of God, and his righteousness; and all these things shall be added unto you." (Matthew vi, 33.)--All these things: namely, food, clothing, all the necessities of life. An error, to put it mildly.... A bit before this God appears as a tailor, at least in certain cases....

"Rejoice ye in that day, and leap for joy: for, behold, your reward is great in heaven: for in the like manner did their fathers unto the prophets." (Luke vi, 23.)--Impudent rabble! It compares itself to the prophets....

"Know ye not that ye are the temple of God, and that the spirit of God dwelleth in you? If any man defile the temple of God, him shall God destroy; for the temple of God is holy, which temple ye are." (Paul, 1 Corinthians iii, 16.[19])--For that sort of thing one cannot have enough contempt....

[19] And 17.

"Do ye not know that the saints shall judge the world? and if the world shall be judged by you, are ye unworthy to judge the smallest matters?" (Paul, 1 Corinthians vi, 2.)--Unfortunately, not merely the speech of a lunatic.... This frightful impostor then proceeds: "Know ye not that we shall judge angels? how much more things that pertain to this life?"...

"Hath not God made foolish the wisdom of this world? For after that in the wisdom of God the world by wisdom knew not God, it pleased God by the foolishness of preaching to save them that believe.... Not many wise men after the flesh, not men mighty, not many noble are called: But God hath chosen the foolish things of the world to confound the wise; and God hath chosen the weak things of the world to confound the things which are mighty; And base things of the world, and things which are despised, hath God chosen, yea, and things which are not, to bring to nought things that are: That no flesh should glory in his presence." (Paul, 1 Corinthians i, 20ff.[20])--In order to understand this passage, a first-rate example of the psychology underlying every Chandala-morality, one should read the first part of my "Genealogy of Morals": there, for the first time, the antagonism between a noble morality and a morality born of ressentiment and impotent vengefulness is exhibited. Paul was the greatest of all apostles of revenge....

[20] Verses 20, 21, 26, 27, 28, 29.

46.

--What follows, then? That one had better put on gloves before reading the New Testament. The presence of so much filth makes it very advisable. One would as little choose "early Christians" for companions as Polish Jews: not that one need seek out an objection to them.... Neither has a pleasant smell.--I have searched the New Testament in vain for a single sympathetic touch; nothing is there that is free, kindly, open-hearted or upright. In it humanity does not even make the first step upward--the instinct for cleanliness is lacking.... Only evil instincts are there, and there is not even the courage of these evil instincts. It is all cowardice; it is all a shutting of the eyes, a self-deception. Every other book becomes clean, once one has read the New Testament: for example, immediately after reading Paul I took up with delight that most charming and wanton of scoffers, Petronius, of whom one may say what Domenico Boccaccio wrote of Cæsar Borgia to the Duke of Parma: "è tutto festo"--immortally healthy, immortally cheerful and sound.... These petty bigots make a capital miscalculation. They attack, but everything they attack is thereby distinguished. Whoever is attacked by an "early Christian" is surely not befouled.... On the contrary, it is an honour to have an "early Christian" as an opponent. One cannot read the New Testament without acquired admiration for whatever it abuses-- not to speak of the "wisdom of this world," which an impudent wind-bag tries to dispose of "by the foolishness of preaching."... Even the scribes and pharisees are benefitted by such opposition: they must certainly have been worth something to have been hated in such an indecent manner. Hypocrisy--as if this were a charge that the "early Christians" dared to make!--After all, they were the privileged, and that

was enough: the hatred of the Chandala needed no other
excuse. The "early Christian"--and also, I fear, the "last
Christian," whom I may perhaps live to see--is a rebel against
all privilege by profound instinct--he lives and makes war for
ever for "equal rights.".... Strictly speaking, he has no
alternative. When a man proposes to represent, in his own
person, the "chosen of God"--or to be a "temple of God," or a
"judge of the angels"--then every other criterion, whether based
upon honesty, upon intellect, upon manliness and pride, or
upon beauty and freedom of the heart, becomes simply
"worldly"--evil in itself.... Moral: every word that comes from
the lips of an "early Christian" is a lie, and his every act is
instinctively dishonest--all his values, all his aims are noxious,
but whoever he hates, whatever he hates, has real value.... The
Christian, and particularly the Christian priest, is thus a
criterion of values.

--Must I add that, in the whole New Testament, there appears
but a solitary figure worthy of honour? Pilate, the Roman
viceroy. To regard a Jewish imbroglio seriously--that was quite
beyond him. One Jew more or less--what did it matter?... The
noble scorn of a Roman, before whom the word "truth" was
shamelessly mishandled, enriched the New Testament with the
only saying that has any value--and that is at once its criticism
and its destruction: "What is truth?..."

47.

--The thing that sets us apart is not that we are unable to find
God, either in history, or in nature, or behind nature--but that
we regard what has been honoured as God, not as "divine," but
as pitiable, as absurd, as injurious; not as a mere error, but as a
crime against life.... We deny that God is God.... If any one

were to show us this Christian God, we'd be still less inclined to believe in him.--In a formula: deus, qualem Paulus creavit, dei negatio.--Such a religion as Christianity, which does not touch reality at a single point and which goes to pieces the moment reality asserts its rights at any point, must be inevitably the deadly enemy of the "wisdom of this world," which is to say, of science--and it will give the name of good to whatever means serve to poison, calumniate and cry down all intellectual discipline, all lucidity and strictness in matters of intellectual conscience, and all noble coolness and freedom of the mind. "Faith," as an imperative, vetoes science--in praxi, lying at any price.... Paul well knew that lying--that "faith"-- was necessary; later on the church borrowed the fact from Paul.--The God that Paul invented for himself, a God who "reduced to absurdity" "the wisdom of this world" (especially the two great enemies of superstition, philology and medicine), is in truth only an indication of Paul's resolute determination to accomplish that very thing himself: to give one's own will the name of God, thora--that is essentially Jewish. Paul wants to dispose of the "wisdom of this world": his enemies are the good philologians and physicians of the Alexandrine school-- on them he makes his war. As a matter of fact no man can be a philologian or a physician without being also Antichrist. That is to say, as a philologian a man sees behind the "holy books," and as a physician he sees behind the physiological degeneration of the typical Christian. The physician says "incurable"; the philologian says "fraud."...

48.

--Has any one ever clearly understood the celebrated story at the beginning of the Bible--of God's mortal terror of science?... No one, in fact, has understood it. This priest-book par

87

excellence opens, as is fitting, with the great inner difficulty of
the priest: he faces only one great danger; ergo, "God" faces
only one great danger.--

The old God, wholly "spirit," wholly the high-priest, wholly
perfect, is promenading his garden: he is bored and trying to
kill time. Against boredom even gods struggle in vain.[21]
What does he do? He creates man--man is entertaining.... But
then he notices that man is also bored. God's pity for the only
form of distress that invades all paradises knows no bounds: so
he forthwith creates other animals. God's first mistake: to man
these other animals were not entertaining--he sought dominion
over them; he did not want to be an "animal" himself.--So God
created woman. In the act he brought boredom to an end--and
also many other things! Woman was the second mistake of
God.--"Woman, at bottom, is a serpent, Heva"--every priest
knows that; "from woman comes every evil in the world"--
every priest knows that, too. Ergo, she is also to blame for
science.... It was through woman that man learned to taste of
the tree of knowledge.--What happened? The old God was
seized by mortal terror. Man himself had been his greatest
blunder; he had created a rival to himself; science makes men
godlike--it is all up with priests and gods when man becomes
scientific!--Moral: science is the forbidden per se; it alone is
forbidden. Science is the first of sins, the germ of all sins, the
original sin. This is all there is of morality.--"Thou shall not
know":--the rest follows from that.--God's mortal terror,
however, did not hinder him from being shrewd. How is one to
protect one's self against science? For a long while this was the
capital problem. Answer: Out of paradise with man!
Happiness, leisure, foster thought--and all thoughts are bad
thoughts!--Man must not think.--And so the priest invents
distress, death, the mortal dangers of childbirth, all sorts of

misery, old age, decrepitude, above all, sickness--nothing but devices for making war on science! The troubles of man don't allow him to think.... Nevertheless--how terrible!--, the edifice of knowledge begins to tower aloft, invading heaven, shadowing the gods--what is to be done?--The old God invents war; he separates the peoples; he makes men destroy one another (--the priests have always had need of war....). War-- among other things, a great disturber of science!--Incredible! Knowledge, deliverance from the priests, prospers in spite of war.--So the old God comes to his final resolution: "Man has become scientific--there is no help for it: he must be drowned!"...

[21] A paraphrase of Schiller's "Against stupidity even gods struggle in vain."

49.

--I have been understood. At the opening of the Bible there is the whole psychology of the priest.--The priest knows of only one great danger: that is science--the sound comprehension of cause and effect. But science flourishes, on the whole, only under favourable conditions--a man must have time, he must have an overflowing intellect, in order to "know.".... "Therefore, man must be made unhappy,"--this has been, in all ages, the logic of the priest.--It is easy to see just what, by this logic, was the first thing to come into the world:--"sin.".... The concept of guilt and punishment, the whole "moral order of the world," was set up against science--against the deliverance of man from priests.... Man must not look outward; he must look inward. He must not look at things shrewdly and cautiously, to learn about them; he must not look at all; he must suffer.... And he must suffer so much that he is always in need of the priest.-- Away with physicians! What is needed is a Saviour.--The concept of guilt and punishment, including the doctrines of "grace," of "salvation," of "forgiveness"--lies through and through, and absolutely without psychological reality--were devised to destroy man's sense of causality: they are an attack upon the concept of cause and effect!--And not an attack with the fist, with the knife, with honesty in hate and love! On the contrary, one inspired by the most cowardly, the most crafty, the most ignoble of instincts! An attack of priests! An attack of parasites! The vampirism of pale, subterranean leeches!... When the natural consequences of an act are no longer "natural," but are regarded as produced by the ghostly creations of superstition--by "God," by "spirits," by "souls"--and reckoned as merely "moral" consequences, as rewards, as punishments, as hints, as lessons, then the whole ground-work of knowledge is destroyed--then the greatest of crimes against humanity has been perpetrated.--I repeat that sin, man's self-desecration par excellence, was invented in order to make science, culture, and every elevation and ennobling of man impossible; the priest rules through the invention of sin.--

50.

--In this place I can't permit myself to omit a psychology of "belief," of the "believer," for the special benefit of "believers." If there remain any today who do not yet know how indecent it is to be "believing"--or how much a sign of décadence, of a broken will to live--then they will know it well enough tomorrow. My voice reaches even the deaf.--It appears, unless I have been incorrectly informed, that there prevails among Christians a sort of criterion of truth that is called "proof by power." "Faith makes blessed: therefore it is true."--It might be objected right here that blessedness is not demonstrated, it is merely promised: it hangs upon "faith" as a condition--one shall be blessed because one believes.... But what of the thing that the priest promises to the believer, the wholly transcendental "beyond"--how is that to be demonstrated?--The "proof by power," thus assumed, is actually no more at bottom than a belief that the effects which faith promises will not fail to appear. In a formula: "I believe that faith makes for blessedness--therefore, it is true."... But this is as far as we may go. This "therefore" would be absurdum itself as a criterion of truth.--But let us admit, for the sake of politeness, that blessedness by faith may be demonstrated (--not merely hoped for, and not merely promised by the suspicious lips of a priest): even so, could blessedness--in a technical term, pleasure--ever be a proof of truth? So little is this true that it is almost a proof against truth when sensations of pleasure influence the answer to the question "What is true?" or, at all events, it is enough to make that "truth" highly suspicious. The proof by "pleasure" is a proof of "pleasure"--nothing more; why in the world should it be assumed that true judgments give more pleasure than false ones, and that, in conformity to some pre-established harmony, they necessarily bring agreeable feelings in their train?--The experience of all disciplined and profound minds teaches the contrary. Man has had to fight for every atom of the truth, and has had to pay for it almost everything that the heart, that human love, that human trust cling to. Greatness of soul is needed for this business: the service of truth is the hardest of all services.--What, then, is the meaning of integrity in things intellectual? It means that a man must be severe with his own heart, that he must scorn "beautiful feelings," and that he makes every Yea and Nay a matter of conscience!--Faith makes blessed: therefore, it lies....

51.

The fact that faith, under certain circumstances, may work for blessedness, but that this blessedness produced by an idée fixe by no means makes the idea itself true, and the fact that faith actually moves no mountains, but instead raises them up where there were none before: all this is made sufficiently clear by a walk through a lunatic asylum. Not, of course, to a priest: for his instincts prompt him to the lie that sickness is not sickness and lunatic asylums not lunatic asylums. Christianity finds sickness necessary, just as the Greek spirit had need of a superabundance of health--the actual ulterior purpose of the whole system of salvation of the church is to make people ill. And the church itself--doesn't it set up a Catholic lunatic asylum as the ultimate ideal?--The whole earth as a madhouse?--The sort of religious man that the church wants is a typical décadent; the moment at which a religious crisis dominates a people is always marked by epidemics of nervous disorder; the "inner world" of the religious man is so much like the "inner world" of the overstrung and exhausted that it is difficult to distinguish between them; the "highest" states of mind, held up before mankind by Christianity as of supreme worth, are actually epileptoid in form--the church has granted the name of holy only to lunatics or to gigantic frauds in majorem dei honorem.... Once I ventured to designate the whole Christian system of training[22] in penance and salvation (now best studied in England) as a method of producing a folie circulaire upon a soil already prepared for it, which is to say, a soil thoroughly unhealthy. Not every one may be a Christian: one is not "converted" to Christianity--one must first be sick enough for it.... We others, who have the courage for health and likewise for contempt,--we may well despise a religion that teaches misunderstanding of the body!

that refuses to rid itself of the superstition about the soul! that makes a "virtue" of insufficient nourishment! that combats health as a sort of enemy, devil, temptation! that persuades itself that it is possible to carry about a "perfect soul" in a cadaver of a body, and that, to this end, had to devise for itself a new concept of "perfection," a pale, sickly, idiotically ecstatic state of existence, so-called "holiness"--a holiness that is itself merely a series of symptoms of an impoverished, enervated and incurably disordered body!... The Christian movement, as a European movement, was from the start no more than a general uprising of all sorts of outcast and refuse elements (--who now, under cover of Christianity, aspire to power). It does not represent the decay of a race; it represents, on the contrary, a conglomeration of décadence products from all directions, crowding together and seeking one another out. It was not, as has been thought, the corruption of antiquity, of noble antiquity, which made Christianity possible; one cannot too sharply challenge the learned imbecility which today maintains that theory. At the time when the sick and rotten Chandala classes in the whole imperium were Christianized, the contrary type, the nobility, reached its finest and ripest development. The majority became master; democracy, with its Christian instincts, triumphed.... Christianity was not "national," it was not based on race--it appealed to all the varieties of men disinherited by life, it had its allies everywhere. Christianity has the rancour of the sick at its very core--the instinct against the healthy, against health. Everything that is well-constituted, proud, gallant and, above all, beautiful gives offence to its ears and eyes. Again I remind you of Paul's priceless saying: "And God hath chosen the weak things of the world, the foolish things of the world, the base things of the world, and things which are despised":[23] this was the formula; in hoc signo the décadence triumphed.--God on the cross--is man always to

93

miss the frightful inner significance of this symbol?--
Everything that suffers, everything that hangs on the cross, is
divine.... We all hang on the cross, consequently we are
divine.... We alone are divine.... Christianity was thus a
victory: a nobler attitude of mind was destroyed by it--
Christianity remains to this day the greatest misfortune of
humanity.--

[22] The word training is in English in the text.

[23] 1 Corinthians i, 27, 28.

52.

Christianity also stands in opposition to all intellectual well-
being,--sick reasoning is the only sort that it can use as
Christian reasoning; it takes the side of everything that is
idiotic; it pronounces a curse upon "intellect," upon the
superbia of the healthy intellect. Since sickness is inherent in
Christianity, it follows that the typically Christian state of
"faith" must be a form of sickness too, and that all straight,
straightforward and scientific paths to knowledge must be
banned by the church as forbidden ways. Doubt is thus a sin
from the start.... The complete lack of psychological
cleanliness in the priest--revealed by a glance at him--is a
phenomenon resulting from décadence,--one may observe in
hysterical women and in rachitic children how regularly the
falsification of instincts, delight in lying for the mere sake of
lying, and incapacity for looking straight and walking straight
are symptoms of décadence. "Faith" means the will to avoid
knowing what is true. The pietist, the priest of either sex, is a
fraud because he is sick: his instinct demands that the truth
shall never be allowed its rights on any point. "Whatever
makes for illness is good; whatever issues from abundance,

from superabundance, from power, is evil": so argues the believer. The impulse to lie--it is by this that I recognize every foreordained theologian.--Another characteristic of the theologian is his unfitness for philology. What I here mean by philology is, in a general sense, the art of reading with profit-- the capacity for absorbing facts without interpreting them falsely, and without losing caution, patience and subtlety in the effort to understand them. Philology as ephexis[24] in interpretation: whether one be dealing with books, with newspaper reports, with the most fateful events or with weather statistics--not to mention the "salvation of the soul."... The way in which a theologian, whether in Berlin or in Rome, is ready to explain, say, a "passage of Scripture," or an experience, or a victory by the national army, by turning upon it the high illumination of the Psalms of David, is always so daring that it is enough to make a philologian run up a wall. But what shall he do when pietists and other such cows from Suabia[25] use the "finger of God" to convert their miserably commonplace and huggermugger existence into a miracle of "grace," a "providence" and an "experience of salvation"? The most modest exercise of the intellect, not to say of decency, should certainly be enough to convince these interpreters of the perfect childishness and unworthiness of such a misuse of the divine digital dexterity. However small our piety, if we ever encountered a god who always cured us of a cold in the head at just the right time, or got us into our carriage at the very instant heavy rain began to fall, he would seem so absurd a god that he'd have to be abolished even if he existed. God as a domestic servant, as a letter carrier, as an almanac-man--at bottom, he is a mere name for the stupidest sort of chance.... "Divine Providence," which every third man in "educated Germany" still believes in, is so strong an argument against God that it

95

would be impossible to think of a stronger. And in any case it is an argument against Germans!...

[24] That is, to say, scepticism. Among the Greeks scepticism was also occasionally called ephecticism.

[25] A reference to the University of Tübingen and its famous school of Biblical criticism. The leader of this school was F. C. Baur, and one of the men greatly influenced by it was Nietzsche's pet abomination, David F. Strauss, himself a Suabian. Vide § 10 and § 28.

53.

--It is so little true that martyrs offer any support to the truth of a cause that I am inclined to deny that any martyr has ever had anything to do with the truth at all. In the very tone in which a martyr flings what he fancies to be true at the head of the world there appears so low a grade of intellectual honesty and such insensibility to the problem of "truth," that it is never necessary to refute him. Truth is not something that one man has and another man has not: at best, only peasants, or peasant-apostles like Luther, can think of truth in any such way. One may rest assured that the greater the degree of a man's intellectual conscience the greater will be his modesty, his discretion, on this point. To know in five cases, and to refuse, with delicacy, to know anything further.... "Truth," as the word is understood by every prophet, every sectarian, every free-thinker, every Socialist and every churchman, is simply a complete proof that not even a beginning has been made in the intellectual discipline and self-control that are necessary to the unearthing of even the smallest truth.--The deaths of the martyrs, it may be said in passing, have been misfortunes of history: they have misled.... The conclusion that all idiots, women and plebeians come to, that there must be something in a cause for which any one goes to his death (or which, as under primitive Christianity, sets off epidemics of death-seeking)--this conclusion has been an unspeakable drag upon the testing of facts, upon the whole spirit of inquiry and investigation. The martyrs have damaged the truth.... Even to this day the crude fact of persecution is enough to give an honourable name to the most empty sort of sectarianism.--But why? Is the worth of a cause altered by the fact that some one had laid down his life for it?--An error that becomes honourable is simply an error that has acquired one seductive charm the more: do you suppose, Messrs. Theologians, that we shall give you the chance to be martyred for your lies?--One best disposes of a cause by respectfully putting it on ice--that is also the best way to dispose of theologians.... This was precisely the world-historical stupidity of all the persecutors: that they gave the appearance of honour to the cause they opposed--that they made it a present of the fascination of martyrdom.... Women are still on their knees before an error because they have been told that some one died on the cross for it. Is the cross, then, an argument?--But about all these things there is one, and one only, who has said what has been needed for thousands of years--Zarathustra.

"They made signs in blood along the way that they went, and their folly taught them that the truth is proved by blood."

"But blood is the worst of all testimonies to the truth; blood poisoneth even the purest teaching and turneth it into madness and hatred in the heart."

"And when one goeth through fire for his teaching--what doth that prove? Verily, it is more when one's teaching cometh out of one's own burning!"[26]

97

Friedrich Nietzsche

[26] The quotations are from "Also sprach Zarathustra" ii, 24: "Of Priests."

54.

Do not let yourself be deceived: great intellects are sceptical. Zarathustra is a sceptic. The strength, the freedom which proceed from intellectual power, from a superabundance of intellectual power, manifest themselves as scepticism. Men of fixed convictions do not count when it comes to determining what is fundamental in values and lack of values. Men of convictions are prisoners. They do not see far enough, they do not see what is below them: whereas a man who would talk to any purpose about value and non-value must be able to see five hundred convictions beneath him--and behind him.... A mind that aspires to great things, and that wills the means thereto, is necessarily sceptical. Freedom from any sort of conviction belongs to strength, and to an independent point of view.... That grand passion which is at once the foundation and the power of a sceptic's existence, and is both more enlightened and more despotic than he is himself, drafts the whole of his intellect into its service; it makes him unscrupulous; it gives him courage to employ unholy means; under certain circumstances it does not begrudge him even convictions. Conviction as a means: one may achieve a good deal by means of a conviction. A grand passion makes use of and uses up convictions; it does not yield to them--it knows itself to be sovereign.--On the contrary, the need of faith, of something unconditioned by yea or nay, of Carlylism, if I may be allowed the word, is a need of weakness. The man of faith, the "believer" of any sort, is necessarily a dependent man--such a man cannot posit himself as a goal, nor can he find goals within himself. The "believer" does not belong to himself; he

98

can only be a means to an end; he must be used up; he needs
some one to use him up. His instinct gives the highest honours
to an ethic of self-effacement; he is prompted to embrace it by
everything: his prudence, his experience, his vanity. Every sort
of faith is in itself an evidence of self-effacement, of self-
estrangement.... When one reflects how necessary it is to the
great majority that there be regulations to restrain them from
without and hold them fast, and to what extent control, or, in a
higher sense, slavery, is the one and only condition which
makes for the well-being of the weak-willed man, and
especially woman, then one at once understands conviction and
"faith." To the man with convictions they are his backbone. To
avoid seeing many things, to be impartial about nothing, to be a
party man through and through, to estimate all values strictly
and infallibly--these are conditions necessary to the existence
of such a man. But by the same token they are antagonists of
the truthful man--of the truth.... The believer is not free to
answer the question, "true" or "not true," according to the
dictates of his own conscience: integrity on this point would
work his instant downfall. The pathological limitations of his
vision turn the man of convictions into a fanatic--Savonarola,
Luther, Rousseau, Robespierre, Saint-Simon--these types stand
in opposition to the strong, emancipated spirit. But the
grandiose attitudes of these sick intellects, these intellectual
epileptics, are of influence upon the great masses--fanatics are
picturesque, and mankind prefers observing poses to listening
to reasons....

55.

--One step further in the psychology of conviction, of "faith." It
is now a good while since I first proposed for consideration the
question whether convictions are not even more dangerous

enemies to truth than lies. ("Human, All-Too-Human," I, aphorism 483.)[27] This time I desire to put the question definitely: is there any actual difference between a lie and a conviction?--All the world believes that there is; but what is not believed by all the world!--Every conviction has its history, its primitive forms, its stage of tentativeness and error: it becomes a conviction only after having been, for a long time, not one, and then, for an even longer time, hardly one. What if falsehood be also one of these embryonic forms of conviction?--Sometimes all that is needed is a change in persons: what was a lie in the father becomes a conviction in the son.--I call it lying to refuse to see what one sees, or to refuse to see it as it is: whether the lie be uttered before witnesses or not before witnesses is of no consequence. The most common sort of lie is that by which a man deceives himself: the deception of others is a relatively rare offence.--Now, this will not to see what one sees, this will not to see it as it is, is almost the first requisite for all who belong to a party of whatever sort: the party man becomes inevitably a liar. For example, the German historians are convinced that Rome was synonymous with despotism and that the Germanic peoples brought the spirit of liberty into the world: what is the difference between this conviction and a lie? Is it to be wondered at that all partisans, including the German historians, instinctively roll the fine phrases of morality upon their tongues--that morality almost owes its very survival to the fact that the party man of every sort has need of it every moment?--"This is our conviction: we publish it to the whole world; we live and die for it--let us respect all who have convictions!"--I have actually heard such sentiments from the mouths of anti-Semites. On the contrary, gentlemen! An anti-Semite surely does not become more respectable because he lies on principle.... The priests, who have more finesse in such matters, and who well understand the objection that lies against

100

the notion of a conviction, which is to say, of a falsehood that becomes a matter of principle because it serves a purpose, have borrowed from the Jews the shrewd device of sneaking in the concepts, "God," "the will of God" and "the revelation of God" at this place. Kant, too, with his categorical imperative, was on the same road: this was his practical reason.[28] There are questions regarding the truth or untruth of which it is not for man to decide; all the capital questions, all the capital problems of valuation, are beyond human reason.... To know the limits of reason--that alone is genuine philosophy.... Why did God make a revelation to man? Would God have done anything superfluous? Man could not find out for himself what was good and what was evil, so God taught him His will.... Moral: the priest does not lie--the question, "true" or "untrue," has nothing to do with such things as the priest discusses; it is impossible to lie about these things. In order to lie here it would be necessary to know what is true. But this is more than man can know; therefore, the priest is simply the mouthpiece of God.--Such a priestly syllogism is by no means merely Jewish and Christian; the right to lie and the shrewd dodge of "revelation" belong to the general priestly type--to the priest of the décadence as well as to the priest of pagan times (--Pagans are all those who say yes to life, and to whom "God" is a word signifying acquiescence in all things).--The "law," the "will of God," the "holy book," and "inspiration"--all these things are merely words for the conditions under which the priest comes to power and with which he maintains his power,--these concepts are to be found at the bottom of all priestly organizations, and of all priestly or priestly-philosophical schemes of governments. The "holy lie"--common alike to Confucius, to the Code of Manu, to Mohammed and to the Christian church--is not even wanting in Plato. "Truth is here": this means, no matter where it is heard, the priest lies....

101

[27] The aphorism, which is headed "The Enemies of Truth," makes the direct statement: "Convictions are more dangerous enemies of truth than lies."

[28] A reference, of course, to Kant's "Kritik der praktischen Vernunft" (Critique of Practical Reason).

56.

--In the last analysis it comes to this: what is the end of lying? The fact that, in Christianity, "holy" ends are not visible is my objection to the means it employs. Only bad ends appear: the poisoning, the calumniation, the denial of life, the despising of the body, the degradation and self-contamination of man by the concept of sin--therefore, its means are also bad.--I have a contrary feeling when I read the Code of Manu, an incomparably more intellectual and superior work, which it would be a sin against the intelligence to so much as name in the same breath with the Bible. It is easy to see why: there is a genuine philosophy behind it, in it, not merely an evil-smelling mess of Jewish rabbinism and superstition,--it gives even the most fastidious psychologist something to sink his teeth into. And, not to forget what is most important, it differs fundamentally from every kind of Bible: by means of it the nobles, the philosophers and the warriors keep the whip-hand over the majority; it is full of noble valuations, it shows a feeling of perfection, an acceptance of life, and triumphant feeling toward self and life--the sun shines upon the whole book.--All the things on which Christianity vents its fathomless vulgarity--for example, procreation, women and marriage--are here handled earnestly, with reverence and with love and confidence. How can any one really put into the hands of children and ladies a book which contains such vile things as this: "to avoid fornication, let every man have his own wife, and let every woman have her own husband; ... it is better to marry than to burn"?[29] And is it possible to be a Christian so long as the origin of man is Christianized, which is to say, befouled, by the doctrine of the immaculata conceptio?... I know of no book in which so many delicate and kindly things are said of women as in the Code of Manu; these old grey-beards and saints have a way of being gallant to women that it would be impossible, perhaps, to surpass. "The mouth of a woman," it says in one place, "the breasts of a maiden, the prayer of a child and the smoke of sacrifice are always pure." In another place: "there is nothing purer than the light of the sun, the shadow cast by a cow, air, water, fire and the breath of a maiden." Finally, in still another place--perhaps this is also a holy lie--: "all the orifices of the body above the navel are pure, and all below are impure. Only in the maiden is the whole body pure."

[29] 1 Corinthians vii, 2, 9.

57.

One catches the unholiness of Christian means in flagranti by the simple process of putting the ends sought by Christianity beside the ends sought by the Code of Manu--by putting these enormously antithetical ends under a strong light. The critic of Christianity cannot evade the necessity of making Christianity contemptible.--A book of laws such as the Code of Manu has the same origin as every other good law-book: it epitomizes the experience, the sagacity and the ethical experimentation of long centuries; it brings things to a conclusion; it no longer creates. The prerequisite to a codification of this sort is recognition of the fact that the means which establish the authority of a slowly and painfully attained truth are fundamentally different from those which one would make use of to prove it. A law-book never recites the utility, the grounds, the casuistical antecedents of a law: for if it did so it would lose the imperative tone, the "thou shall," on which obedience is based. The problem lies exactly here.--At a certain point in the evolution of a people, the class within it of the greatest insight, which is to say, the greatest hindsight and foresight, declares that the series of experiences determining how all shall live--or can live--has come to an end. The object now is to reap as rich and as complete a harvest as possible from the days of experiment and hard experience. In consequence, the thing that is to be avoided above everything is further experimentation-- the continuation of the state in which values are fluent, and are tested, chosen and criticized ad infinitum. Against this a double wall is set up: on the one hand, revelation, which is the assumption that the reasons lying behind the laws are not of human origin, that they were not sought out and found by a slow process and after many errors, but that they are of divine ancestry, and came into being complete, perfect, without a history, as a free gift, a miracle...; and on the other hand, tradition, which is the assumption that the law has stood unchanged from time immemorial, and that it is impious and a crime against one's forefathers to bring it into question. The authority of the law is thus grounded on the thesis: God gave it, and the fathers lived it.--The higher motive of such procedure lies in the design to distract consciousness, step by step, from its concern with notions of right living (that is to say, those that have been proved to be right by wide and carefully considered experience), so that instinct attains to a perfect automatism--a primary necessity to every sort of mastery, to every sort of perfection in the art of life. To draw up such a law-book as Manu's means to lay before a people the possibility of future mastery, of attainable perfection--it permits them to aspire to the highest reaches of the art of life. To that end the thing must be made unconscious: that is the aim of every holy lie.--The order of castes, the highest, the dominating law, is merely the ratification of an order of nature, of a natural law of the first rank, over which no arbitrary fiat, no "modern idea," can exert any influence. In every healthy society there are three physiological types, gravitating toward differentiation but mutually conditioning one another, and each of these has its own hygiene, its own sphere of work, its own special mastery and feeling of perfection. It is not Manu but nature that sets off in one class those who are chiefly intellectual, in another those who are marked by muscular strength and temperament, and in a third those who are distinguished in neither one way or the other, but show only mediocrity--the last-named represents the great majority, and the first two the select. The superior caste--I call it the fewest--has, as the most perfect, the privileges of the few: it stands for happiness, for beauty, for everything good upon earth. Only the most intellectual of men have any right to beauty, to the beautiful; only in them can goodness escape being weakness. Pulchrum est paucorum hominum:[30] goodness is a privilege. Nothing could be more unbecoming to them than uncouth manners or a pessimistic look, or an eye that sees ugliness--or indignation against the general aspect of things. Indignation is the privilege of the Chandala; so is pessimism. "The world is perfect"--so prompts the instinct of the intellectual, the instinct of the man who says yes to life. "Imperfection, whatever is inferior to us, distance, the pathos of distance, even the Chandala themselves are parts of this perfection." The most intelligent men, like the strongest, find their happiness where others would find only disaster: in the labyrinth, in being hard with themselves and with others, in effort; their delight is in self-mastery; in them asceticism

105

becomes second nature, a necessity, an instinct. They regard a difficult task as a privilege; it is to them a recreation to play with burdens that would crush all others.... Knowledge--a form of asceticism.--They are the most honourable kind of men: but that does not prevent them being the most cheerful and most amiable. They rule, not because they want to, but because they are; they are not at liberty to play second.--The second caste: to this belong the guardians of the law, the keepers of order and security, the more noble warriors, above all, the king as the highest form of warrior, judge and preserver of the law. The second in rank constitute the executive arm of the intellectuals, the next to them in rank, taking from them all that is rough in the business of ruling--their followers, their right hand, their most apt disciples.--In all this, I repeat, there is nothing arbitrary, nothing "made up"; whatever is to the contrary is made up--by it nature is brought to shame.... The order of castes, the order of rank, simply formulates the supreme law of life itself; the separation of the three types is necessary to the maintenance of society, and to the evolution of higher types, and the highest types--the inequality of rights is essential to the existence of any rights at all.--A right is a privilege. Every one enjoys the privileges that accord with his state of existence. Let us not underestimate the privileges of the mediocre. Life is always harder as one mounts the heights--the cold increases, responsibility increases. A high civilization is a pyramid: it can stand only on a broad base; its primary prerequisite is a strong and soundly consolidated mediocrity. The handicrafts, commerce, agriculture, science, the greater part of art, in brief, the whole range of occupational activities, are compatible only with mediocre ability and aspiration; such callings would be out of place for exceptional men; the instincts which belong to them stand as much opposed to aristocracy as to anarchism. The fact that a man is publicly useful, that he is a wheel, a function, is evidence of a natural predisposition; it is not society, but the only sort of happiness that the majority are capable of, that makes them intelligent machines. To the mediocre mediocrity is a form of happiness; they have a natural instinct for mastering one thing, for specialization. It would be altogether unworthy of a profound intellect to see anything objectionable in mediocrity in itself. It is, in fact, the first prerequisite to the appearance of the exceptional: it is a necessary condition to a high degree of civilization. When the exceptional man handles the mediocre man with more delicate fingers than he applies to himself or to his equals, this is not merely kindness of heart--it is simply his duty.... Whom do I hate most heartily among the rabbles of today? The rabble of Socialists, the apostles to the Chandala, who undermine the workingman's instincts, his pleasure, his feeling of contentment with his petty existence--who make him envious and teach him revenge.... Wrong never lies in unequal rights; it lies in the assertion of "equal" rights.... What is bad? But I have already answered: all that proceeds from weakness, from envy, from revenge.--The anarchist and the Christian have the same ancestry....

[30] Few men are noble.

58.

In point of fact, the end for which one lies makes a great difference: whether one preserves thereby or destroys. There is a perfect likeness between Christian and anarchist: their object, their instinct, points only toward destruction. One need only turn to history for a proof of this: there it appears with appalling distinctness. We have just studied a code of religious legislation whose object it was to convert the conditions which

cause life to flourish into an "eternal" social organization,--
Christianity found its mission in putting an end to such an
organization, because life flourished under it. There the
benefits that reason had produced during long ages of
experiment and insecurity were applied to the most remote
uses, and an effort was made to bring in a harvest that should
be as large, as rich and as complete as possible; here, on the
contrary, the harvest is blighted overnight.... That which stood
there aere perennis, the imperium Romanum, the most
magnificent form of organization under difficult conditions that
has ever been achieved, and compared to which everything
before it and after it appears as patchwork, bungling,
dilletantism--those holy anarchists made it a matter of "piety"
to destroy "the world," which is to say, the imperium
Romanum, so that in the end not a stone stood upon another--
and even Germans and other such louts were able to become its
masters.... The Christian and the anarchist: both are décadents;
both are incapable of any act that is not disintegrating,
poisonous, degenerating, blood-sucking; both have an instinct
of mortal hatred of everything that stands up, and is great, and
has durability, and promises life a future.... Christianity was the
vampire of the imperium Romanum,--overnight it destroyed
the vast achievement of the Romans: the conquest of the soil
for a great culture that could await its time. Can it be that this
fact is not yet understood? The imperium Romanum that we
know, and that the history of the Roman provinces teaches us
to know better and better,--this most admirable of all works of
art in the grand manner was merely the beginning, and the
structure to follow was not to prove its worth for thousands of
years. To this day, nothing on a like scale sub specie aeterni
has been brought into being, or even dreamed of!--This
organization was strong enough to withstand bad emperors: the
accident of personality has nothing to do with such things--the

first principle of all genuinely great architecture. But it was not strong enough to stand up against the corruptest of all forms of corruption--against Christians.... These stealthy worms, which under the cover of night, mist and duplicity, crept upon every individual, sucking him dry of all earnest interest in real things, of all instinct for reality--this cowardly, effeminate and sugar-coated gang gradually alienated all "souls," step by step, from that colossal edifice, turning against it all the meritorious, manly and noble natures that had found in the cause of Rome their own cause, their own serious purpose, their own pride. The sneakishness of hypocrisy, the secrecy of the conventicle, concepts as black as hell, such as the sacrifice of the innocent, the unio mystica in the drinking of blood, above all, the slowly rekindled fire of revenge, of Chandala revenge--all that sort of thing became master of Rome: the same kind of religion which, in a pre-existent form, Epicurus had combatted. One has but to read Lucretius to know what Epicurus made war upon--not paganism, but "Christianity," which is to say, the corruption of souls by means of the concepts of guilt, punishment and immortality.--He combatted the subterranean cults, the whole of latent Christianity--to deny immortality was already a form of genuine salvation.--Epicurus had triumphed, and every respectable intellect in Rome was Epicurean--when Paul appeared ... Paul, the Chandala hatred of Rome, of "the world," in the flesh and inspired by genius--the Jew, the eternal Jew par excellence.... What he saw was how, with the aid of the small sectarian Christian movement that stood apart from Judaism, a "world conflagration" might be kindled; how, with the symbol of "God on the cross," all secret seditions, all the fruits of anarchistic intrigues in the empire, might be amalgamated into one immense power. "Salvation is of the Jews."--Christianity is the formula for exceeding and summing up the subterranean cults of all varieties, that of Osiris, that of the Great Mother, that of Mithras, for instance: in his discernment of this fact the genius of Paul showed itself. His instinct was here so sure that, with reckless violence to the truth, he put the ideas which lent fascination to every sort of Chandala religion into the mouth of the "Saviour" as his own inventions, and not only into the mouth--he made out of him something that even a priest of Mithras could understand.... This was his revelation at Damascus: he grasped the fact that he needed the belief in immortality in order to rob "the world" of its value, that the concept of "hell" would master Rome--that the notion of a "beyond" is the death of life.... Nihilist and Christian: they rhyme in German, and they do more than rhyme....

59.

The whole labour of the ancient world gone for naught: I have no word to describe the feelings that such an enormity arouses in me.--And, considering the fact that its labour was merely preparatory, that with adamantine self-consciousness it laid only the foundations for a work to go on for thousands of years, the whole meaning of antiquity disappears!... To what end the Greeks? to what end the Romans?--All the prerequisites to a learned culture, all the methods of science, were already there; man had already perfected the great and incomparable art of reading profitably--that first necessity to the tradition of culture, the unity of the sciences; the natural sciences, in alliance with mathematics and mechanics, were on the right road,--the sense of fact, the last and more valuable of all the senses, had its schools, and its traditions were already centuries old! Is all this properly understood? Every essential to the beginning of the work was ready:--and the most essential, it cannot be said too often, are methods, and also the most difficult to develop, and the longest opposed by habit and laziness. What we have today reconquered, with unspeakable self-discipline, for ourselves--for certain bad instincts, certain Christian instincts, still lurk in our bodies--that is to say, the keen eye for reality, the cautious hand, patience and seriousness in the smallest things, the whole integrity of knowledge--all these things were already there, and had been there for two thousand years! More, there was also a refined and excellent tact and taste! Not as mere brain-drilling! Not as "German" culture, with its loutish manners! But as body, as bearing, as instinct--in short, as reality.... All gone for naught! Overnight it became merely a memory!--The Greeks! The Romans! Instinctive nobility, taste, methodical inquiry, genius for organization and administration, faith in and the will to secure the future of man, a great yes to everything entering into the imperium Romanum and palpable to all the senses, a grand style that was beyond mere art, but had become reality, truth, life....--All overwhelmed in a night, but not by a convulsion of nature! Not trampled to death by Teutons and others of heavy hoof! But brought to shame by crafty, sneaking, invisible, anæmic vampires! Not conquered,--only sucked dry!... Hidden vengefulness, petty envy, became master! Everything wretched, intrinsically ailing, and invaded by bad feelings, the whole ghetto-world of the soul, was at once on top!--One needs but read any of the Christian agitators, for example, St. Augustine, in order to realize, in order to smell, what filthy fellows came to the top. It would be an error, however, to assume that there was any lack of understanding in the leaders of the Christian movement:--ah, but they were clever, clever to the point of holiness, these fathers of the church! What they lacked was something quite different. Nature neglected-- perhaps forgot--to give them even the most modest endowment of respectable, of upright, of cleanly instincts.... Between ourselves, they are not even men.... If Islam despises

111

Christianity, it has a thousandfold right to do so: Islam at least assumes that it is dealing with men....

60.

Christianity destroyed for us the whole harvest of ancient civilization, and later it also destroyed for us the whole harvest of Mohammedan civilization. The wonderful culture of the Moors in Spain, which was fundamentally nearer to us and appealed more to our senses and tastes than that of Rome and Greece, was trampled down (--I do not say by what sort of feet--) Why? Because it had to thank noble and manly instincts for its origin--because it said yes to life, even to the rare and refined luxuriousness of Moorish life!... The crusaders later made war on something before which it would have been more fitting for them to have grovelled in the dust--a civilization beside which even that of our nineteenth century seems very poor and very "senile."--What they wanted, of course, was booty: the orient was rich.... Let us put aside our prejudices! The crusades were a higher form of piracy, nothing more! The German nobility, which is fundamentally a Viking nobility, was in its element there: the church knew only too well how the German nobility was to be won.... The German noble, always the "Swiss guard" of the church, always in the service of every bad instinct of the church--but well paid.... Consider the fact that it is precisely the aid of German swords and German blood and valour that has enabled the church to carry through its war to the death upon everything noble on earth! At this point a host of painful questions suggest themselves. The German nobility stands outside the history of the higher civilization: the reason is obvious.... Christianity, alcohol--the two great means of corruption.... Intrinsically there should be no more choice between Islam and Christianity than there is between an Arab and a Jew. The decision is already reached; nobody remains at liberty to choose here. Either a man is a Chandala or he is not.... "War to the knife with Rome! Peace and friendship with Islam!": this was the feeling, this was the act, of that great free spirit, that genius among German emperors, Frederick II. What! must a German first be a genius, a free spirit, before he can feel decently? I can't make out how a German could ever feel Christian....

61.

Here it becomes necessary to call up a memory that must be a hundred times more painful to Germans. The Germans have destroyed for Europe the last great harvest of civilization that Europe was ever to reap--the Renaissance. Is it understood at last, will it ever be understood, what the Renaissance was? The transvaluation of Christian values,--an attempt with all available means, all instincts and all the resources of genius to bring about a triumph of the opposite values, the more noble values.... This has been the one great war of the past; there has never been a more critical question than that of the Renaissance--it is my question too--; there has never been a form of attack more fundamental, more direct, or more violently delivered by a whole front upon the center of the enemy! To attack at the critical place, at the very seat of Christianity, and there enthrone the more noble values--that is to say, to insinuate them into the instincts, into the most fundamental needs and appetites of those sitting there ... I see before me the possibility of a perfectly heavenly enchantment and spectacle:--it seems to me to scintillate with all the vibrations of a fine and delicate beauty, and within it there is an art so divine, so infernally divine, that one might search in vain for thousands of years for another such possibility; I see a

spectacle so rich in significance and at the same time so
wonderfully full of paradox that it should arouse all the gods
on Olympus to immortal laughter--Cæsar Borgia as pope!...
Am I understood?... Well then, that would have been the sort of
triumph that I alone am longing for today--: by it Christianity
would have been swept away!--What happened? A German
monk, Luther, came to Rome. This monk, with all the vengeful
instincts of an unsuccessful priest in him, raised a rebellion
against the Renaissance in Rome.... Instead of grasping, with
profound thanksgiving, the miracle that had taken place: the
conquest of Christianity at its capital--instead of this, his hatred
was stimulated by the spectacle. A religious man thinks only of
himself.--Luther saw only the depravity of the papacy at the
very moment when the opposite was becoming apparent: the
old corruption, the peccatum originale, Christianity itself, no
longer occupied the papal chair! Instead there was life! Instead
there was the triumph of life! Instead there was a great yea to
all lofty, beautiful and daring things!... And Luther restored the
church: he attacked it.... The Renaissance--an event without
meaning, a great futility!--Ah, these Germans, what they have
not cost us! Futility--that has always been the work of the
Germans.--The Reformation; Leibnitz; Kant and so-called
German philosophy; the war of "liberation"; the empire--every
time a futile substitute for something that once existed, for
something irrecoverable.... These Germans, I confess, are my
enemies: I despise all their uncleanliness in concept and
valuation, their cowardice before every honest yea and nay. For
nearly a thousand years they have tangled and confused
everything their fingers have touched; they have on their
conscience all the half-way measures, all the three-eighths-way
measures, that Europe is sick of,--they also have on their
conscience the uncleanest variety of Christianity that exists,
and the most incurable and indestructible--Protestantism.... If

114

mankind never manages to get rid of Christianity the Germans will be to blame....

62.

--With this I come to a conclusion and pronounce my judgment. I condemn Christianity; I bring against the Christian church the most terrible of all the accusations that an accuser has ever had in his mouth. It is, to me, the greatest of all imaginable corruptions; it seeks to work the ultimate corruption, the worst possible corruption. The Christian church has left nothing untouched by its depravity; it has turned every value into worthlessness, and every truth into a lie, and every integrity into baseness of soul. Let any one dare to speak to me of its "humanitarian" blessings! Its deepest necessities range it against any effort to abolish distress; it lives by distress; it creates distress to make itself immortal.... For example, the worm of sin: it was the church that first enriched mankind with this misery!--The "equality of souls before God"--this fraud, this pretext for the rancunes of all the base-minded--this explosive concept, ending in revolution, the modern idea, and the notion of overthrowing the whole social order--this is Christian dynamite.... The "humanitarian" blessings of Christianity forsooth! To breed out of humanitas a self-contradiction, an art of self-pollution, a will to lie at any price, an aversion and contempt for all good and honest instincts! All this, to me, is the "humanitarianism" of Christianity!--Parasitism as the only practice of the church; with its anæmic and "holy" ideals, sucking all the blood, all the love, all the hope out of life; the beyond as the will to deny all reality; the cross as the distinguishing mark of the most subterranean conspiracy ever heard of,--against health, beauty, well-being, intellect, kindness of soul--against life itself....

115

This eternal accusation against Christianity I shall write upon all walls, wherever walls are to be found--I have letters that even the blind will be able to see.... I call Christianity the one great curse, the one great intrinsic depravity, the one great instinct of revenge, for which no means are venomous enough, or secret, subterranean and small enough,--I call it the one immortal blemish upon the human race....

And mankind reckons time from the dies nefastus when this fatality befell--from the first day of Christianity!--Why not rather from its last?--From today?--The transvaluation of all values!...

BOOKS PUBLISHED
BY
FREDERICK ELLIS
(New Hardbacks)

Buy Direct @ 35% Discount – e-mail >> frederick659@yahoo.com

Author - Jack London

MARTIN EDEN

WAR OF THE CLASSES

JOHN BARLEYCORN

THE PEOPLE OF THE ABYSS

JACK LONDON ON THE ROAD

THE ASSASSINATION BUREAU, LTD.

THE IRON HEEL

Author – Bruno Traven

GENERAL FROM THE JUNGLE

THE DEATH SHIP

THE REBELLION OF THE HANGED

THE WHITE ROSE

THE BRIDGE IN THE JUNGLE

MARCH TO THE MONTERIA

THE TREASURE OF THE SIERRA MADRE

1

Author – Carl Frederick

est PLAYING THE GAME THE NEW WAY

Authors - Frederick Ellis & Carl Frederick

THE OAKLAND STATEMENT

Author – Mao Tsetung

QUOTATIONS FROM CHAIRMAN MAO TSETUNG

Author – Upton Sinclair

OUR LADY

OIL

THE JUNGLE

DRAGON'S TEETH (Pulitzer Prize Winner)

THE FLIVVER KING: THE STORY OF FORD-AMERICA

ONE HUNDRED PERCENT: THE STORY OF A
PATRIOT

WORLD'S END I

WORLD'S END II

THE SECRET LIFE OF JESUS

THE MONEYCHANGERS

MENTAL RADIO

THE MILLENIUM

A PERSONAL JESUS

PROFITS OF RELIGION

THEY CALL ME CARPENTER: A TALE OF
THE SECOND COMING

Author – Thomas Paine

COMMON SENSE, THE RIGHTS OF MAN
& THE AGE OF REASON

THE AMERICAN CRISIS

Author – Karl Marx

DAS KAPITAL

THE COMMUNIST MANIFESTO &
WAGES, PRICE AND PROFIT

WAGE-LABOUR AND CAPITAL
& VALUE, PRICE AND PROFIT

Author – W. E. B. Du Bois

THE SOULS OF BLACK FOLK

Author – Eugene Debs

WALLS AND BARS

Author – Jean-Jacques Rousseau

THE SOCIAL CONTRACT

Author – John Reed

TEN DAYS THAT SHOOK THE WORLD

INSURGENT MEXICO

Author – Antonio Gramsci

THE MODERN PRINCE AND
SELECTED WRITINGS

Author – V. I. Lenin

THE STATE AND REVOLUTION

FIGHT AGAINST STALINISM & IMPERIALISM: THE HIGHEST
STAGE OF CAPITALISM

Author – John Dewey

HOW WE THINK & EDUCATION AND EXPERIENCE

Author – David Ricardo

PRINCIPLES OF POLITICAL ECONOMY
AND TAXATION

Author – Thomas Jefferson

BIOGRAPHY OF THOMAS JEFFERSON & THE LIFE AND
MORALS OF JESUS OF NAZARETH

Author – Emma Goldman

ANARCHISM AND OTHER WRITINGS

Author – Rosa Luxemburg

REFORM OR REVOLUTION & THE MASS STRIKE

Author – Leon Trotsky

THE REVOLUTION BETRAYED

Author – John Stuart Mill

ON SOCIALISM & THE SUBJECTION OF WOMEN

Author – Friedrich Nietzsche

BEYOND GOOD AND EVIL

THE BIRTH OF TRAGEDY & SEVENTY-FIVE APHORISMS & THE ANTI-CHRIST

Author – John Quincy Adams

THE AMISTAD ARGUMENT & THE STATE OF THE UNION ADDRESSES

Authors – James Madison, Alexander Hamilton and John Jay

THE FEDERALIST PAPERS

Author – Alexander Hamilton

THE WORKS OF ALEXANDER HAMILTON

www.ingramcontent.com/pod-product-compliance
Lightning Source LLC
Chambersburg PA
CBHW020403100426
42812CB00001B/180